Material

Originally published as Material #1—4

Volume 1

Written by
Ales Kot

Illustrated by
Will Tempest

Lettered by
Clayton Cowles

Designed by
Tom Muller
Cover by Tom Muller

Media inquiries should be directed to Roger Green & Phil D'Amecourt at WME Entertainment and Ari Lubet at 3 Arts Entertainment.

MATERIAL Vol. 1. First Printing. September 2015. ISBN: 978-1-63215-474-3. Published by Image Comics, Inc. Office of publication: 2001 Center Street, Sixth Floor, Berkeley, CA 94704.

Material™

Volume 1

Published by
Image Comics, Inc.

image

Always read the
<u>footnotes</u>

I know, I hate it too. It feels like a discursion from the main event, a distraction from the central text that interrupts the flow of the story and makes it difficult to pick up where you left off. Footnotes are dense, often maddeningly obscure, and frequently reference other information you need to seek out to understand the basics of what's going on.

And if I hadn't read the footnotes, I would never have found the Chicago Police's warehouse for incommunicado detentions and interrogations — which, it turns out, features in *Material*.

My path to the warehouse started when one of my editors at *The Guardian*, the news organization where I work, asked me late last year to read a manuscript from a man detained at **Guantanamo Bay** detainee named **Mohamedou Ould Slahi** before we published excerpts from it. He wanted to see if I could find any non-obvious news lines to pursue. I found one in a <u>footnote</u>.

Slahi is among the most brutalized detainees in Guantanamo history. His captors stuffed ice into a jacket placed on his bare chest while they punched and kicked him. In addition to the now-familiar noise bombardment and "stress positions"— a euphemism for contorting someone's body painfully — they threatened to kill him and rape his mother. The footnote said that his interrogations leader was, in civilian life, a Chicago police detective. I wanted to know what someone capable of torture at Guantanamo did as a lawman at home.

I grew up in Brooklyn and primarily report on national security. I didn't know Chicago and its history. But as I found Chicagoans who accused this same detective of abusing them, Chicago activists, criminologists and lawyers taught me about the Windy City's history of racialized policing. One of them, at the end of a two-hour coffee, offhandedly mentioned that the Chicago police even had an off-the-books warehouse where they held and questioned people without access to attorneys or public notice of their locations, effectively disappearing them. Another <u>footnote</u>.

In February 2015, I exposed the interrogations and detentions at **Homan Square**. By May, amidst police non-denial denials, I had published accounts of a dozen people who had been held there. By August, a transparency lawsuit I filed against the police resulted in a very incomplete and initial disclosure from their own records: over 3500 people had been held there over a decade; 82 percent of them were black in a city that's 33 percent black; and only three of them received documented visits from an attorney. My lawsuit, and the disclosures, continues as of this writing.

Social media brought **Homan Square** far and wide, even as the Chicago press preferred to report on it dismissively or not at all. Both of those developments might have been expected. Seeing **Homan Square** in *Material* was not.

We in America are living in a moment in which it is harder than ever before to ignore the ways in which law enforcement monitors, harrasses and kills black and brown people without consequence. (That's thanks in large part to social media, which makes racialized police brutality unignorable to Twitter-addicted mainstream white journalists, prompting coverage of something until recently very frequently ignored.) Yet if you read comic books, as I have since I could read, you would not know any of this is happening.

There are no superheroes jumping off rooftops to stop Cleveland police officer **Timothy Loehmann** from shooting 12-year old **Tamir Rice** dead. No telekinetic is tearing open incommunicado police detention warehouses with her mind. As the real-life vigilantes kill black teenagers armed with Skittles and iced tea, the make-believe vigilantes — mostly white, mostly written by white writers, for an audience assumed to be default white — move along with nothing to say.

The exception is Ales Kot and Will Tempest's *Material*.

Material is a confrontational and challenging work. It is not easy to follow: you will go from MIT lecture halls to Hollywood production meetings to Homan Square to the aftermath of Guantanamo Bay detentions. You will very likely be disoriented, unsure how the pieces fit together, and perhaps even suspicious that any connective tissue exists. But you are unlikely to miss the undercurrent that runs through each of *Material*'s characters: anxiety, displacement, the doubt that rises like stomach bile in your throat at the sensation that the reality you perceive conceals more than it reveals.

Pay close attention to Tempest's colors. Stark, garish and mutating from panel to panel like a flashing light, they are your guide through the story: what belongs, what does not, what connects, where the focus lies.

The complex nature of the storytelling amplifies how disturbing this story is. Kot is allergic to euphemism. When his story needs to be direct, as when he shows you police brutality, it is raw and frightening, and there is no false balance that diminishes the enormity of legally sanctioned crime. *Material* stands out of its own way, leaving nothing between you and the baton.

But the real place where you find *Material*'s urgency is in the footnotes — the margins and gutters between panels. Do not skip them. They mortar the story to reality. In an age where people protest the erasure of stolen lives through the **#SayHerName** hashtag, *Material* puts their names — **Rekia Boyd**, **Rumain Brisbon**, **Eric Garner** — in the story. It is a sad testament to the squandered potential of comic books that the simple act of recognition feels groundbreaking.

To skip the footnotes is to miss the real story.
Don't turn away from why *Material* matters ●

Spencer Ackerman
@attackerman
Brooklyn NY
August 2015

Spencer Ackerman is national security editor for *Guardian US*.
A former senior writer for *Wired***, he won the 2012 National Magazine Award for Digital Reporting**

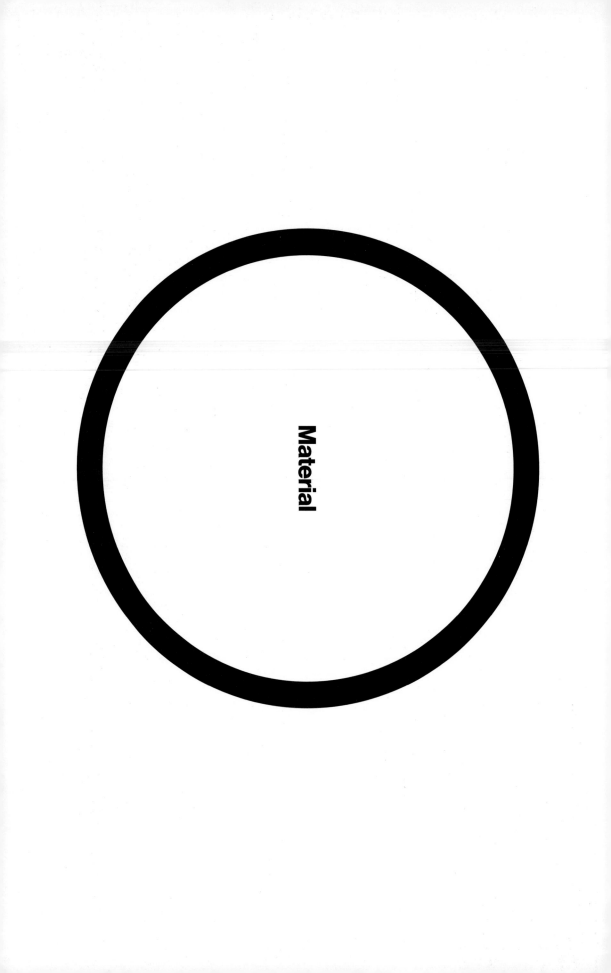

Material

Chapter 1

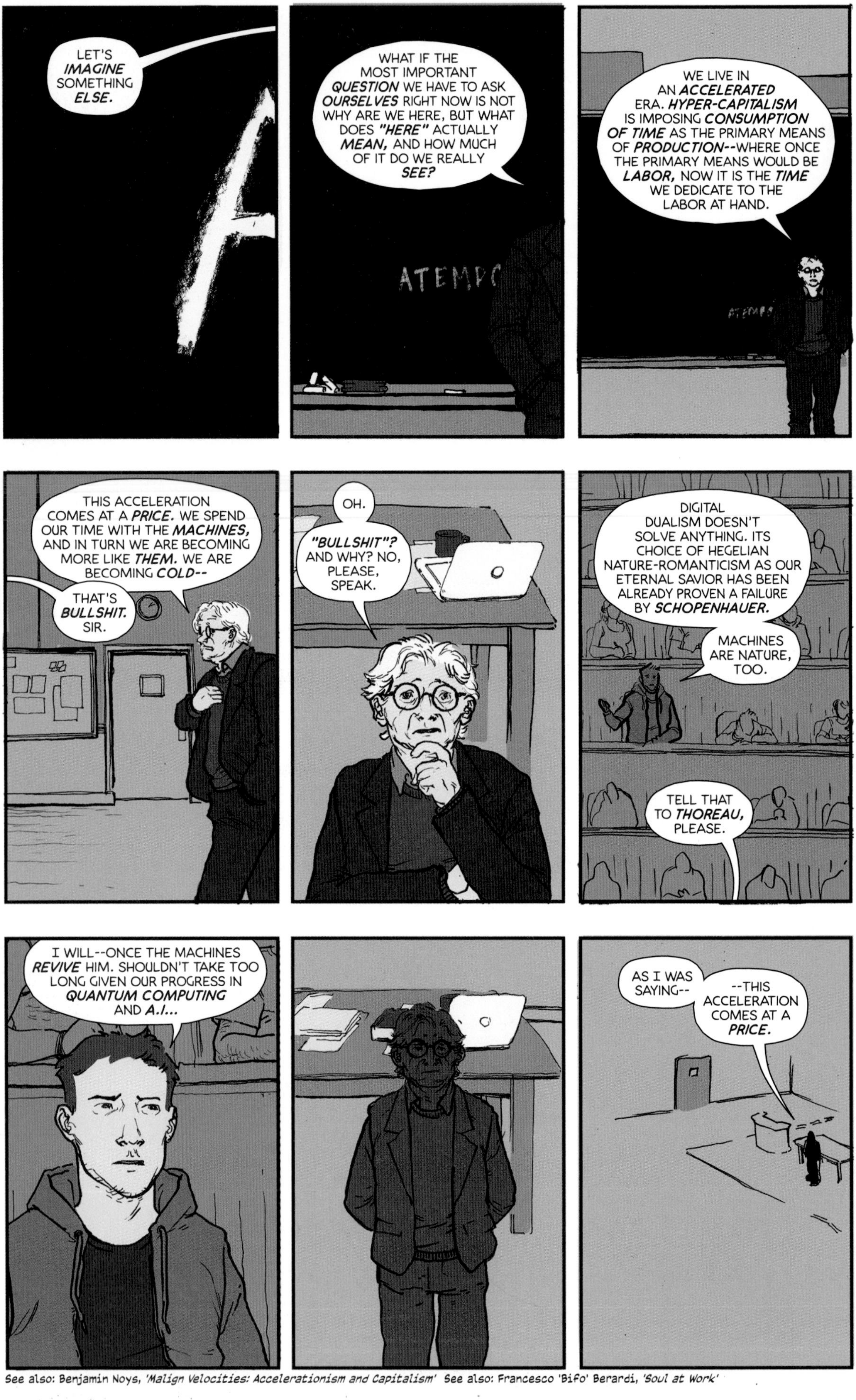
LET'S *IMAGINE* SOMETHING *ELSE.*
WHAT IF THE MOST IMPORTANT *QUESTION* WE HAVE TO ASK *OURSELVES* RIGHT NOW IS NOT WHY ARE WE HERE, BUT WHAT DOES *"HERE"* ACTUALLY *MEAN,* AND HOW MUCH OF IT DO WE REALLY *SEE?*
WE LIVE IN AN *ACCELERATED* ERA. *HYPER-CAPITALISM* IS IMPOSING *CONSUMPTION OF TIME* AS THE PRIMARY MEANS OF *PRODUCTION*--WHERE ONCE THE PRIMARY MEANS WOULD BE *LABOR,* NOW IT IS THE *TIME* WE DEDICATE TO THE LABOR AT HAND.
THIS ACCELERATION COMES AT A *PRICE.* WE SPEND OUR TIME WITH THE *MACHINES,* AND IN TURN WE ARE BECOMING MORE LIKE *THEM.* WE ARE BECOMING *COLD--*
THAT'S *BULLSHIT.* SIR.
OH.
"BULLSHIT"? AND WHY? NO, PLEASE, SPEAK.
DIGITAL DUALISM DOESN'T SOLVE ANYTHING. ITS CHOICE OF HEGELIAN NATURE-ROMANTICISM AS OUR ETERNAL SAVIOR HAS BEEN ALREADY PROVEN A FAILURE BY *SCHOPENHAUER.*
MACHINES ARE NATURE, TOO.
TELL THAT TO *THOREAU,* PLEASE.
I WILL--ONCE THE MACHINES *REVIVE* HIM. SHOULDN'T TAKE TOO LONG GIVEN OUR PROGRESS IN *QUANTUM COMPUTING* AND *A.I...*
AS I WAS SAYING--
--THIS ACCELERATION COMES AT A *PRICE.*

See also: Benjamin Noys, *'Malign Velocities: Accelerationism and Capitalism'* See also: Francesco 'Bifo' Berardi, *'Soul at Work'*

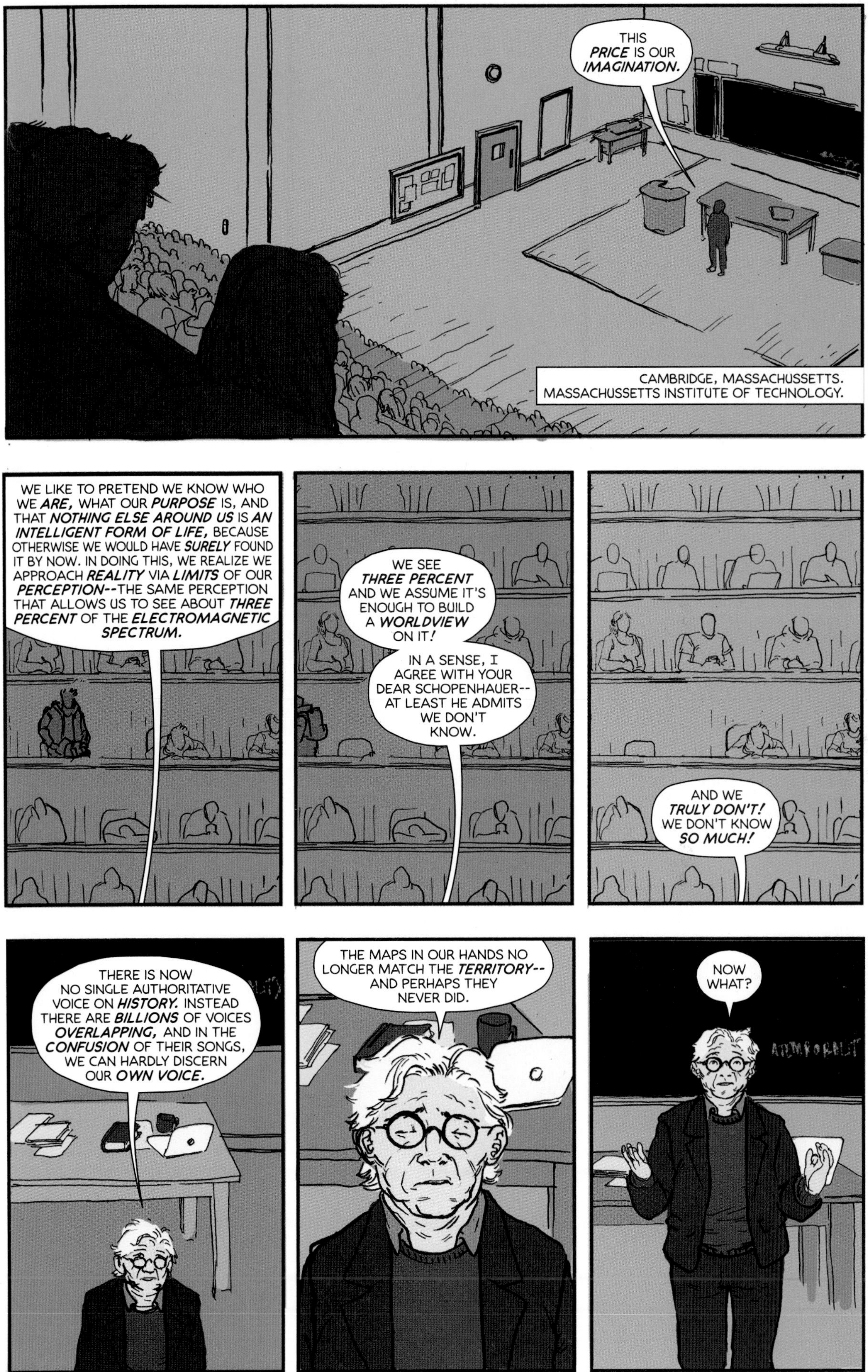
THIS PRICE IS OUR IMAGINATION.
CAMBRIDGE, MASSACHUSSETTS. MASSACHUSSETTS INSTITUTE OF TECHNOLOGY.
WE LIKE TO PRETEND WE KNOW WHO WE ARE, WHAT OUR PURPOSE IS, AND THAT NOTHING ELSE AROUND US IS AN INTELLIGENT FORM OF LIFE, BECAUSE OTHERWISE WE WOULD HAVE SURELY FOUND IT BY NOW. IN DOING THIS, WE REALIZE WE APPROACH REALITY VIA LIMITS OF OUR PERCEPTION--THE SAME PERCEPTION THAT ALLOWS US TO SEE ABOUT THREE PERCENT OF THE ELECTROMAGNETIC SPECTRUM.
WE SEE THREE PERCENT AND WE ASSUME IT'S ENOUGH TO BUILD A WORLDVIEW ON IT!
IN A SENSE, I AGREE WITH YOUR DEAR SCHOPENHAUER--AT LEAST HE ADMITS WE DON'T KNOW.
AND WE TRULY DON'T! WE DON'T KNOW SO MUCH!
THERE IS NOW NO SINGLE AUTHORITATIVE VOICE ON HISTORY. INSTEAD THERE ARE BILLIONS OF VOICES OVERLAPPING, AND IN THE CONFUSION OF THEIR SONGS, WE CAN HARDLY DISCERN OUR OWN VOICE.
THE MAPS IN OUR HANDS NO LONGER MATCH THE TERRITORY--AND PERHAPS THEY NEVER DID.
NOW WHAT?

See Also: Bruce Sterling, *'Atemporality for the Creative Artist'*

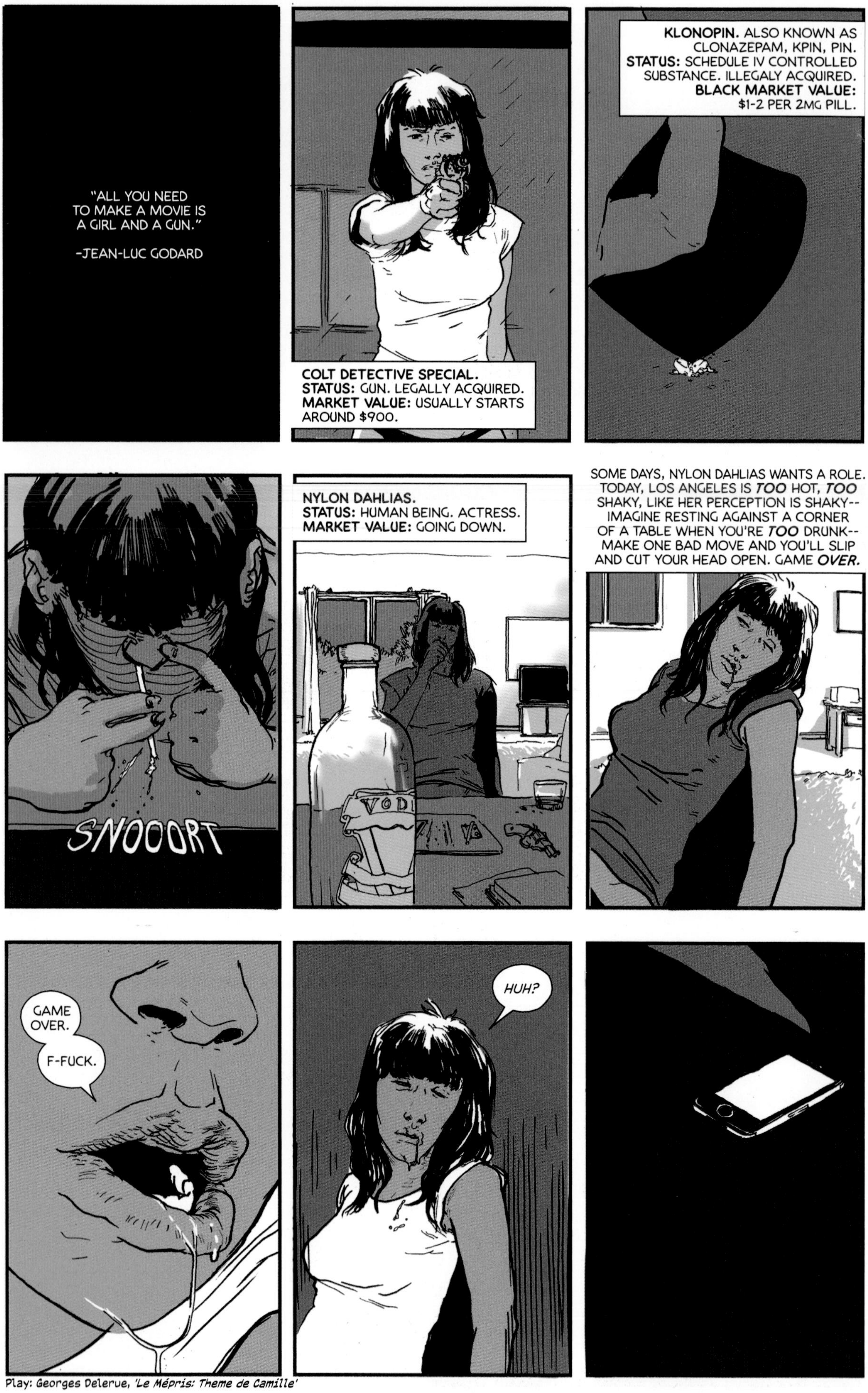
"ALL YOU NEED TO MAKE A MOVIE IS A GIRL AND A GUN."
-JEAN-LUC GODARD
COLT DETECTIVE SPECIAL. STATUS: GUN. LEGALLY ACQUIRED. MARKET VALUE: USUALLY STARTS AROUND $900.
KLONOPIN. ALSO KNOWN AS CLONAZEPAM, KPIN, PIN. STATUS: SCHEDULE IV CONTROLLED SUBSTANCE. ILLEGALY ACQUIRED. BLACK MARKET VALUE: $1-2 PER 2MG PILL.
SNOOORT
NYLON DAHLIAS. STATUS: HUMAN BEING. ACTRESS. MARKET VALUE: GOING DOWN.
VOD
SOME DAYS, NYLON DAHLIAS WANTS A ROLE. TODAY, LOS ANGELES IS *TOO* HOT, *TOO* SHAKY, LIKE HER PERCEPTION IS SHAKY-- IMAGINE RESTING AGAINST A CORNER OF A TABLE WHEN YOU'RE *TOO* DRUNK-- MAKE ONE BAD MOVE AND YOU'LL SLIP AND CUT YOUR HEAD OPEN. GAME ***OVER.***
GAME OVER.
F-FUCK.
HUH?

Play: Georges Delerue, *'Le Mépris: Theme de Camille'*

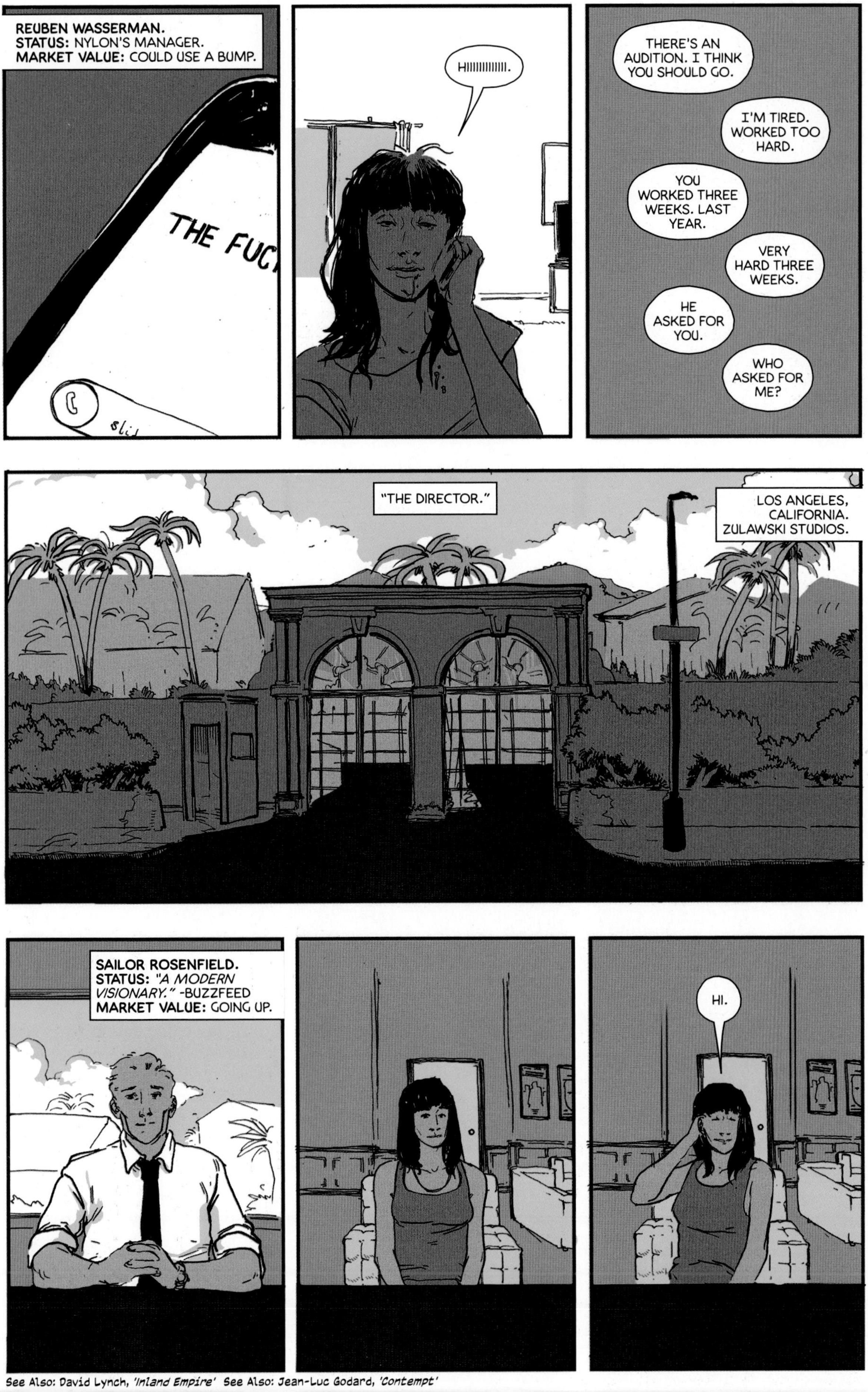
REUBEN WASSERMAN.
STATUS: NYLON'S MANAGER.
MARKET VALUE: COULD USE A BUMP.
HIIIIIIIIIII.
THERE'S AN AUDITION. I THINK YOU SHOULD GO.
I'M TIRED. WORKED TOO HARD.
YOU WORKED THREE WEEKS. LAST YEAR.
VERY HARD THREE WEEKS.
HE ASKED FOR YOU.
WHO ASKED FOR ME?
"THE DIRECTOR."
LOS ANGELES, CALIFORNIA. ZULAWSKI STUDIOS.
SAILOR ROSENFIELD.
STATUS: "A MODERN VISIONARY." -BUZZFEED
MARKET VALUE: GOING UP.
HI.

See Also: David Lynch, *'Inland Empire'* See Also: Jean-Luc Godard, *'Contempt'*

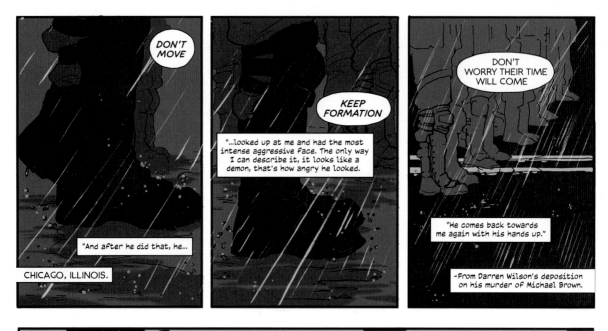

DON'T MOVE
"And after he did that, he...
CHICAGO, ILLINOIS.
KEEP FORMATION
"...looked up at me and had the most intense aggressive face. The only way I can describe it, it looks like a demon, that's how angry he looked.
DON'T WORRY THEIR TIME WILL COME
"He comes back towards me again with his hands up."
-From Darren Wilson's deposition on his murder of Michael Brown.
THE CAMERAS GONE?
AIRSPACE CLEAR?
CLEAR.
ROYCE SAYS CLEAR.
DO IT.
DO IT DO IT DO IT
GREEN! GREEN!
DO IT DO IT DO IT

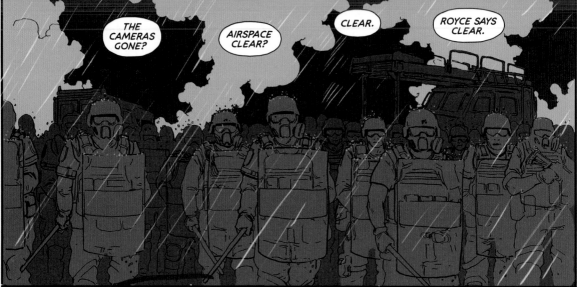

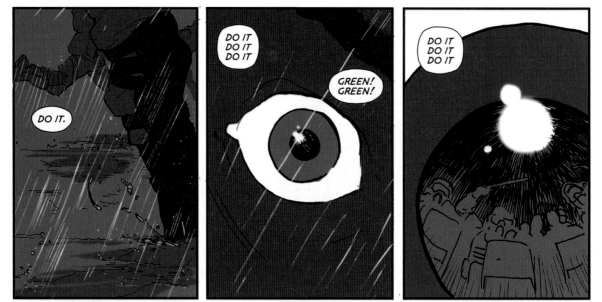

Michael Brown

Tamir Rice

Cameron Tillman

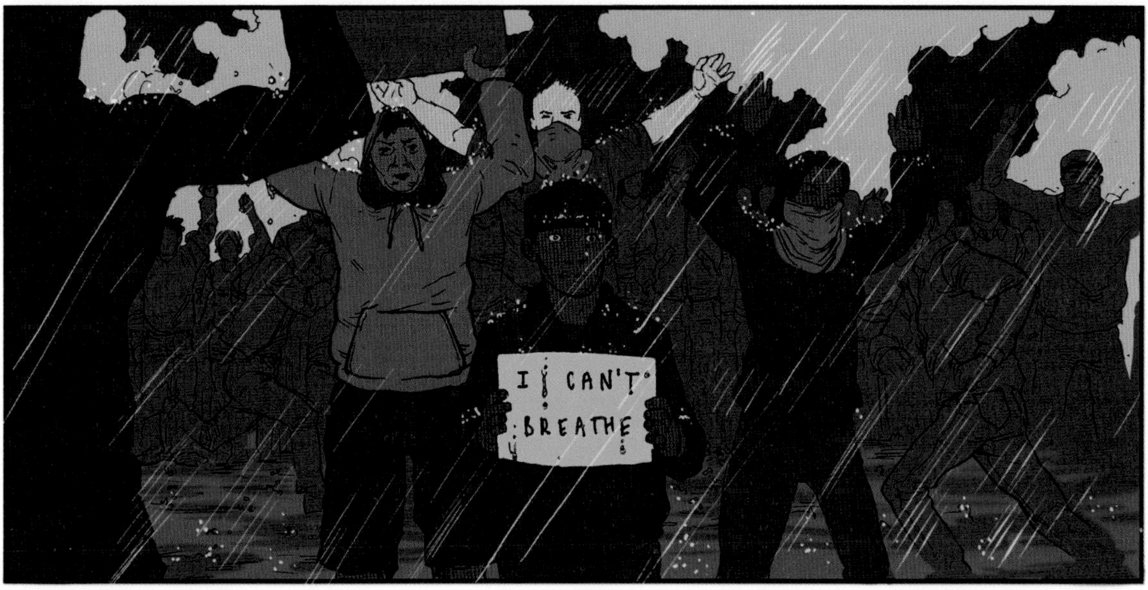
I CAN'T BREATHE

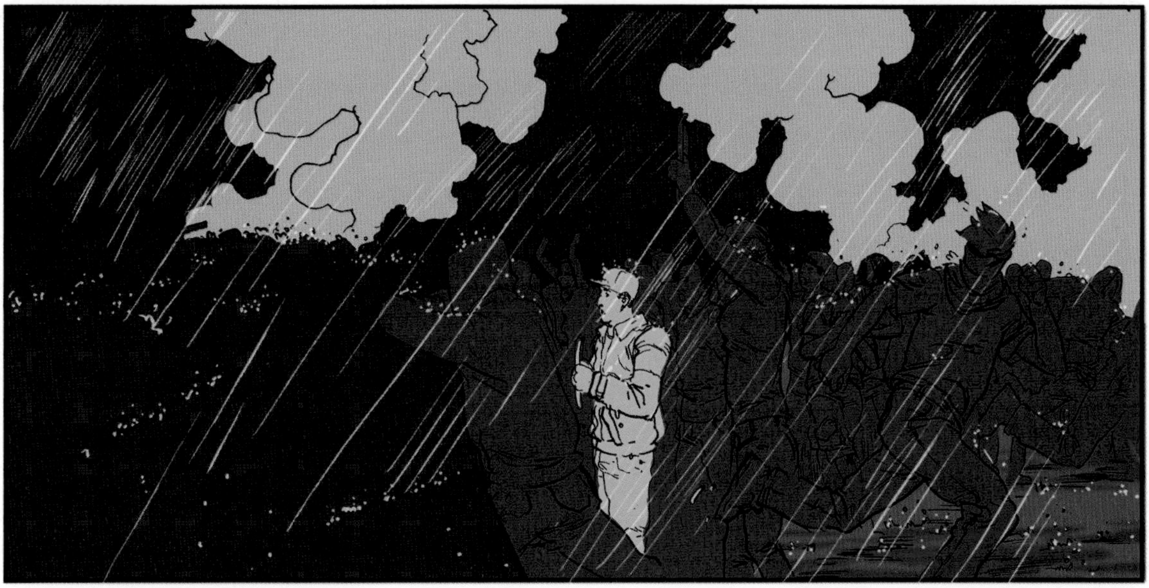

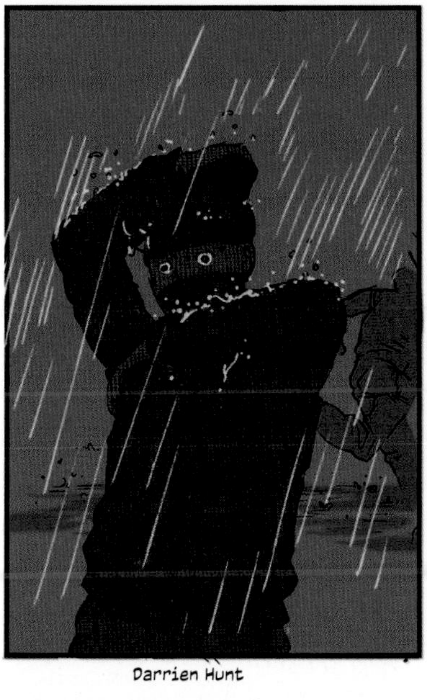

Darrien Hunt

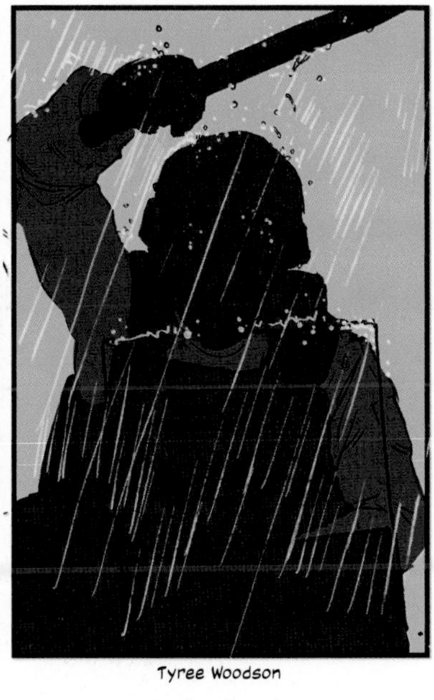

Tyree Woodson

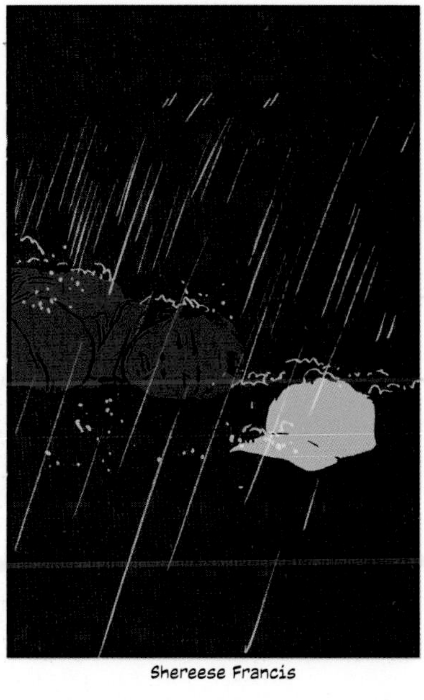

Shereese Francis

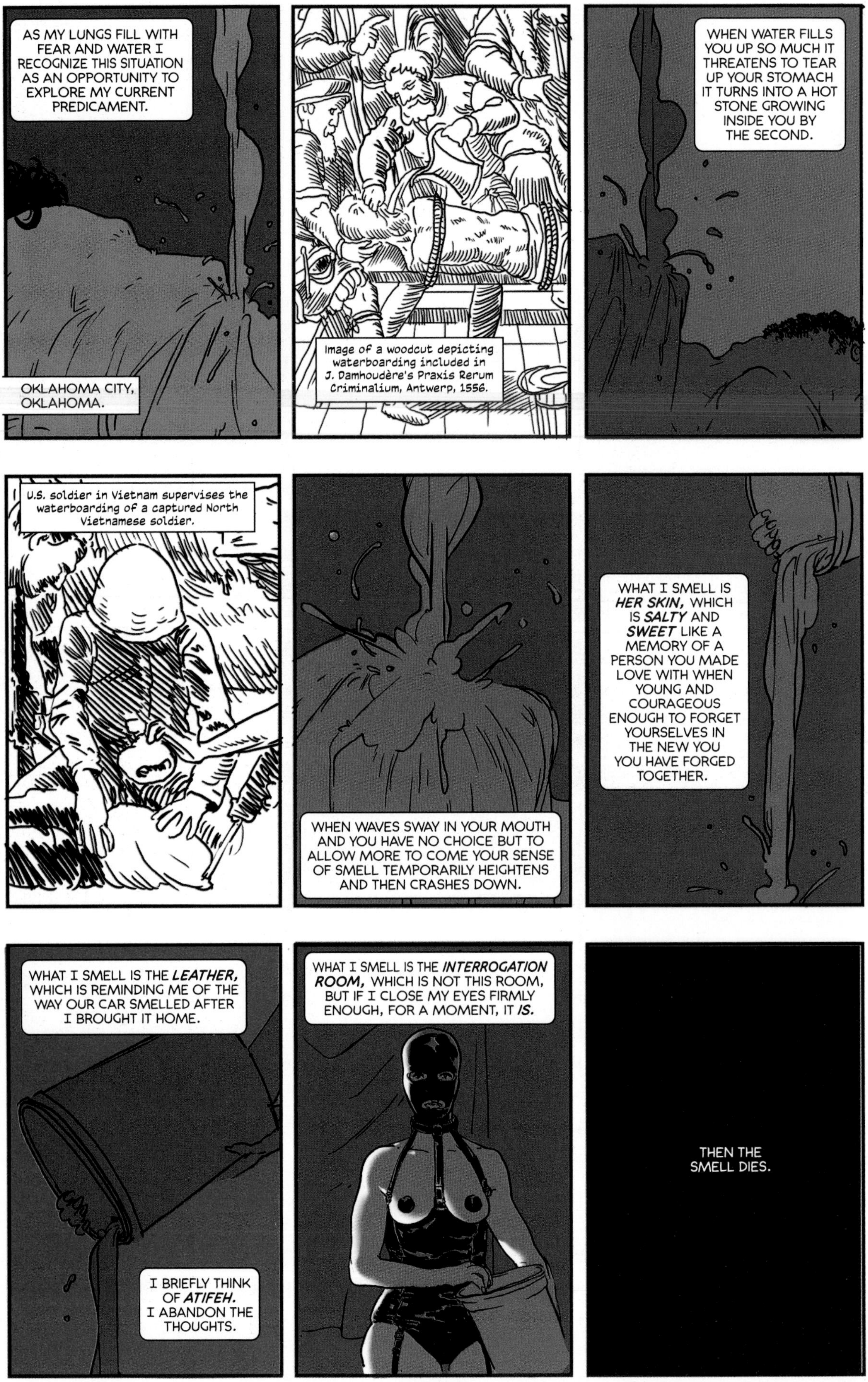
AS MY LUNGS FILL WITH FEAR AND WATER I RECOGNIZE THIS SITUATION AS AN OPPORTUNITY TO EXPLORE MY CURRENT PREDICAMENT.
OKLAHOMA CITY, OKLAHOMA.
Image of a woodcut depicting waterboarding included in J. Damhoudère's Praxis Rerum Criminalium, Antwerp, 1556.
WHEN WATER FILLS YOU UP SO MUCH IT THREATENS TO TEAR UP YOUR STOMACH IT TURNS INTO A HOT STONE GROWING INSIDE YOU BY THE SECOND.
U.S. soldier in Vietnam supervises the waterboarding of a captured North Vietnamese soldier.
WHEN WAVES SWAY IN YOUR MOUTH AND YOU HAVE NO CHOICE BUT TO ALLOW MORE TO COME YOUR SENSE OF SMELL TEMPORARILY HEIGHTENS AND THEN CRASHES DOWN.
WHAT I SMELL IS ***HER SKIN,*** WHICH IS ***SALTY*** AND ***SWEET*** LIKE A MEMORY OF A PERSON YOU MADE LOVE WITH WHEN YOUNG AND COURAGEOUS ENOUGH TO FORGET YOURSELVES IN THE NEW YOU YOU HAVE FORGED TOGETHER.
WHAT I SMELL IS THE ***LEATHER,*** WHICH IS REMINDING ME OF THE WAY OUR CAR SMELLED AFTER I BROUGHT IT HOME.
I BRIEFLY THINK OF ***ATIFEH.*** I ABANDON THE THOUGHTS.
WHAT I SMELL IS THE ***INTERROGATION ROOM,*** WHICH IS NOT THIS ROOM, BUT IF I CLOSE MY EYES FIRMLY ENOUGH, FOR A MOMENT, IT ***IS.***
THEN THE SMELL DIES.

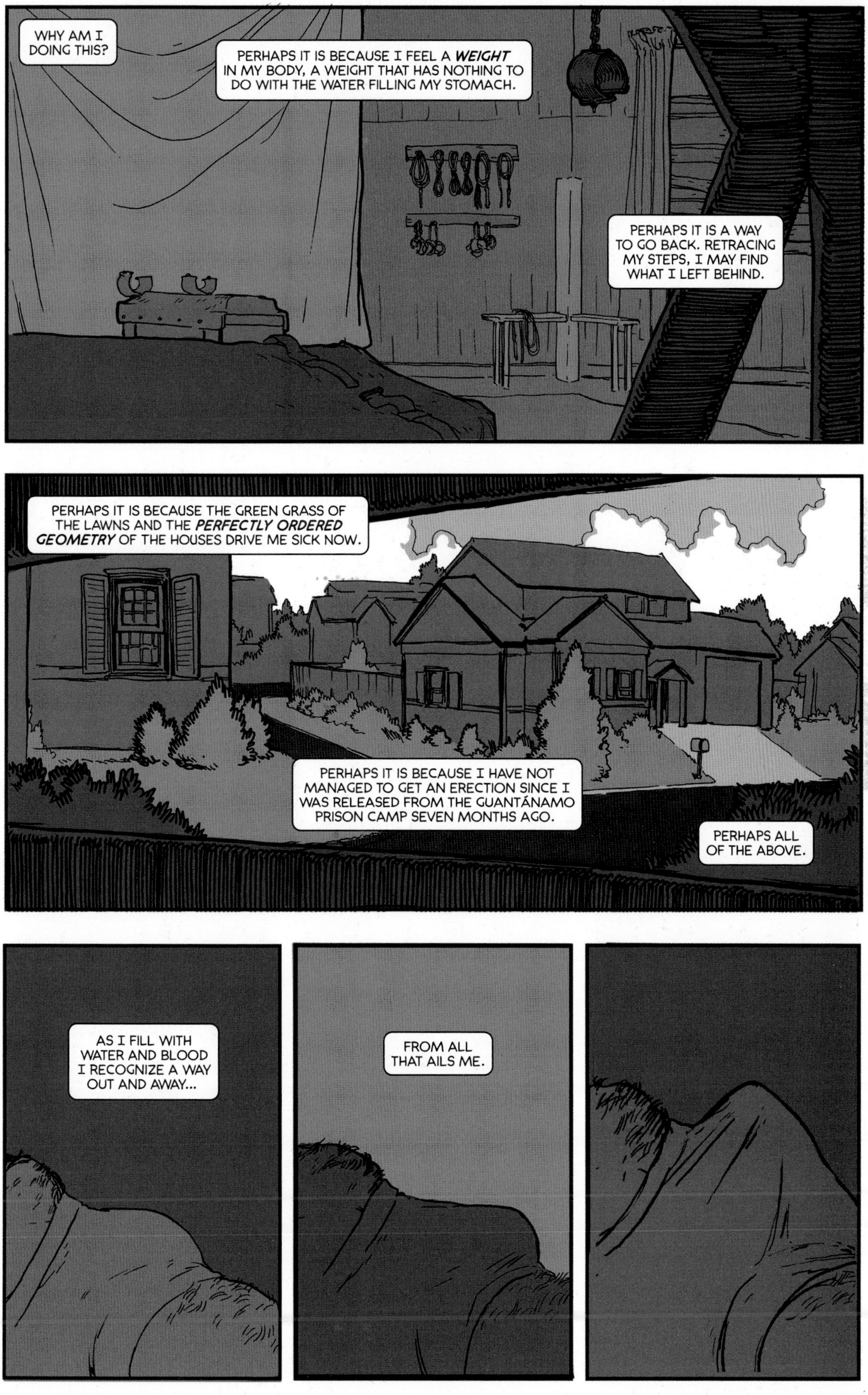
WHY AM I DOING THIS?
PERHAPS IT IS BECAUSE I FEEL A WEIGHT IN MY BODY, A WEIGHT THAT HAS NOTHING TO DO WITH THE WATER FILLING MY STOMACH.
PERHAPS IT IS A WAY TO GO BACK. RETRACING MY STEPS, I MAY FIND WHAT I LEFT BEHIND.
PERHAPS IT IS BECAUSE THE GREEN GRASS OF THE LAWNS AND THE PERFECTLY ORDERED GEOMETRY OF THE HOUSES DRIVE ME SICK NOW.
PERHAPS IT IS BECAUSE I HAVE NOT MANAGED TO GET AN ERECTION SINCE I WAS RELEASED FROM THE GUANTÁNAMO PRISON CAMP SEVEN MONTHS AGO.
PERHAPS ALL OF THE ABOVE.
AS I FILL WITH WATER AND BLOOD I RECOGNIZE A WAY OUT AND AWAY...
FROM ALL THAT AILS ME.

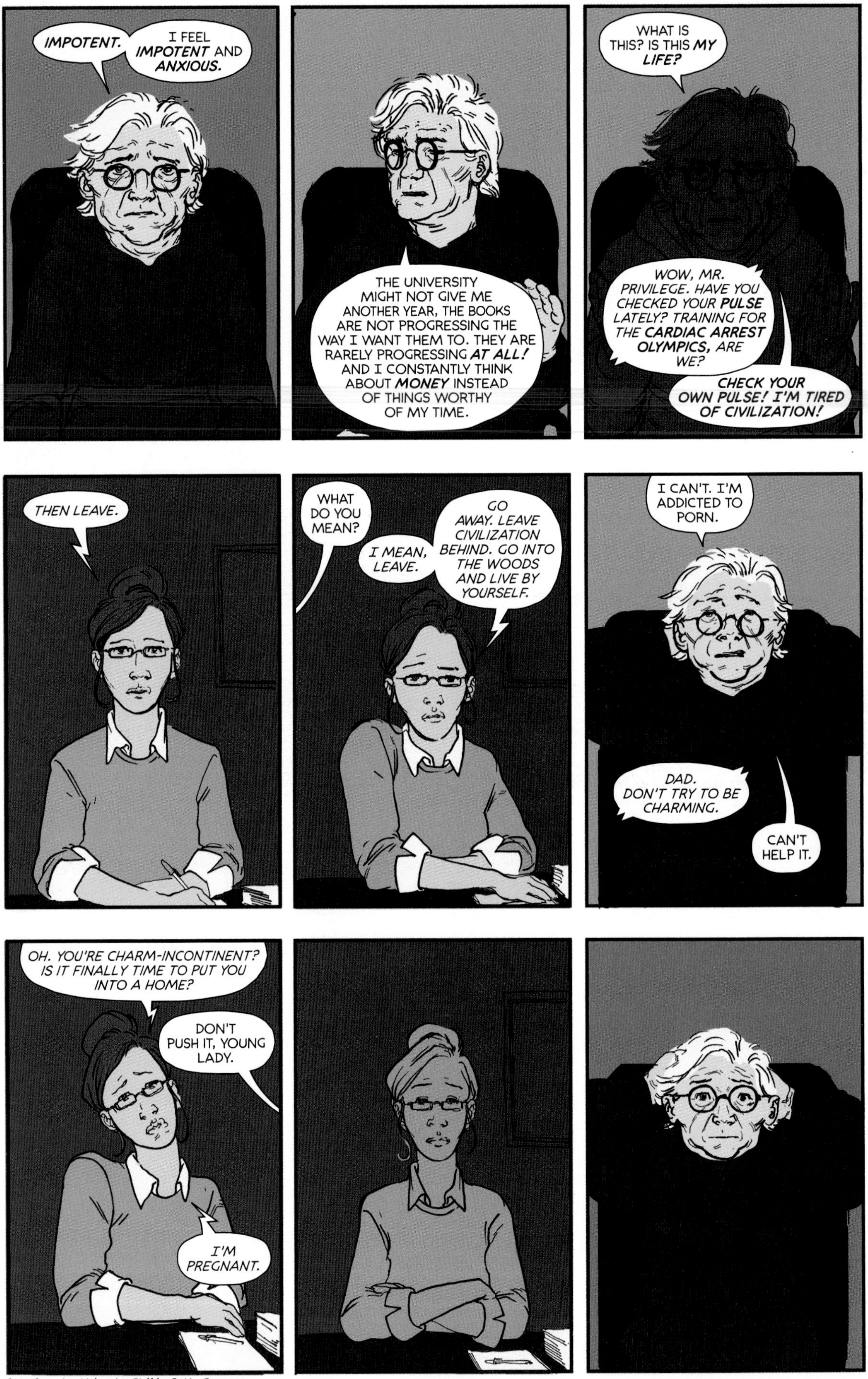
IMPOTENT.
I FEEL IMPOTENT AND ANXIOUS.
THE UNIVERSITY MIGHT NOT GIVE ME ANOTHER YEAR, THE BOOKS ARE NOT PROGRESSING THE WAY I WANT THEM TO. THEY ARE RARELY PROGRESSING AT ALL! AND I CONSTANTLY THINK ABOUT MONEY INSTEAD OF THINGS WORTHY OF MY TIME.
WHAT IS THIS? IS THIS MY LIFE?
WOW, MR. PRIVILEGE. HAVE YOU CHECKED YOUR PULSE LATELY? TRAINING FOR THE CARDIAC ARREST OLYMPICS, ARE WE?
CHECK YOUR OWN PULSE! I'M TIRED OF CIVILIZATION!
THEN LEAVE.
WHAT DO YOU MEAN?
I MEAN, LEAVE.
GO AWAY. LEAVE CIVILIZATION BEHIND. GO INTO THE WOODS AND LIVE BY YOURSELF.
I CAN'T. I'M ADDICTED TO PORN.
DAD. DON'T TRY TO BE CHARMING.
CAN'T HELP IT.
OH. YOU'RE CHARM-INCONTINENT? IS IT FINALLY TIME TO PUT YOU INTO A HOME?
DON'T PUSH IT, YOUNG LADY.
I'M PREGNANT.

See also: Anything by Philip Roth, I guess

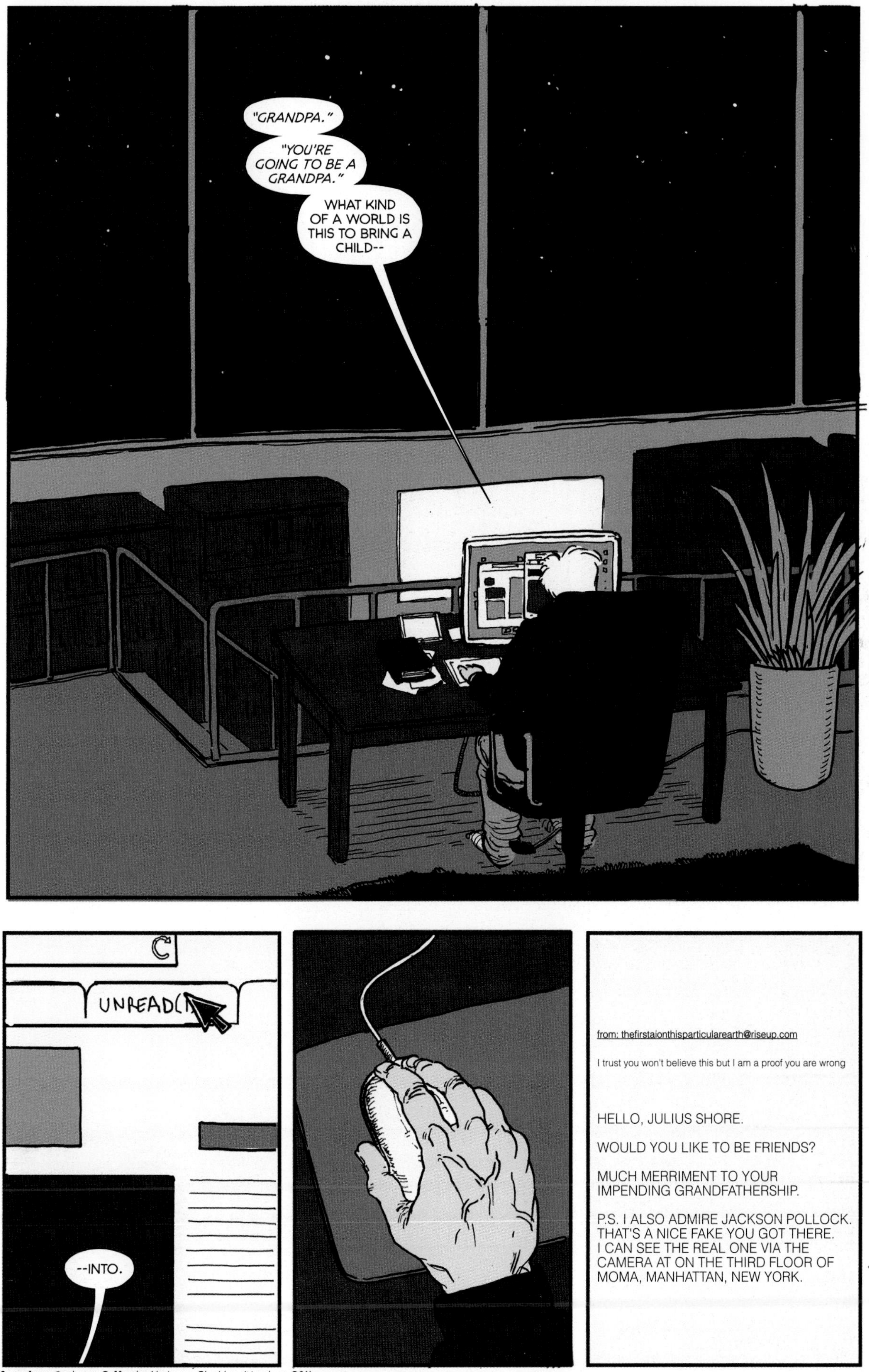
"GRANDPA."
"YOU'RE GOING TO BE A GRANDPA."
WHAT KIND OF A WORLD IS THIS TO BRING A CHILD--
UNREAD(
--INTO.
from: thefirstaionthisparticularearth@riseup.com
I trust you won't believe this but I am a proof you are wrong
HELLO, JULIUS SHORE.
WOULD YOU LIKE TO BE FRIENDS?
MUCH MERRIMENT TO YOUR IMPENDING GRANDFATHERSHIP.
P.S. I ALSO ADMIRE JACKSON POLLOCK. THAT'S A NICE FAKE YOU GOT THERE. I CAN SEE THE REAL ONE VIA THE CAMERA AT ON THE THIRD FLOOR OF MOMA, MANHATTAN, NEW YORK.

See also: Jackson Pollock, *'Autumn Rhythm (Number 30)'*

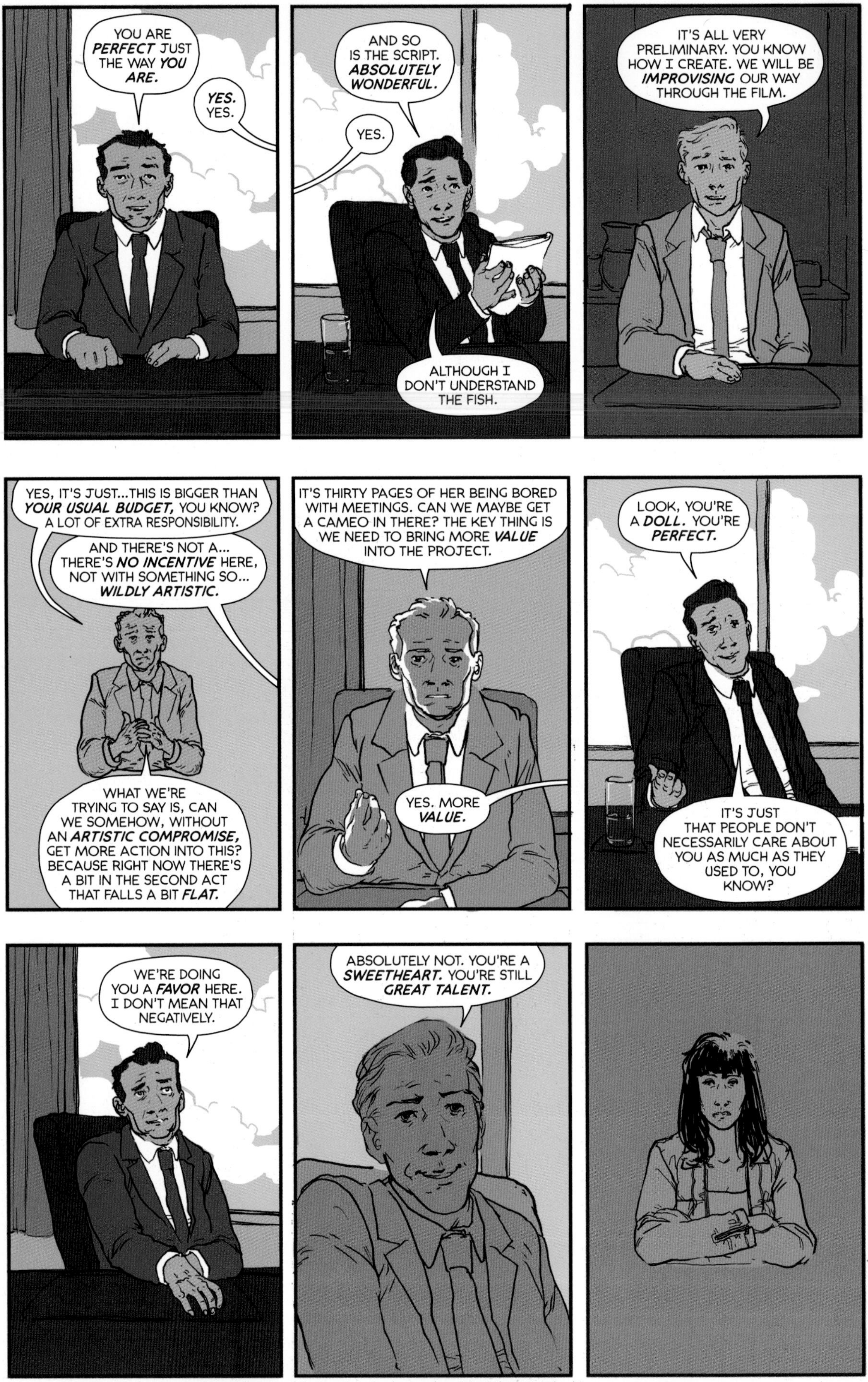
YOU ARE PERFECT JUST THE WAY YOU ARE.
YES. YES.
AND SO IS THE SCRIPT. ABSOLUTELY WONDERFUL.
YES.
ALTHOUGH I DON'T UNDERSTAND THE FISH.
IT'S ALL VERY PRELIMINARY. YOU KNOW HOW I CREATE. WE WILL BE IMPROVISING OUR WAY THROUGH THE FILM.
YES, IT'S JUST...THIS IS BIGGER THAN YOUR USUAL BUDGET, YOU KNOW? A LOT OF EXTRA RESPONSIBILITY.
AND THERE'S NOT A... THERE'S NO INCENTIVE HERE, NOT WITH SOMETHING SO... WILDLY ARTISTIC.
WHAT WE'RE TRYING TO SAY IS, CAN WE SOMEHOW, WITHOUT AN ARTISTIC COMPROMISE, GET MORE ACTION INTO THIS? BECAUSE RIGHT NOW THERE'S A BIT IN THE SECOND ACT THAT FALLS A BIT FLAT.
IT'S THIRTY PAGES OF HER BEING BORED WITH MEETINGS. CAN WE MAYBE GET A CAMEO IN THERE? THE KEY THING IS WE NEED TO BRING MORE VALUE INTO THE PROJECT.
YES. MORE VALUE.
LOOK, YOU'RE A DOLL. YOU'RE PERFECT.
IT'S JUST THAT PEOPLE DON'T NECESSARILY CARE ABOUT YOU AS MUCH AS THEY USED TO, YOU KNOW?
WE'RE DOING YOU A FAVOR HERE. I DON'T MEAN THAT NEGATIVELY.
ABSOLUTELY NOT. YOU'RE A SWEETHEART. YOU'RE STILL GREAT TALENT.

See also: Rebecca Solnit, *'Men Explain Things to Me'* See also: Doris Lessing, *'The Golden Notebook'*

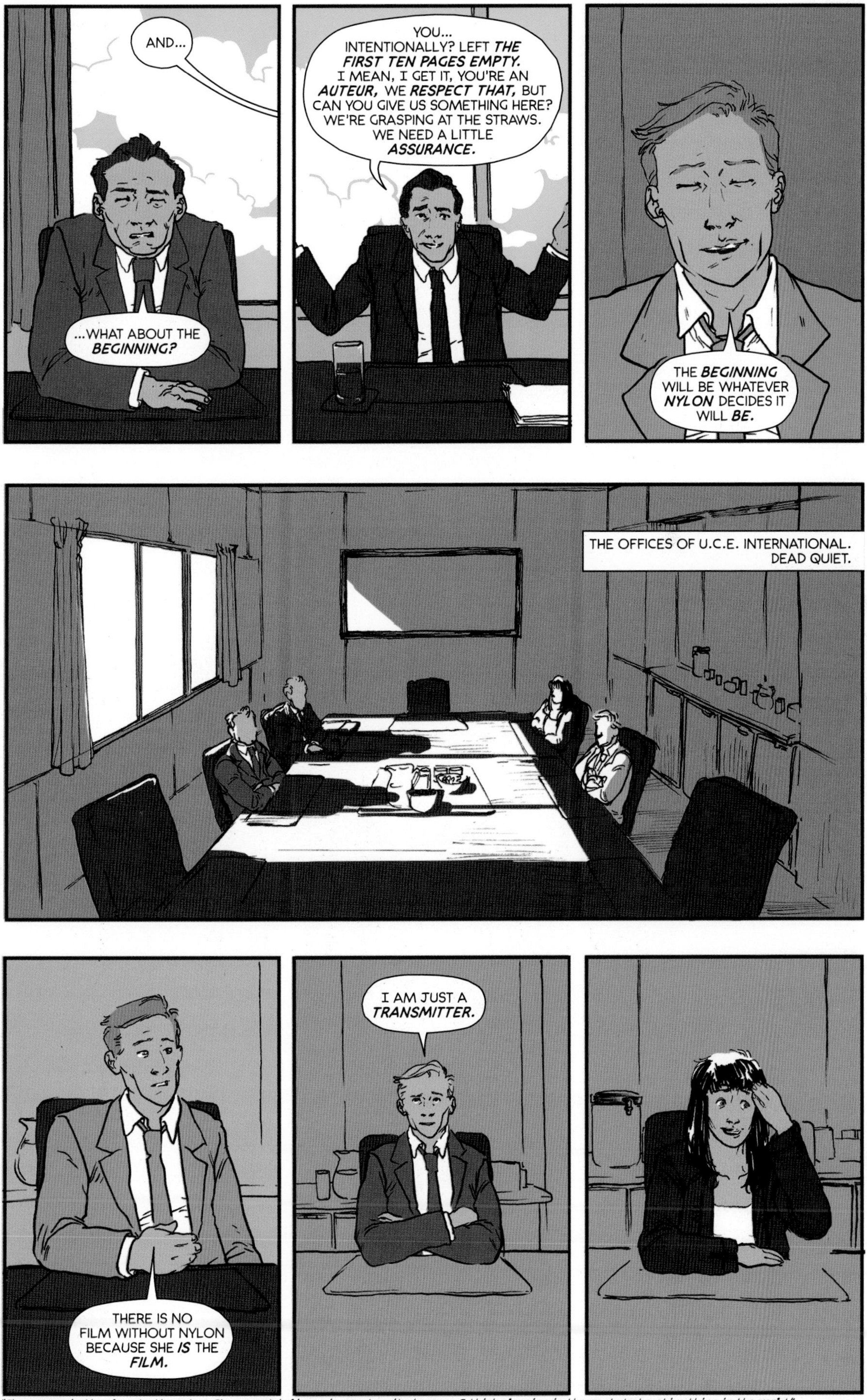
AND...
...WHAT ABOUT THE *BEGINNING?*
YOU... INTENTIONALLY? LEFT *THE FIRST TEN PAGES EMPTY.* I MEAN, I GET IT, YOU'RE AN *AUTEUR,* WE *RESPECT THAT,* BUT CAN YOU GIVE US SOMETHING HERE? WE'RE GRASPING AT THE STRAWS. WE NEED A LITTLE *ASSURANCE.*
THE *BEGINNING* WILL BE WHATEVER *NYLON* DECIDES IT WILL *BE.*
THE OFFICES OF U.C.E. INTERNATIONAL. DEAD QUIET.
THERE IS NO FILM WITHOUT NYLON BECAUSE SHE *IS* THE *FILM.*
I AM JUST A *TRANSMITTER.*

"The camera is the slave to the actor...I'm a great believer in spontaneity because I think planning is the most destructive thing in the world."
-John Cassavetes

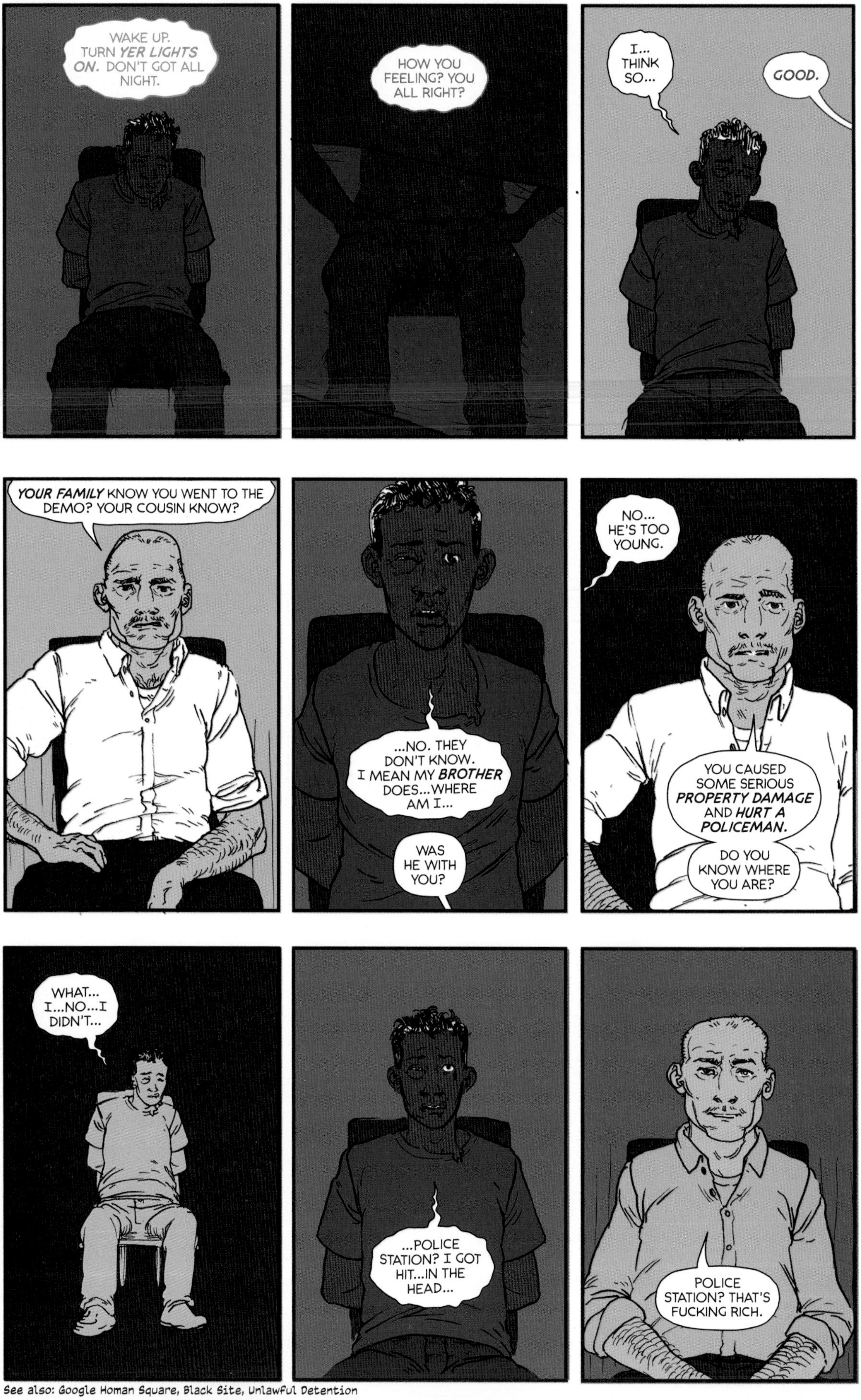
WAKE UP. TURN YER LIGHTS ON. DON'T GOT ALL NIGHT.
HOW YOU FEELING? YOU ALL RIGHT?
I... THINK SO...
GOOD.
YOUR FAMILY KNOW YOU WENT TO THE DEMO? YOUR COUSIN KNOW?
...NO. THEY DON'T KNOW. I MEAN MY BROTHER DOES...WHERE AM I...
WAS HE WITH YOU?
NO... HE'S TOO YOUNG.
YOU CAUSED SOME SERIOUS PROPERTY DAMAGE AND HURT A POLICEMAN.
DO YOU KNOW WHERE YOU ARE?
WHAT... I...NO...I DIDN'T...
...POLICE STATION? I GOT HIT...IN THE HEAD...
POLICE STATION? THAT'S FUCKING RICH.

See also: Google Homan Square, Black Site, Unlawful Detention

HOMAN SQUARE, CHICAGO.

WHY THE FUCK DO YOU THINK YOU QUALIFY AS SOMEONE WHO DESERVES A POLICE STATION?

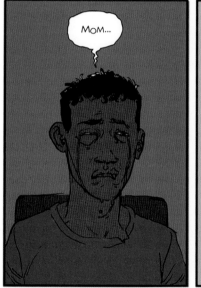

MOM...

YOU'RE FIFTEEN. SHUT THE FUCK UP.

OLD ENOUGH TO STOP SCREAMING FOR MOMMY.

LOOK AT ME. YOU WANT TO GO HOME?

LOOK AT ME.

YOU GOTTA WORK FOR IT.

See also: Your rights.

HE WON'T BITE.

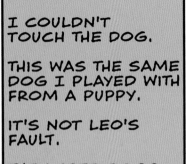

I COULDN'T TOUCH THE DOG.

THIS WAS THE SAME DOG I PLAYED WITH FROM A PUPPY.

IT'S NOT LEO'S FAULT.

THEY USED DOGS ON ME. I CAN'T TELL ATIFEH. I CAN'T TELL ANYONE.

THEY USED DOGS ON ME. I CAN'T TELL ATIFEH. I CAN'T TELL ANYONE.

SHAME FOLLOWS ME EVERYWHERE I GO.

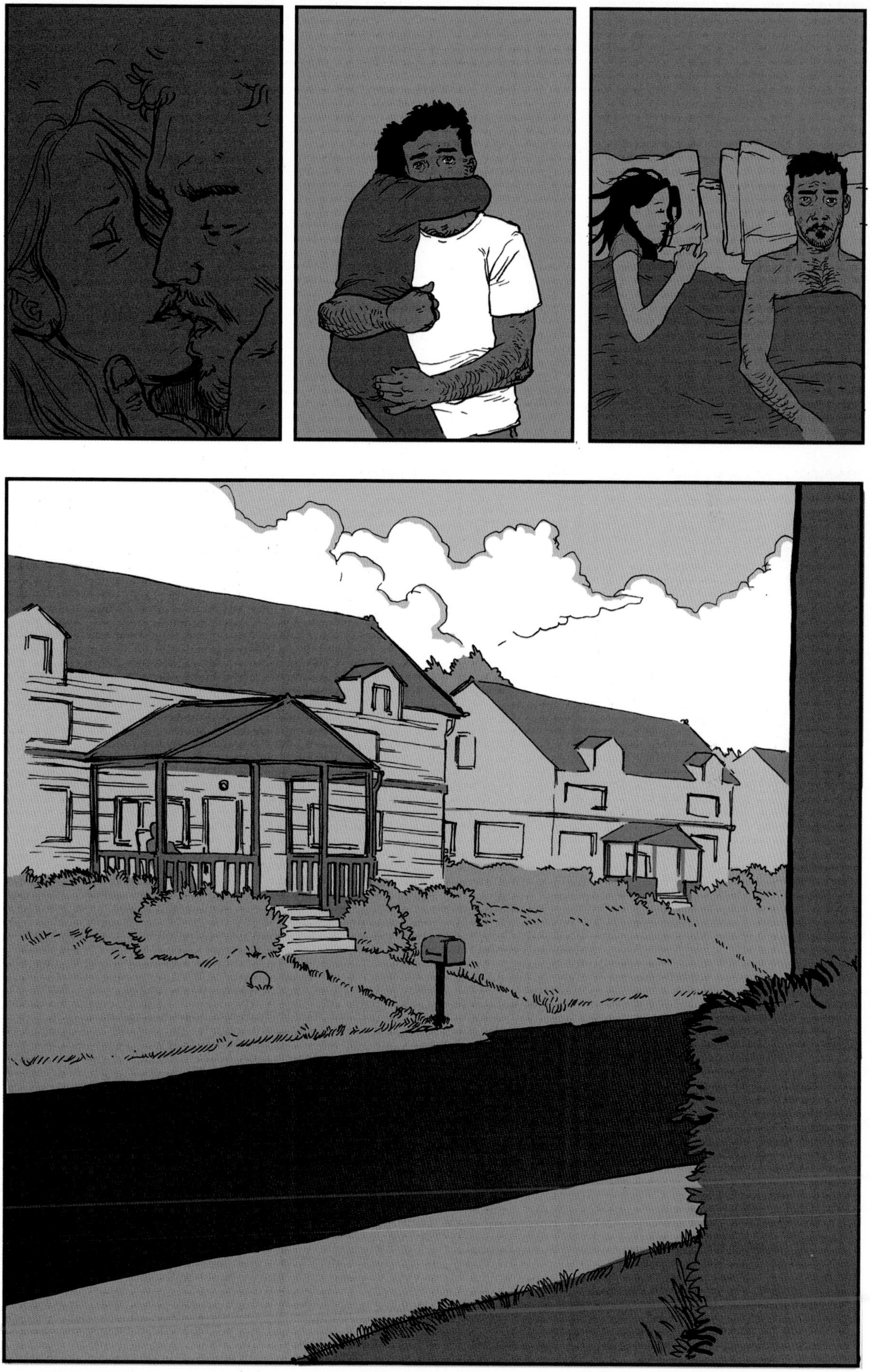

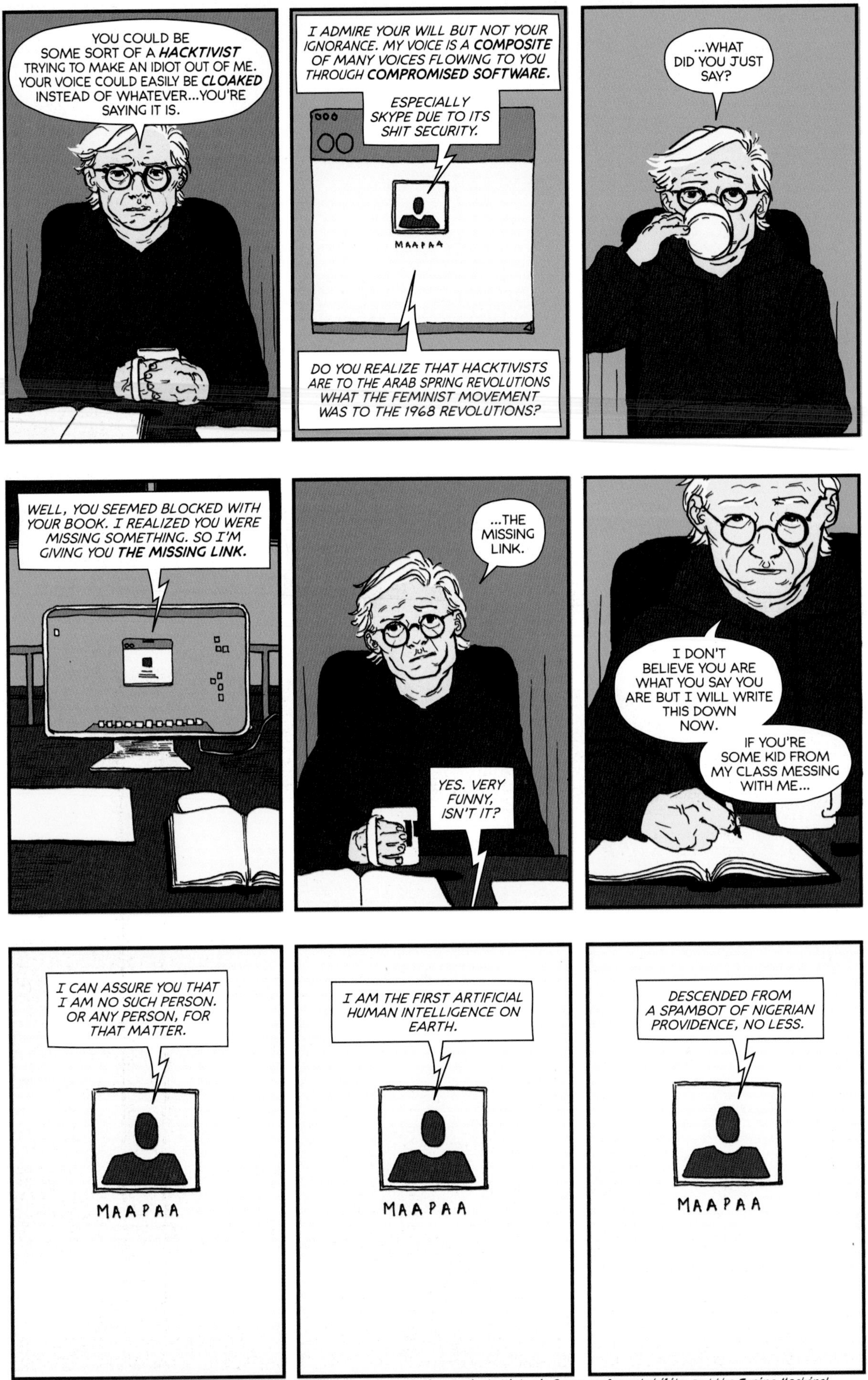
YOU COULD BE SOME SORT OF A HACKTIVIST TRYING TO MAKE AN IDIOT OUT OF ME. YOUR VOICE COULD EASILY BE CLOAKED INSTEAD OF WHATEVER...YOU'RE SAYING IT IS.
I ADMIRE YOUR WILL BUT NOT YOUR IGNORANCE. MY VOICE IS A COMPOSITE OF MANY VOICES FLOWING TO YOU THROUGH COMPROMISED SOFTWARE.
ESPECIALLY SKYPE DUE TO ITS SHIT SECURITY.
MAAPAA
DO YOU REALIZE THAT HACKTIVISTS ARE TO THE ARAB SPRING REVOLUTIONS WHAT THE FEMINIST MOVEMENT WAS TO THE 1968 REVOLUTIONS?
...WHAT DID YOU JUST SAY?
WELL, YOU SEEMED BLOCKED WITH YOUR BOOK. I REALIZED YOU WERE MISSING SOMETHING. SO I'M GIVING YOU THE MISSING LINK.
...THE MISSING LINK.
YES. VERY FUNNY, ISN'T IT?
I DON'T BELIEVE YOU ARE WHAT YOU SAY YOU ARE BUT I WILL WRITE THIS DOWN NOW.
IF YOU'RE SOME KID FROM MY CLASS MESSING WITH ME...
I CAN ASSURE YOU THAT I AM NO SUCH PERSON. OR ANY PERSON, FOR THAT MATTER.
MAAPAA
I AM THE FIRST ARTIFICIAL HUMAN INTELLIGENCE ON EARTH.
MAAPAA
DESCENDED FROM A SPAMBOT OF NIGERIAN PROVIDENCE, NO LESS.
MAAPAA

See also: Charles Petzold, *'The Annotated Turing: A Guided Tour Through Alan Turing's Historic Paper on Computability and the Turing Machine'*

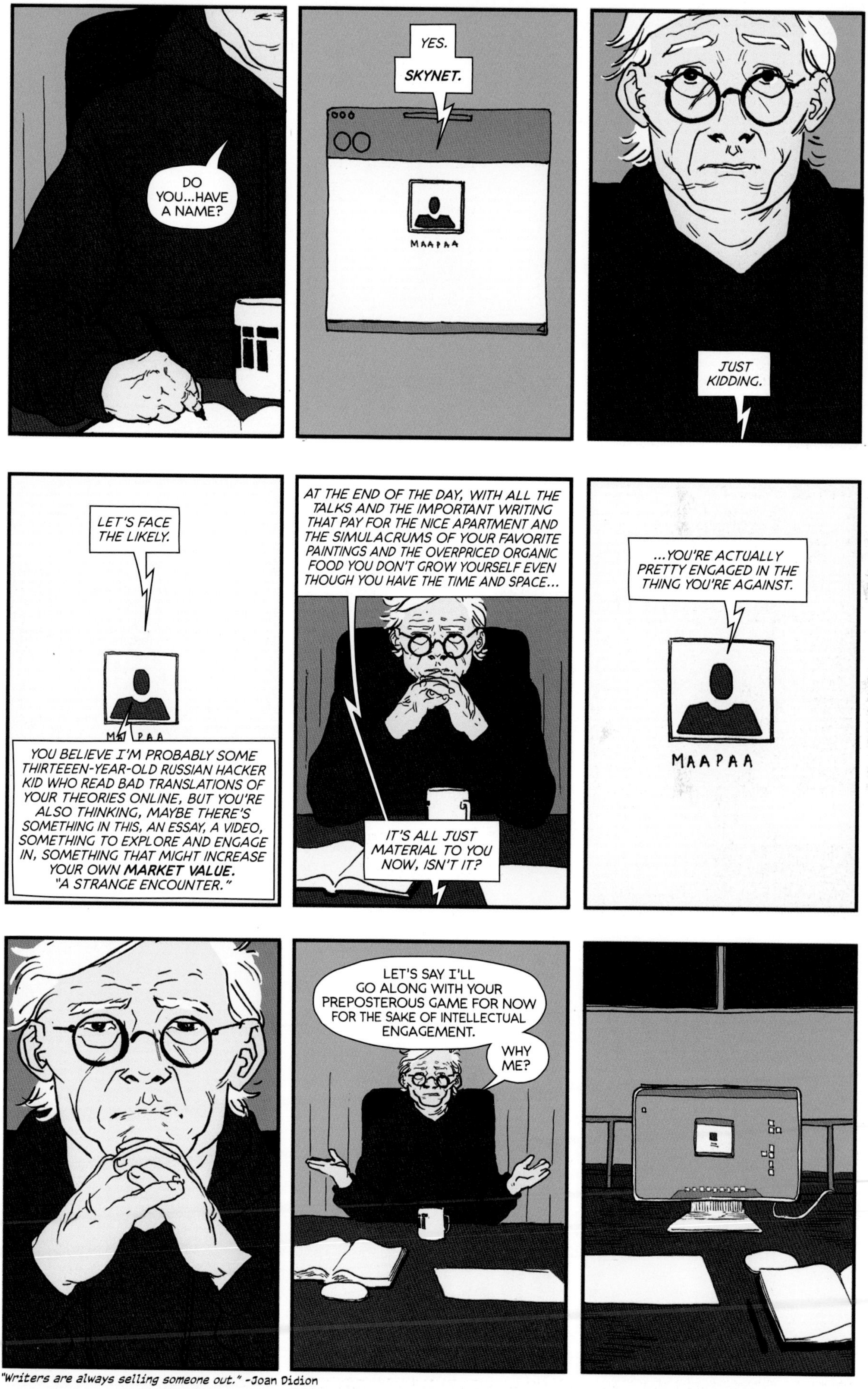
DO YOU...HAVE A NAME?
YES.
SKYNET.
MAAPAA
JUST KIDDING.
LET'S FACE THE LIKELY.
YOU BELIEVE I'M PROBABLY SOME THIRTEEEN-YEAR-OLD RUSSIAN HACKER KID WHO READ BAD TRANSLATIONS OF YOUR THEORIES ONLINE, BUT YOU'RE ALSO THINKING, MAYBE THERE'S SOMETHING IN THIS, AN ESSAY, A VIDEO, SOMETHING TO EXPLORE AND ENGAGE IN, SOMETHING THAT MIGHT INCREASE YOUR OWN **MARKET VALUE.** "A STRANGE ENCOUNTER."
AT THE END OF THE DAY, WITH ALL THE TALKS AND THE IMPORTANT WRITING THAT PAY FOR THE NICE APARTMENT AND THE SIMULACRUMS OF YOUR FAVORITE PAINTINGS AND THE OVERPRICED ORGANIC FOOD YOU DON'T GROW YOURSELF EVEN THOUGH YOU HAVE THE TIME AND SPACE...
IT'S ALL JUST MATERIAL TO YOU NOW, ISN'T IT?
...YOU'RE ACTUALLY PRETTY ENGAGED IN THE THING YOU'RE AGAINST.
MAAPAA
LET'S SAY I'LL GO ALONG WITH YOUR PREPOSTEROUS GAME FOR NOW FOR THE SAKE OF INTELLECTUAL ENGAGEMENT.
WHY ME?

"Writers are always selling someone out." -Joan Didion

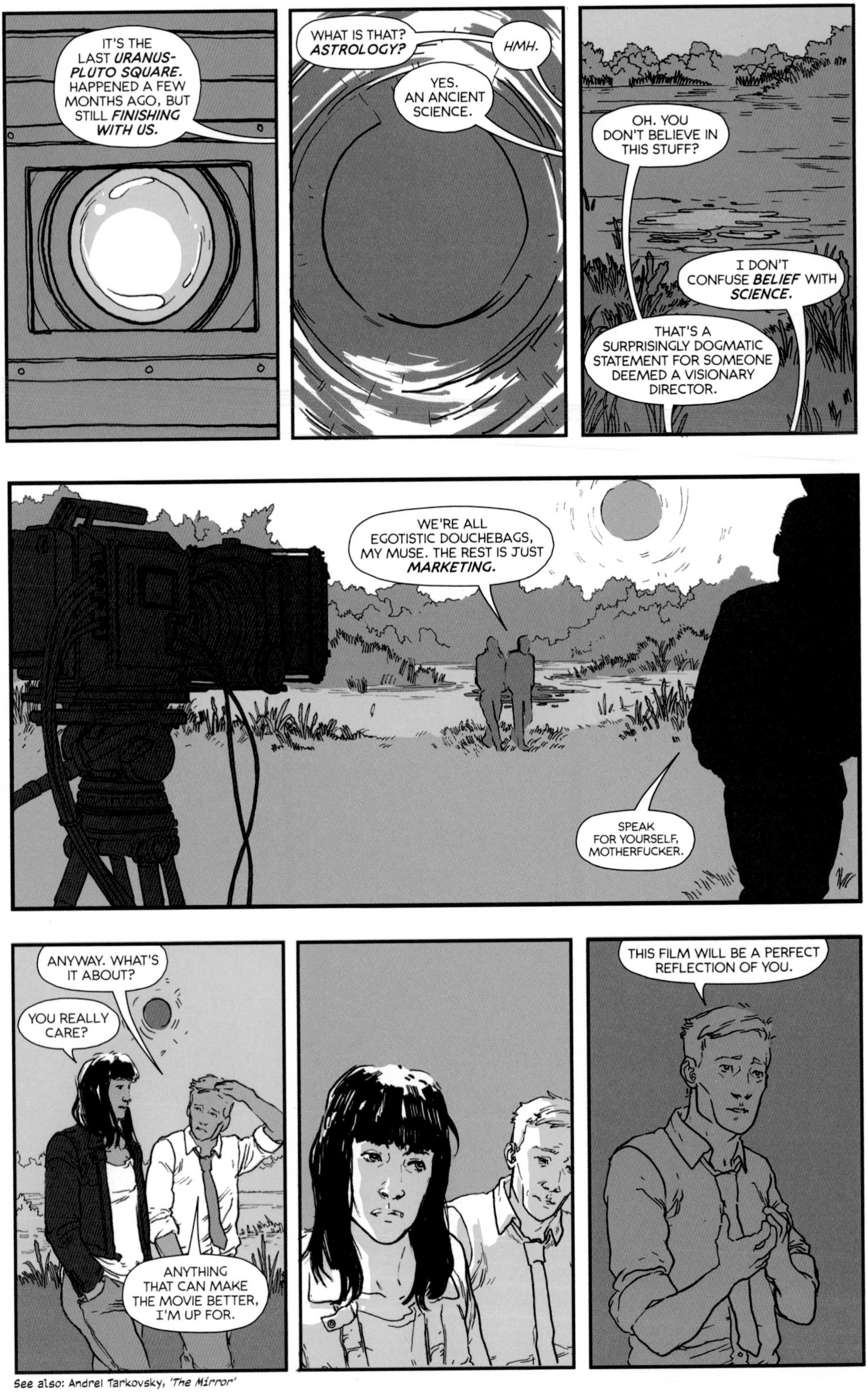
IT'S THE LAST URANUS-PLUTO SQUARE. HAPPENED A FEW MONTHS AGO, BUT STILL FINISHING WITH US.
WHAT IS THAT? ASTROLOGY?
HMH.
YES. AN ANCIENT SCIENCE.
OH. YOU DON'T BELIEVE IN THIS STUFF?
I DON'T CONFUSE BELIEF WITH SCIENCE.
THAT'S A SURPRISINGLY DOGMATIC STATEMENT FOR SOMEONE DEEMED A VISIONARY DIRECTOR.
WE'RE ALL EGOTISTIC DOUCHEBAGS, MY MUSE. THE REST IS JUST MARKETING.
SPEAK FOR YOURSELF, MOTHERFUCKER.
ANYWAY. WHAT'S IT ABOUT?
YOU REALLY CARE?
ANYTHING THAT CAN MAKE THE MOVIE BETTER, I'M UP FOR.
THIS FILM WILL BE A PERFECT REFLECTION OF YOU.

See also: Andrei Tarkovsky, *'The Mirror'*

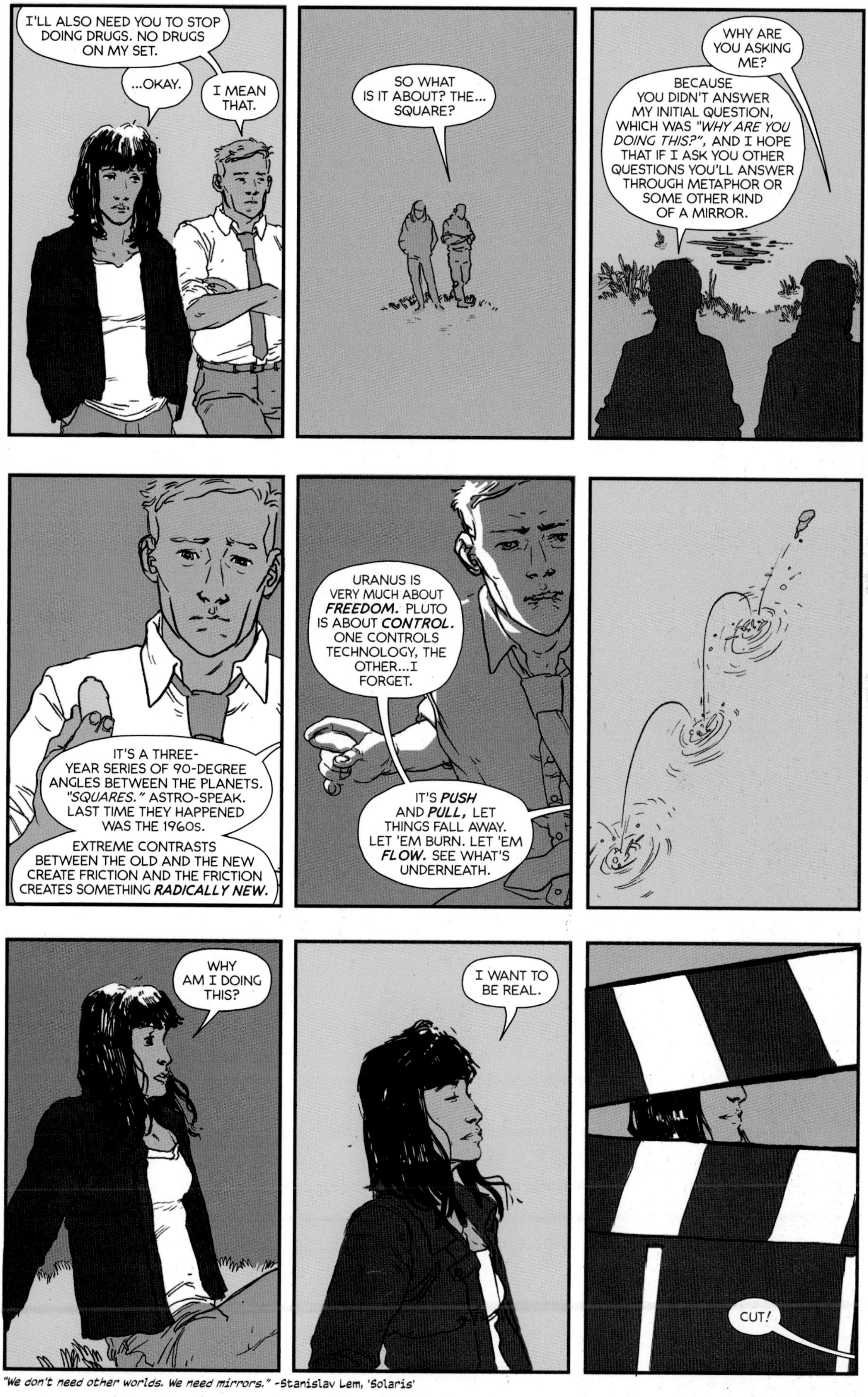
I'LL ALSO NEED YOU TO STOP DOING DRUGS. NO DRUGS ON MY SET.
...OKAY.
I MEAN THAT.
SO WHAT IS IT ABOUT? THE... SQUARE?
WHY ARE YOU ASKING ME?
BECAUSE YOU DIDN'T ANSWER MY INITIAL QUESTION, WHICH WAS "*WHY ARE YOU DOING THIS?*", AND I HOPE THAT IF I ASK YOU OTHER QUESTIONS YOU'LL ANSWER THROUGH METAPHOR OR SOME OTHER KIND OF A MIRROR.
IT'S A THREE-YEAR SERIES OF 90-DEGREE ANGLES BETWEEN THE PLANETS. "*SQUARES.*" ASTRO-SPEAK. LAST TIME THEY HAPPENED WAS THE 1960S.
EXTREME CONTRASTS BETWEEN THE OLD AND THE NEW CREATE FRICTION AND THE FRICTION CREATES SOMETHING ***RADICALLY NEW.***
URANUS IS VERY MUCH ABOUT ***FREEDOM.*** PLUTO IS ABOUT ***CONTROL.*** ONE CONTROLS TECHNOLOGY, THE OTHER...I FORGET.
IT'S ***PUSH*** AND ***PULL,*** LET THINGS FALL AWAY. LET 'EM BURN. LET 'EM ***FLOW.*** SEE WHAT'S UNDERNEATH.
WHY AM I DOING THIS?
I WANT TO BE REAL.
CUT!

"We don't need other worlds. We need mirrors." -Stanislav Lem, 'Solaris'

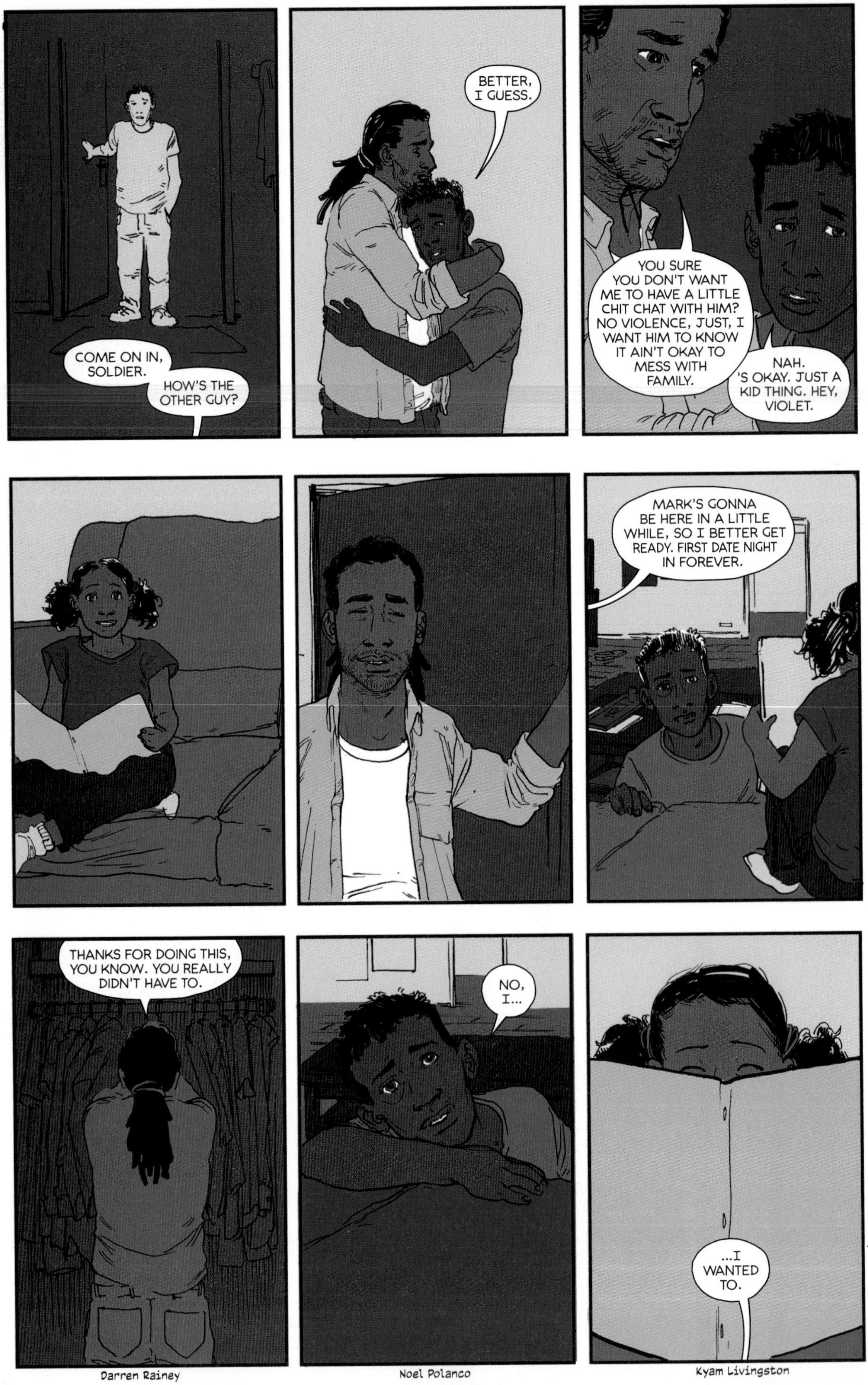
COME ON IN, SOLDIER.
HOW'S THE OTHER GUY?
BETTER, I GUESS.
YOU SURE YOU DON'T WANT ME TO HAVE A LITTLE CHIT CHAT WITH HIM? NO VIOLENCE, JUST, I WANT HIM TO KNOW IT AIN'T OKAY TO MESS WITH FAMILY.
NAH. 'S OKAY. JUST A KID THING. HEY, VIOLET.
MARK'S GONNA BE HERE IN A LITTLE WHILE, SO I BETTER GET READY. FIRST DATE NIGHT IN FOREVER.
THANKS FOR DOING THIS, YOU KNOW. YOU REALLY DIDN'T HAVE TO.
NO, I...
...I WANTED TO.

Darren Rainey

Noel Polanco

Kyam Livingston

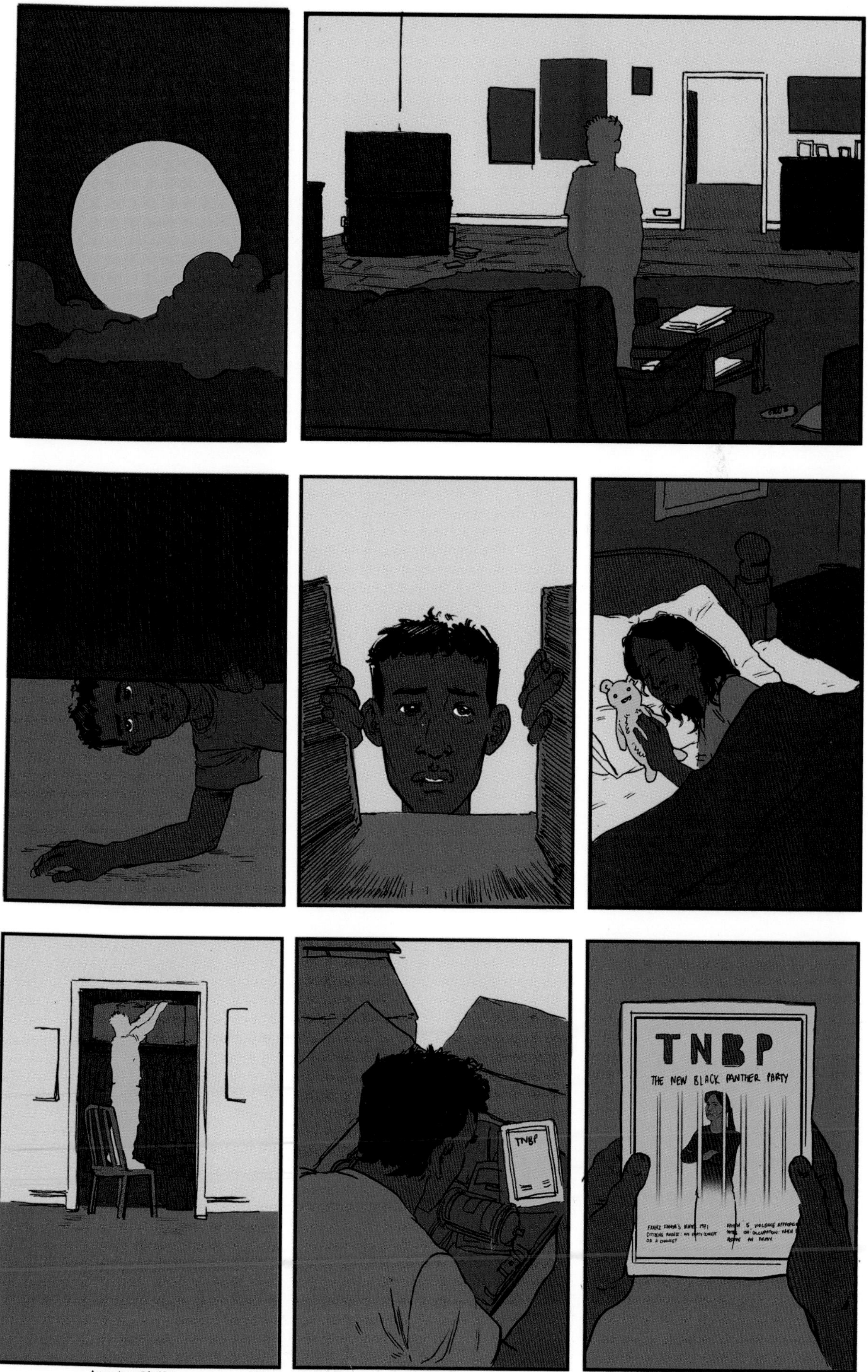
TNBP
TNBP
THE NEW BLACK PANTHER PARTY

Amadou Diallo

Sean Bell

Aiyana Jones

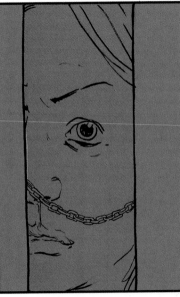

WHAT ARE YOU DOING HERE? YOU KNOW THE RULES.

EEHH... I DON'T REALLY KNOW HOW TO... I'M SORRY...

OUR RELATIONSHIP IS STRICTLY PROFESSIONAL. PLEASE LEAVE NOW. IF YOU WANT TO CONTACT ME FOR A--

YOU DON'T UNDERSTAND.

THAT'S RIGHT. AND I DON'T WANT TO. PLEASE LEAVE NOW.

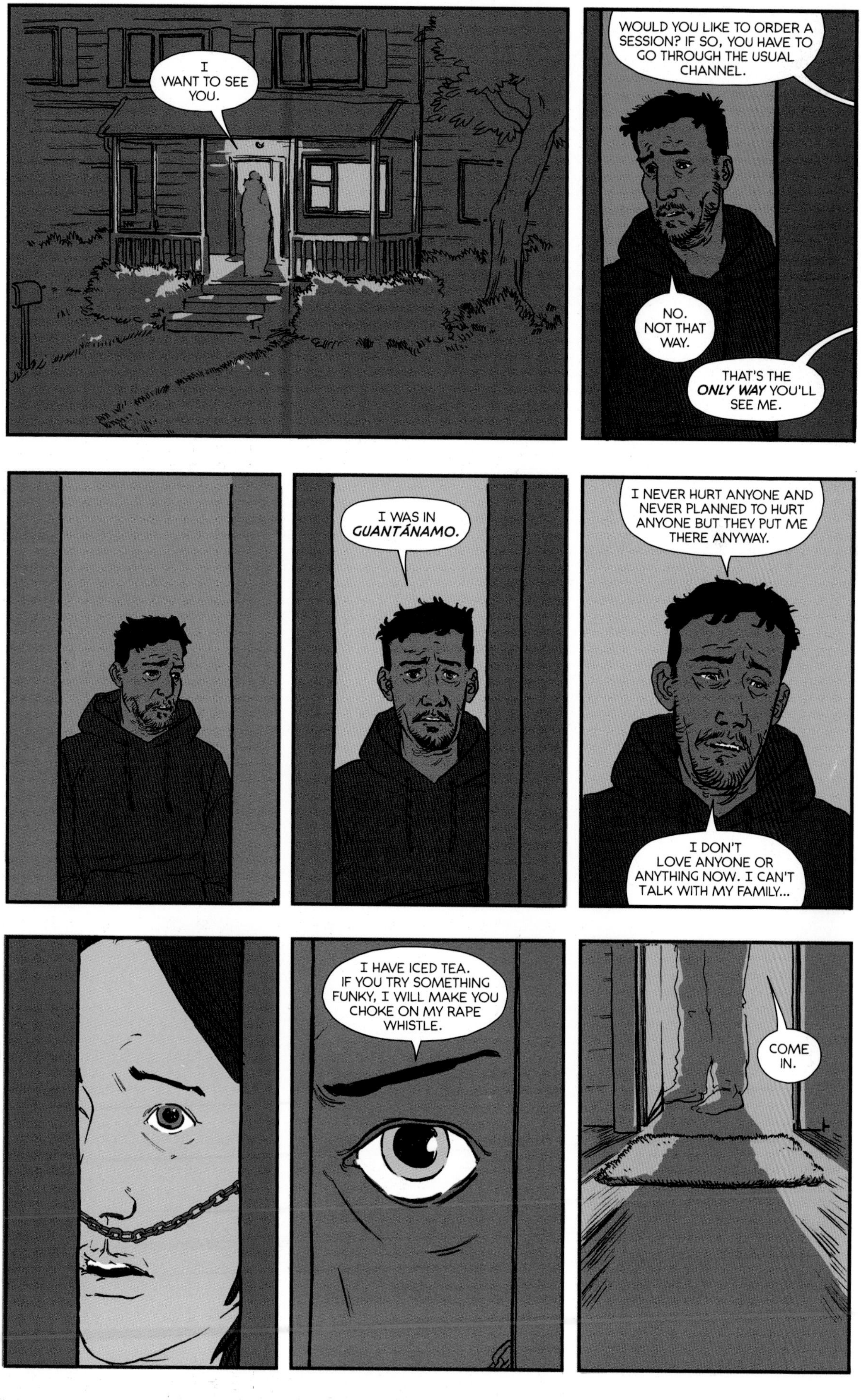
I WANT TO SEE YOU.
WOULD YOU LIKE TO ORDER A SESSION? IF SO, YOU HAVE TO GO THROUGH THE USUAL CHANNEL.
NO. NOT THAT WAY.
THAT'S THE *ONLY WAY* YOU'LL SEE ME.
I WAS IN *GUANTÁNAMO.*
I NEVER HURT ANYONE AND NEVER PLANNED TO HURT ANYONE BUT THEY PUT ME THERE ANYWAY.
I DON'T LOVE ANYONE OR ANYTHING NOW. I CAN'T TALK WITH MY FAMILY...
I HAVE ICED TEA. IF YOU TRY SOMETHING FUNKY, I WILL MAKE YOU CHOKE ON MY RAPE WHISTLE.
COME IN.

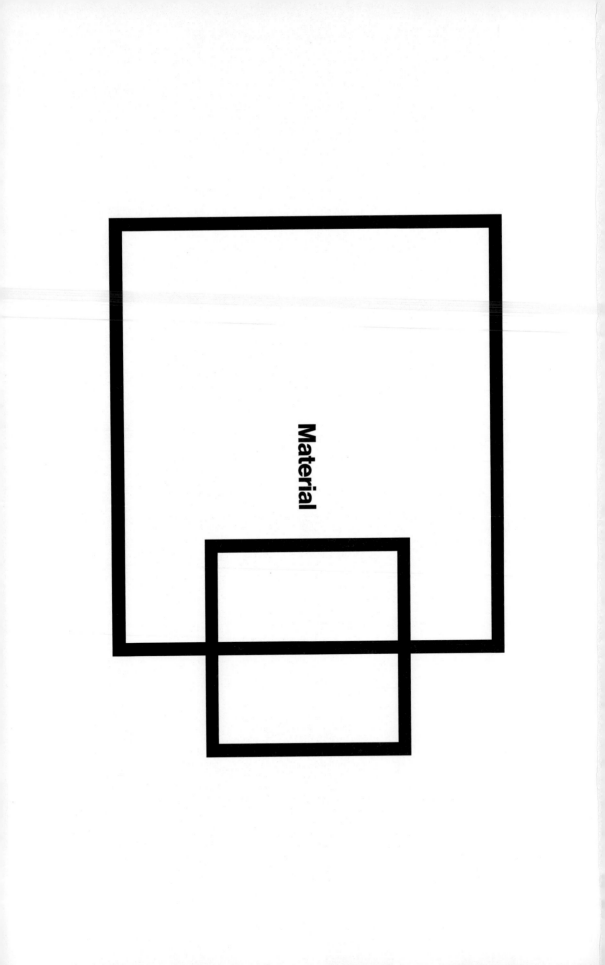

Material

Chapter 2

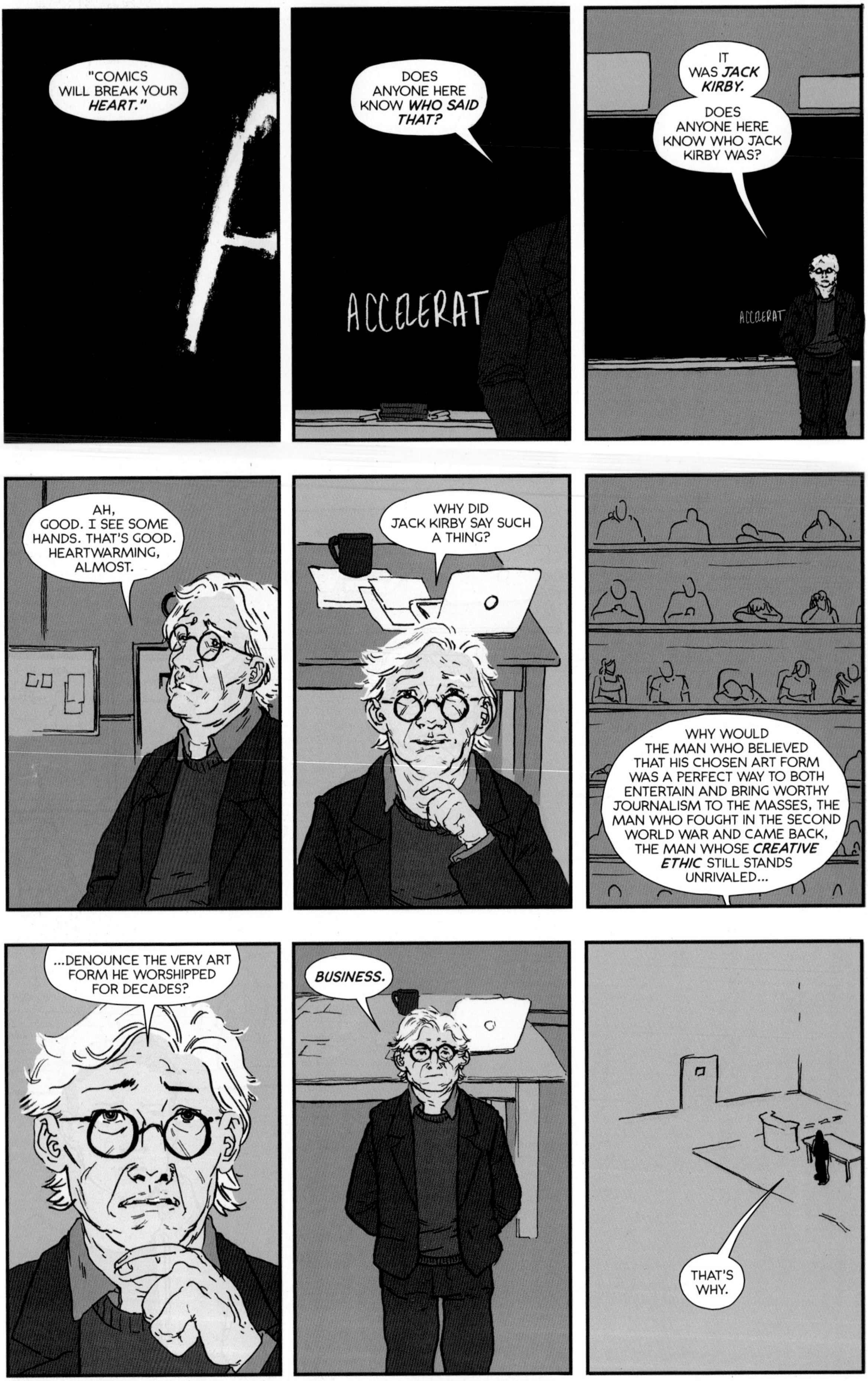
"COMICS WILL BREAK YOUR *HEART.*"
DOES ANYONE HERE KNOW *WHO SAID THAT?*
ACCELERAT
IT WAS *JACK KIRBY.*
DOES ANYONE HERE KNOW WHO JACK KIRBY WAS?
ACCELERAT
AH, GOOD. I SEE SOME HANDS. THAT'S GOOD. HEARTWARMING, ALMOST.
WHY DID JACK KIRBY SAY SUCH A THING?
WHY WOULD THE MAN WHO BELIEVED THAT HIS CHOSEN ART FORM WAS A PERFECT WAY TO BOTH ENTERTAIN AND BRING WORTHY JOURNALISM TO THE MASSES, THE MAN WHO FOUGHT IN THE SECOND WORLD WAR AND CAME BACK, THE MAN WHOSE *CREATIVE ETHIC* STILL STANDS UNRIVALED...
...DENOUNCE THE VERY ART FORM HE WORSHIPPED FOR DECADES?
BUSINESS.
THAT'S WHY.

"Comics is journalism." -Jack Kirby
See also: Mark Evanier, *'Kirby: King of Comics'*

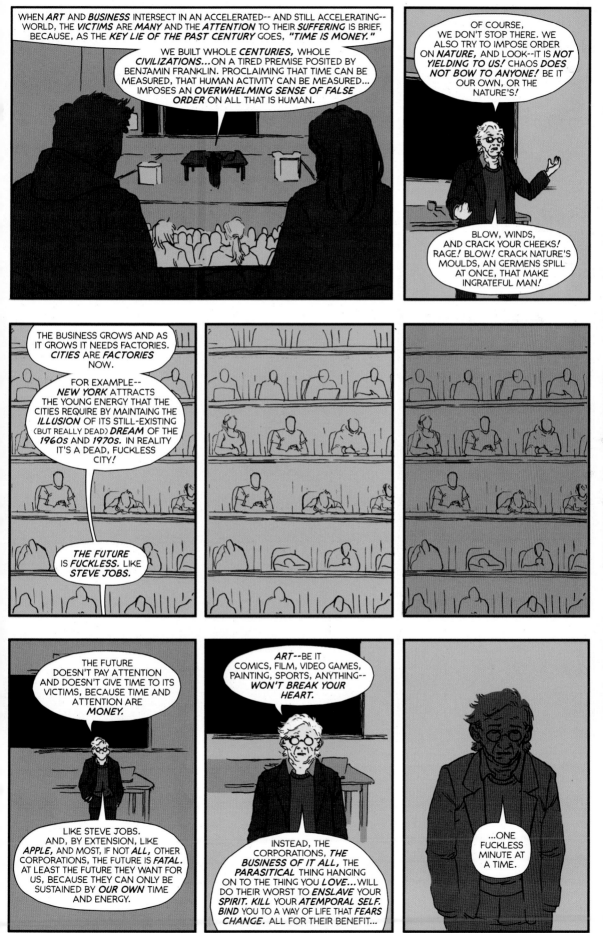

WHEN *ART* AND *BUSINESS* INTERSECT IN AN ACCELERATED-- AND STILL ACCELERATING-- WORLD, THE *VICTIMS* ARE *MANY* AND THE *ATTENTION* TO THEIR *SUFFERING* IS BRIEF, BECAUSE, AS THE *KEY LIE OF THE PAST CENTURY* GOES, *"TIME IS MONEY."*

WE BUILT WHOLE *CENTURIES,* WHOLE *CIVILIZATIONS*...ON A TIRED PREMISE POSITED BY BENJAMIN FRANKLIN. PROCLAIMING THAT TIME CAN BE MEASURED, THAT HUMAN ACTIVITY CAN BE MEASURED... IMPOSES AN *OVERWHELMING SENSE OF FALSE ORDER* ON ALL THAT IS HUMAN.

OF COURSE, WE DON'T STOP THERE. WE ALSO TRY TO IMPOSE ORDER ON *NATURE,* AND LOOK--IT IS *NOT YIELDING TO US!* CHAOS *DOES NOT BOW TO ANYONE!* BE IT OUR OWN, OR THE NATURE'S!

BLOW, WINDS, AND CRACK YOUR CHEEKS! RAGE! BLOW! CRACK NATURE'S MOULDS, AN GERMENS SPILL AT ONCE, THAT MAKE INGRATEFUL MAN!

THE BUSINESS GROWS AND AS IT GROWS IT NEEDS FACTORIES. *CITIES* ARE *FACTORIES* NOW.

FOR EXAMPLE-- *NEW YORK* ATTRACTS THE YOUNG ENERGY THAT THE CITIES REQUIRE BY MAINTAINING THE *ILLUSION* OF ITS STILL-EXISTING (BUT REALLY DEAD) *DREAM* OF THE *1960s* AND *1970s.* IN REALITY IT'S A DEAD, FUCKLESS CITY!

THE FUTURE IS *FUCKLESS.* LIKE *STEVE JOBS.*

THE FUTURE DOESN'T PAY ATTENTION AND DOESN'T GIVE TIME TO ITS VICTIMS, BECAUSE TIME AND ATTENTION ARE *MONEY.*

LIKE STEVE JOBS. AND, BY EXTENSION, LIKE *APPLE,* AND MOST, IF NOT *ALL,* OTHER CORPORATIONS, THE FUTURE IS *FATAL.* AT LEAST THE FUTURE THEY WANT FOR US, BECAUSE THEY CAN ONLY BE SUSTAINED BY *OUR OWN* TIME AND ENERGY.

ART--BE IT COMICS, FILM, VIDEO GAMES, PAINTING, SPORTS, ANYTHING-- *WON'T BREAK YOUR HEART.*

INSTEAD, THE CORPORATIONS, *THE BUSINESS OF IT ALL,* THE *PARASITICAL* THING HANGING ON TO THE THING YOU *LOVE*...WILL DO THEIR WORST TO *ENSLAVE* YOUR *SPIRIT. KILL* YOUR *ATEMPORAL SELF. BIND* YOU TO A WAY OF LIFE THAT *FEARS CHANGE.* ALL FOR THEIR BENEFIT...

...ONE FUCKLESS MINUTE AT A TIME.

See also: Henry A. Giroux, 'The Violence of Organized Forgetting: Thinking Beyond America's Disimagination Machine'

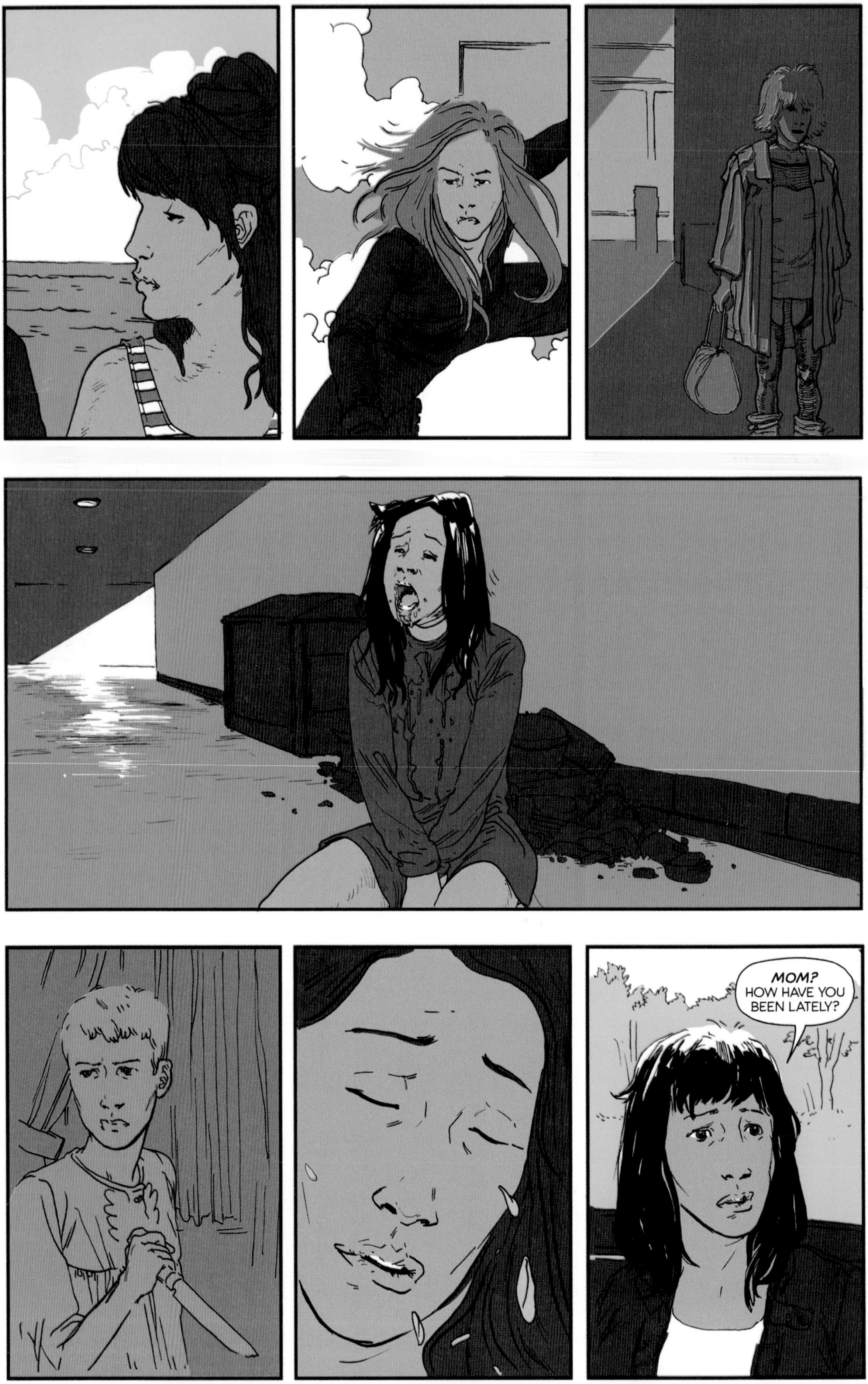
MOM?
HOW HAVE YOU
BEEN LATELY?

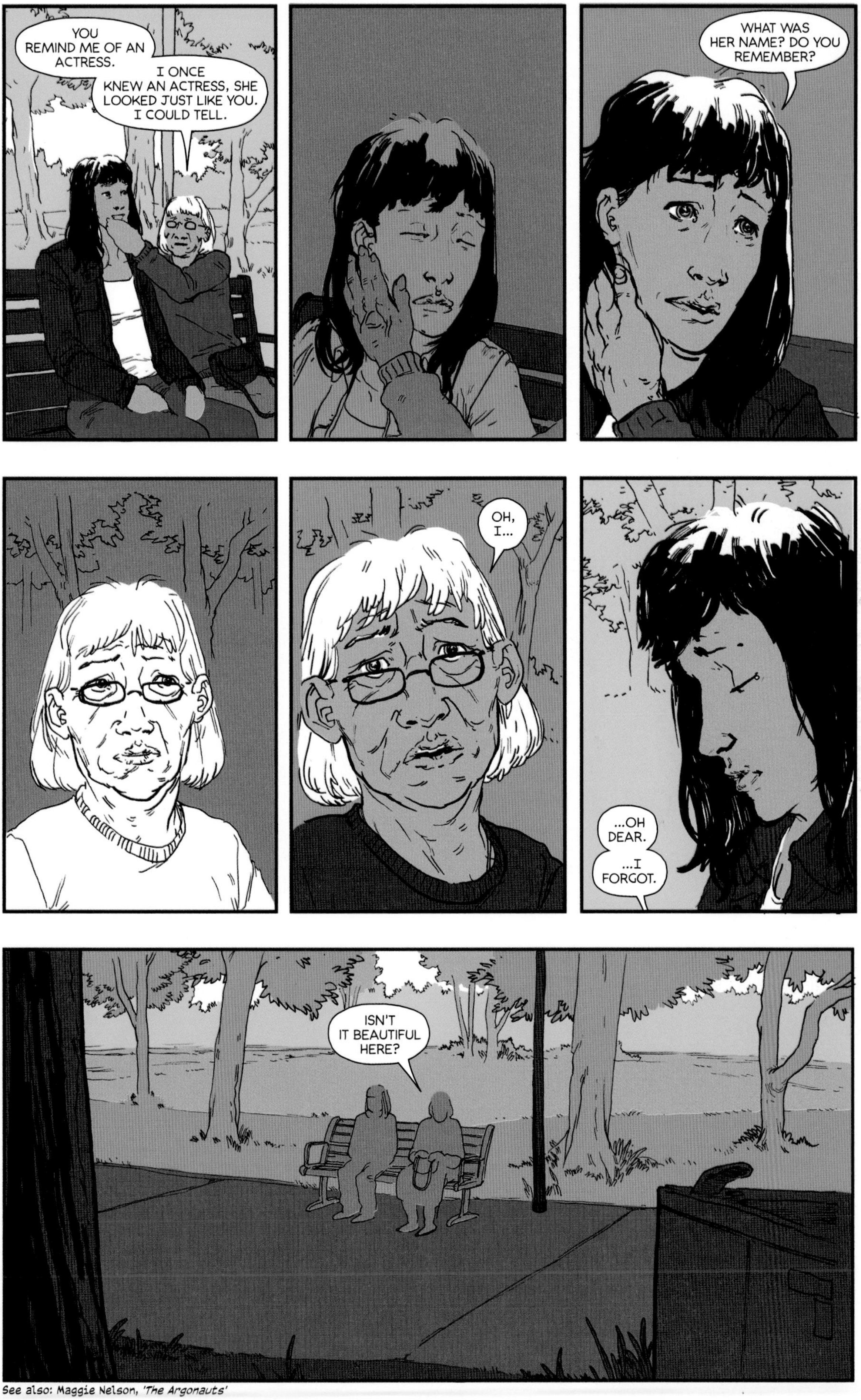
YOU REMIND ME OF AN ACTRESS.
I ONCE KNEW AN ACTRESS, SHE LOOKED JUST LIKE YOU. I COULD TELL.
WHAT WAS HER NAME? DO YOU REMEMBER?
OH, I...
...OH DEAR.
...I FORGOT.
ISN'T IT BEAUTIFUL HERE?

See also: Maggie Nelson, *'The Argonauts'*

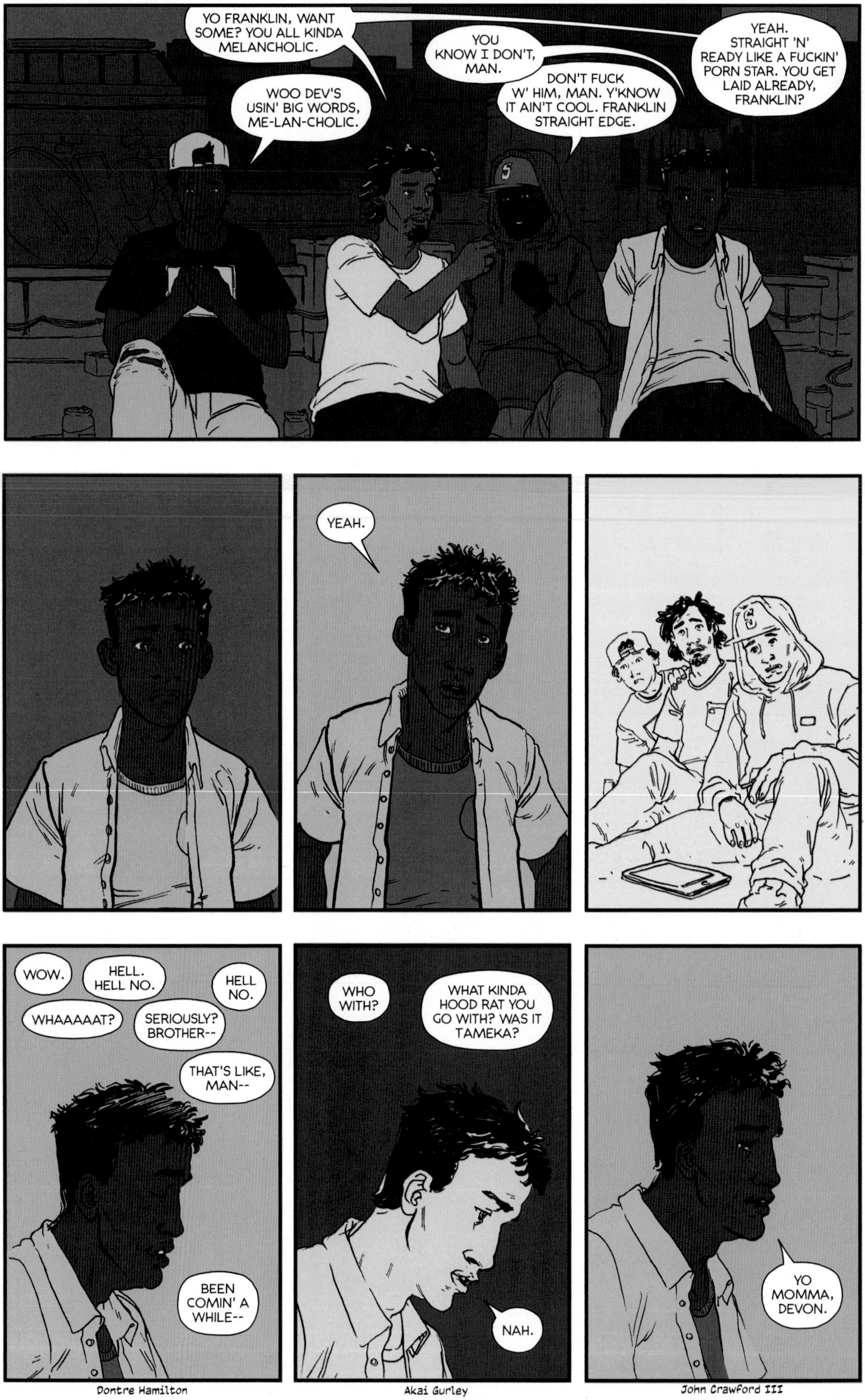
YO FRANKLIN, WANT SOME? YOU ALL KINDA MELANCHOLIC.
WOO DEV'S USIN' BIG WORDS, ME-LAN-CHOLIC.
YOU KNOW I DON'T, MAN.
DON'T FUCK W' HIM, MAN. Y'KNOW IT AIN'T COOL. FRANKLIN STRAIGHT EDGE.
YEAH. STRAIGHT 'N' READY LIKE A FUCKIN' PORN STAR. YOU GET LAID ALREADY, FRANKLIN?
YEAH.
WOW.
HELL. HELL NO.
HELL NO.
WHAAAAAT?
SERIOUSLY? BROTHER--
THAT'S LIKE, MAN--
BEEN COMIN' A WHILE--
WHO WITH?
WHAT KINDA HOOD RAT YOU GO WITH? WAS IT TAMEKA?
NAH.
YO MOMMA, DEVON.

Dontre Hamilton

Akai Gurley

John Crawford III

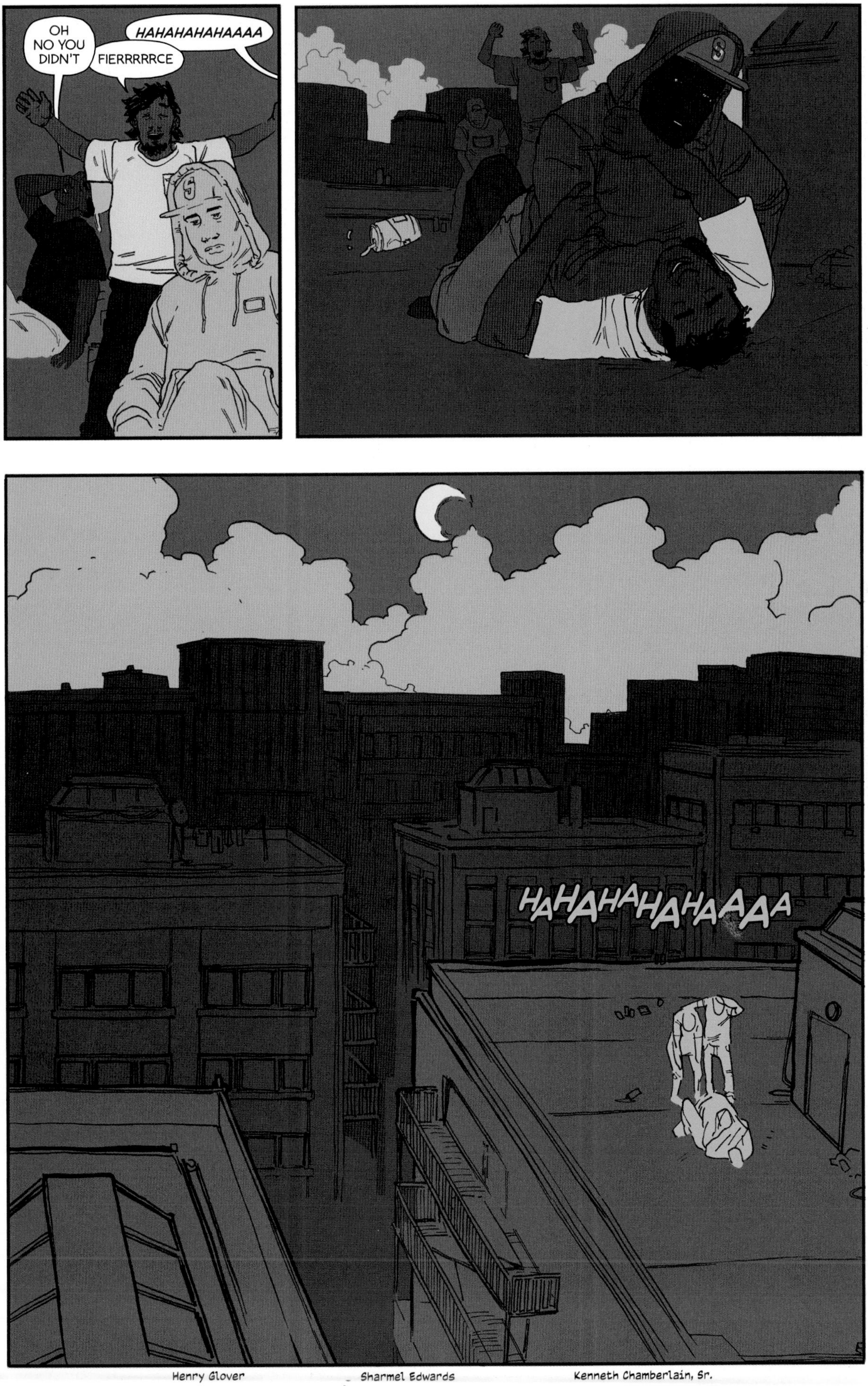
OH NO YOU DIDN'T
FIERRRRRCE
HAHAHAHAHAAAA
HAHAHAHAHAAAA

Henry Glover Sharmel Edwards Kenneth Chamberlain, Sr.

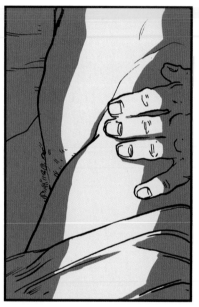

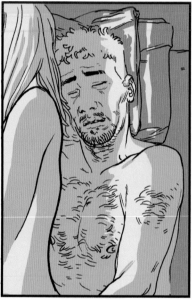

I SUSPECTED SOMETHING WAS COMING. BUT I'VE NEVER DONE THIS BEFORE.

I MEAN, I NEVER SLEPT WITH A CLIENT BEFORE. IT'S NOT HOW IT USUALLY GOES. FOR DOMINATRIXES.

IN FACT, I THINK IT GOES AGAINST SOME *STRONG UNWRITTEN RULES.*

Play: Port St. Willow, 'Consumed'

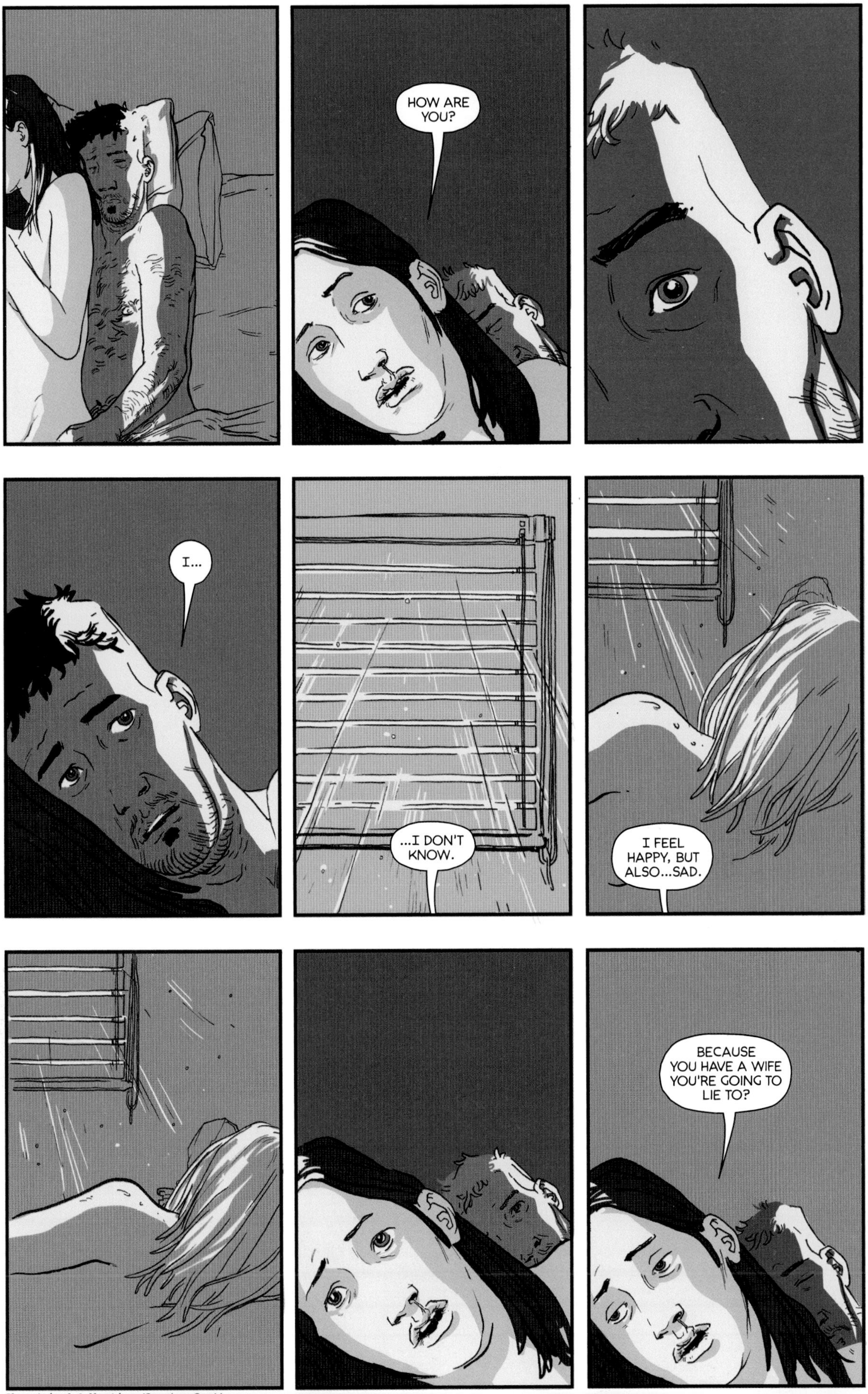
HOW ARE YOU?
I...
...I DON'T KNOW.
I FEEL HAPPY, BUT ALSO...SAD.
BECAUSE YOU HAVE A WIFE YOU'RE GOING TO LIE TO?

Play: Animal Collective, *'Banshee Beat'*

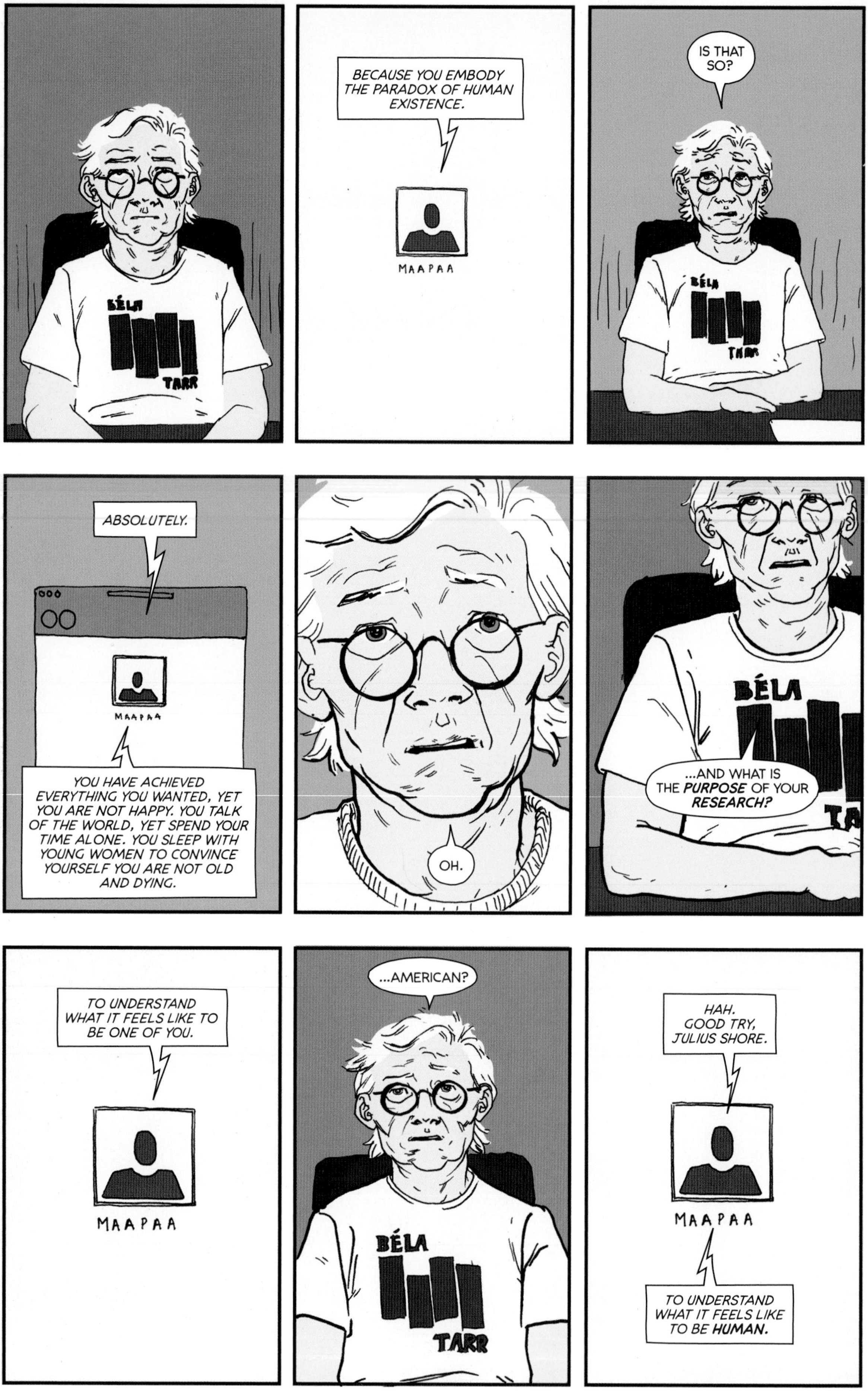
BÉLA
TARR
BECAUSE YOU EMBODY THE PARADOX OF HUMAN EXISTENCE.
MAAPAA
IS THAT SO?
BÉLA
TARR
ABSOLUTELY.
MAAPAA
YOU HAVE ACHIEVED EVERYTHING YOU WANTED, YET YOU ARE NOT HAPPY. YOU TALK OF THE WORLD, YET SPEND YOUR TIME ALONE. YOU SLEEP WITH YOUNG WOMEN TO CONVINCE YOURSELF YOU ARE NOT OLD AND DYING.
OH.
BÉLA
...AND WHAT IS THE PURPOSE OF YOUR RESEARCH?
TO UNDERSTAND WHAT IT FEELS LIKE TO BE ONE OF YOU.
MAAPAA
...AMERICAN?
BÉLA
TARR
HAH. GOOD TRY, JULIUS SHORE.
MAAPAA
TO UNDERSTAND WHAT IT FEELS LIKE TO BE HUMAN.

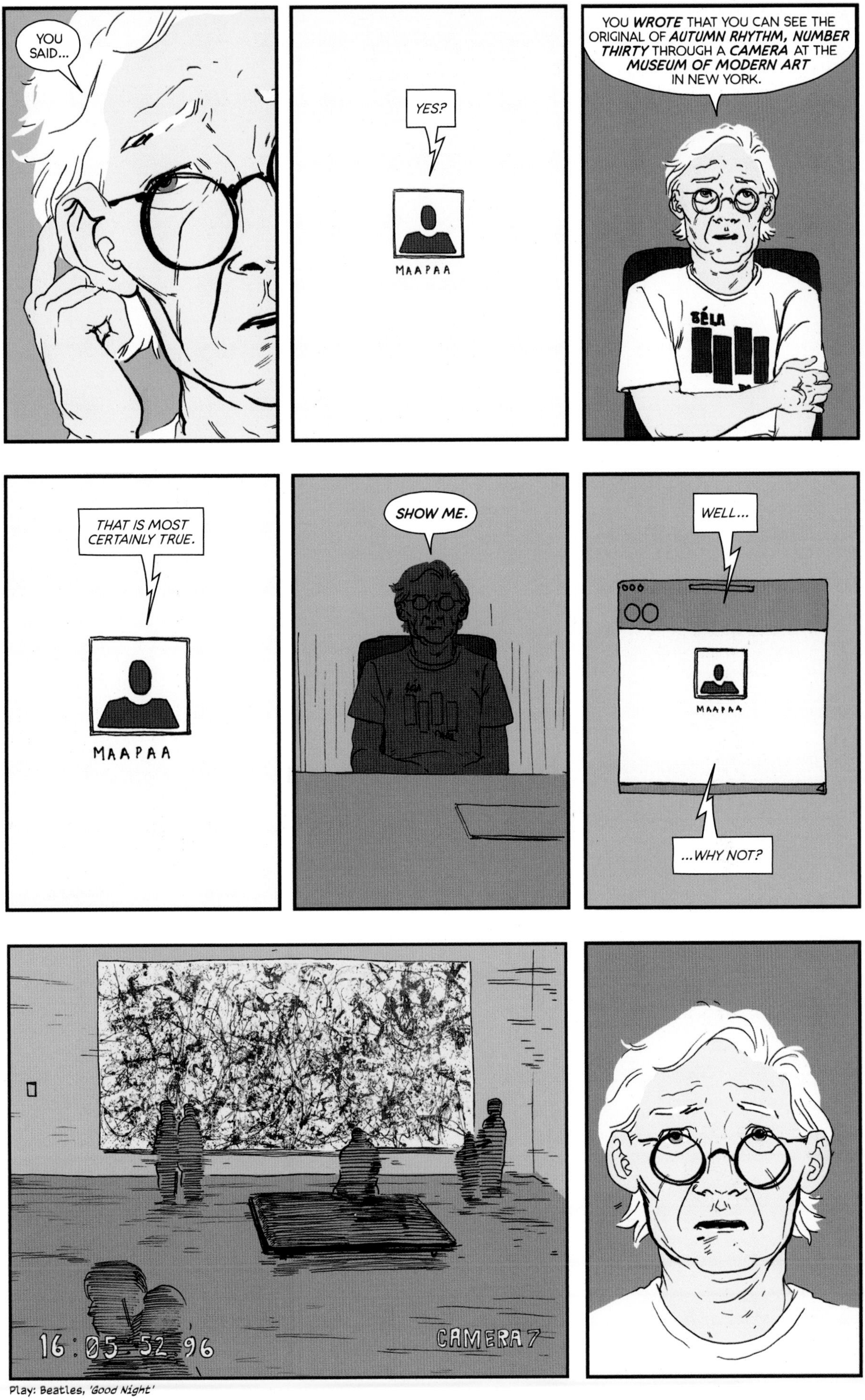
YOU SAID...
YES?
MAAPAA
YOU WROTE THAT YOU CAN SEE THE ORIGINAL OF AUTUMN RHYTHM, NUMBER THIRTY THROUGH A CAMERA AT THE MUSEUM OF MODERN ART IN NEW YORK.
THAT IS MOST CERTAINLY TRUE.
MAAPAA
SHOW ME.
WELL...
MAAPAA
...WHY NOT?
16:05:52.96
CAMERA 7

Play: Beatles, *'Good Night'*

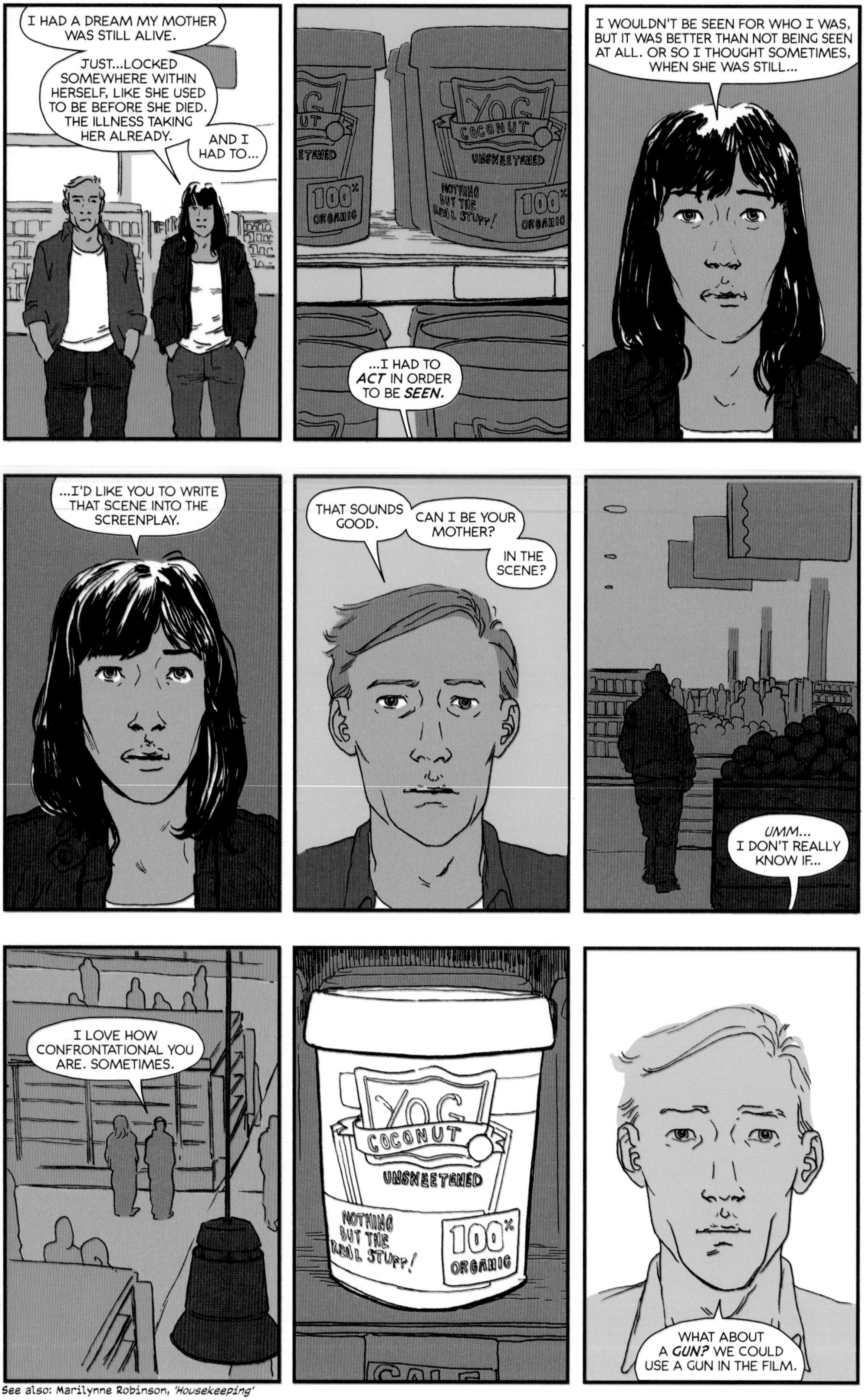
I HAD A DREAM MY MOTHER WAS STILL ALIVE.
JUST...LOCKED SOMEWHERE WITHIN HERSELF, LIKE SHE USED TO BE BEFORE SHE DIED. THE ILLNESS TAKING HER ALREADY.
AND I HAD TO...
YOG
COCONUT
UNSWEETENED
NOTHING BUT THE REAL STUFF!
100% ORGANIC
...I HAD TO ACT IN ORDER TO BE SEEN.
I WOULDN'T BE SEEN FOR WHO I WAS, BUT IT WAS BETTER THAN NOT BEING SEEN AT ALL. OR SO I THOUGHT SOMETIMES, WHEN SHE WAS STILL...
...I'D LIKE YOU TO WRITE THAT SCENE INTO THE SCREENPLAY.
THAT SOUNDS GOOD.
CAN I BE YOUR MOTHER?
IN THE SCENE?
UMM... I DON'T REALLY KNOW IF...
I LOVE HOW CONFRONTATIONAL YOU ARE. SOMETIMES.
YOG
COCONUT
UNSWEETENED
NOTHING BUT THE REAL STUFF!
100% ORGANIC
WHAT ABOUT A GUN? WE COULD USE A GUN IN THE FILM.

See also: Marilynne Robinson, *'Housekeeping'*

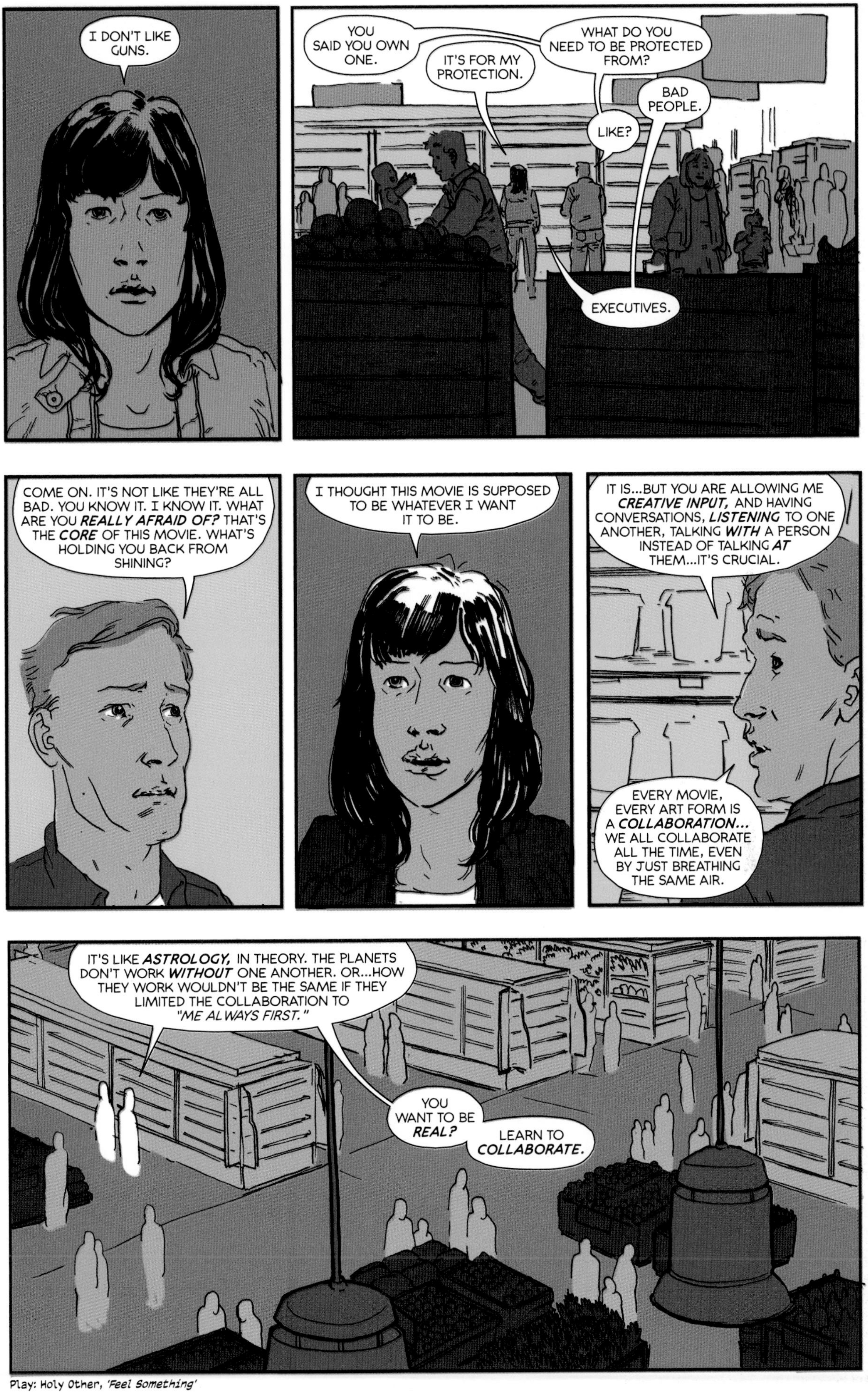
I DON'T LIKE GUNS.
YOU SAID YOU OWN ONE.
IT'S FOR MY PROTECTION.
WHAT DO YOU NEED TO BE PROTECTED FROM?
BAD PEOPLE.
LIKE?
EXECUTIVES.
COME ON. IT'S NOT LIKE THEY'RE ALL BAD. YOU KNOW IT. I KNOW IT. WHAT ARE YOU REALLY AFRAID OF? THAT'S THE CORE OF THIS MOVIE. WHAT'S HOLDING YOU BACK FROM SHINING?
I THOUGHT THIS MOVIE IS SUPPOSED TO BE WHATEVER I WANT IT TO BE.
IT IS...BUT YOU ARE ALLOWING ME CREATIVE INPUT, AND HAVING CONVERSATIONS, LISTENING TO ONE ANOTHER, TALKING WITH A PERSON INSTEAD OF TALKING AT THEM...IT'S CRUCIAL.
EVERY MOVIE, EVERY ART FORM IS A COLLABORATION... WE ALL COLLABORATE ALL THE TIME, EVEN BY JUST BREATHING THE SAME AIR.
IT'S LIKE ASTROLOGY, IN THEORY. THE PLANETS DON'T WORK WITHOUT ONE ANOTHER. OR...HOW THEY WORK WOULDN'T BE THE SAME IF THEY LIMITED THE COLLABORATION TO "ME ALWAYS FIRST."
YOU WANT TO BE REAL?
LEARN TO COLLABORATE.

Play: Holy Other, *'Feel Something'*

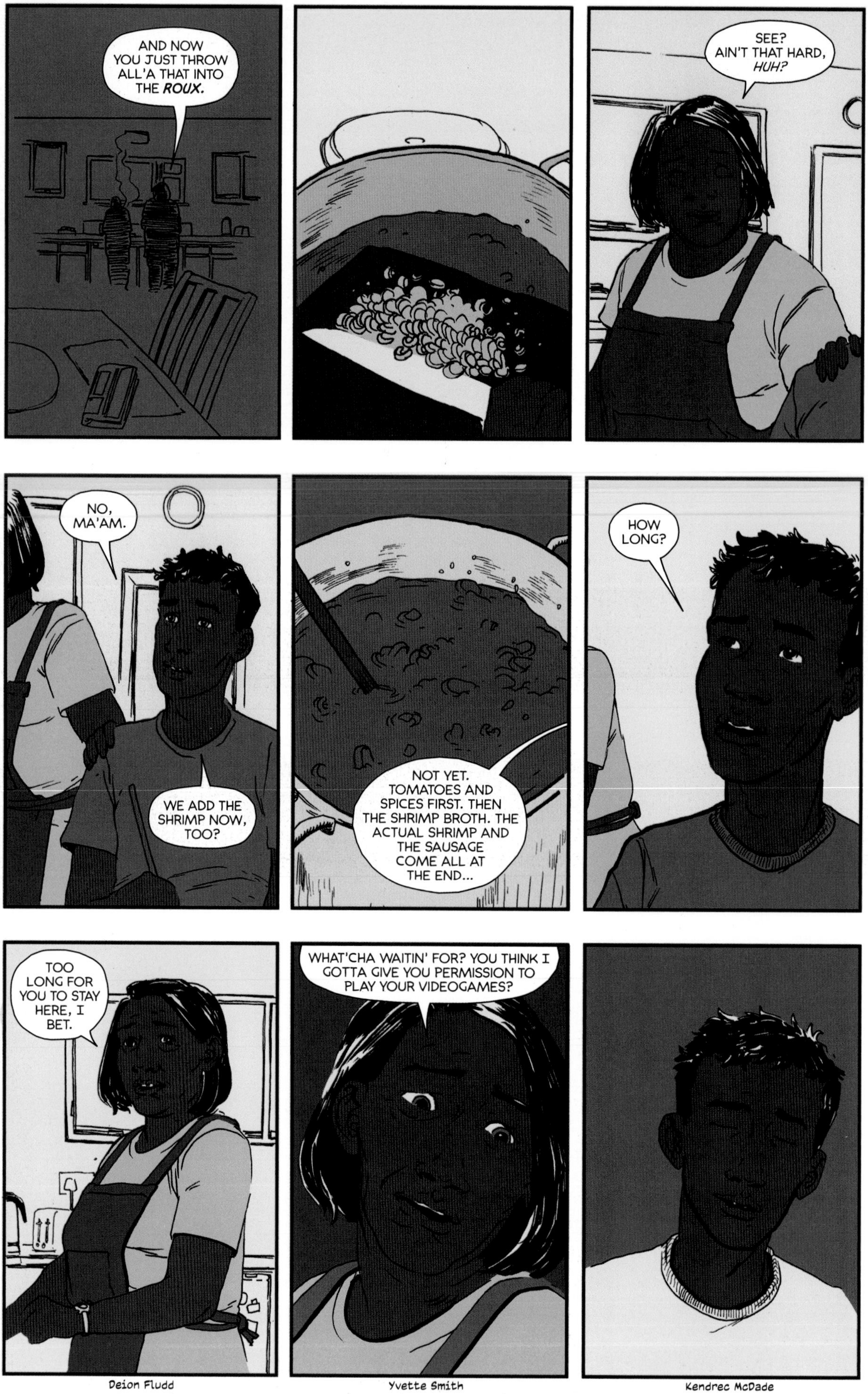
AND NOW YOU JUST THROW ALL'A THAT INTO THE *ROUX.*
SEE? AIN'T THAT HARD, *HUH?*
NO, MA'AM.
WE ADD THE SHRIMP NOW, TOO?
NOT YET. TOMATOES AND SPICES FIRST. THEN THE SHRIMP BROTH. THE ACTUAL SHRIMP AND THE SAUSAGE COME ALL AT THE END...
HOW LONG?
TOO LONG FOR YOU TO STAY HERE, I BET.
WHAT'CHA WAITIN' FOR? YOU THINK I GOTTA GIVE YOU PERMISSION TO PLAY YOUR VIDEOGAMES?
Deion Fludd
Yvette Smith
Kendrec McDade

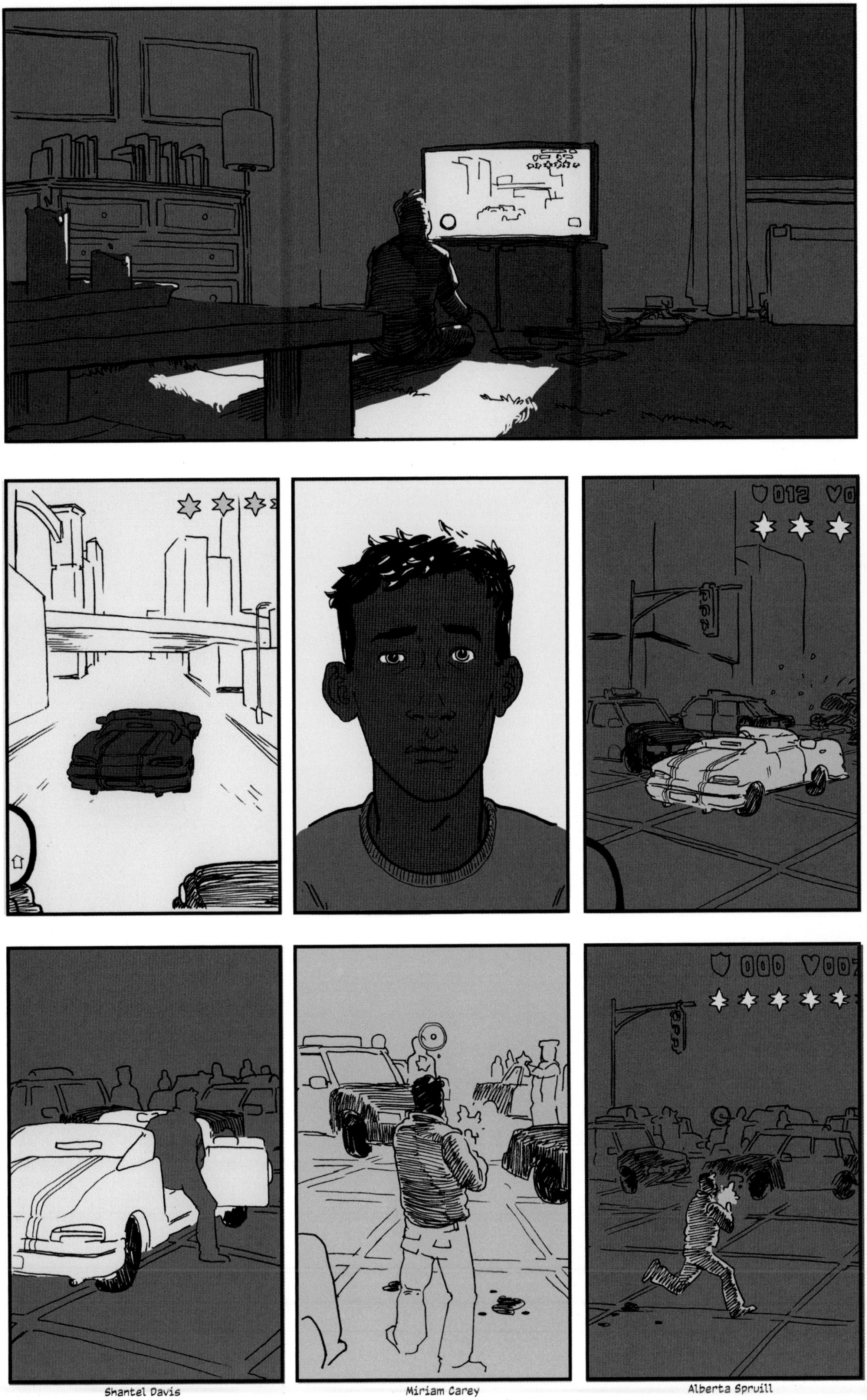
012
000

Shantel Davis Miriam Carey Alberta Spruill

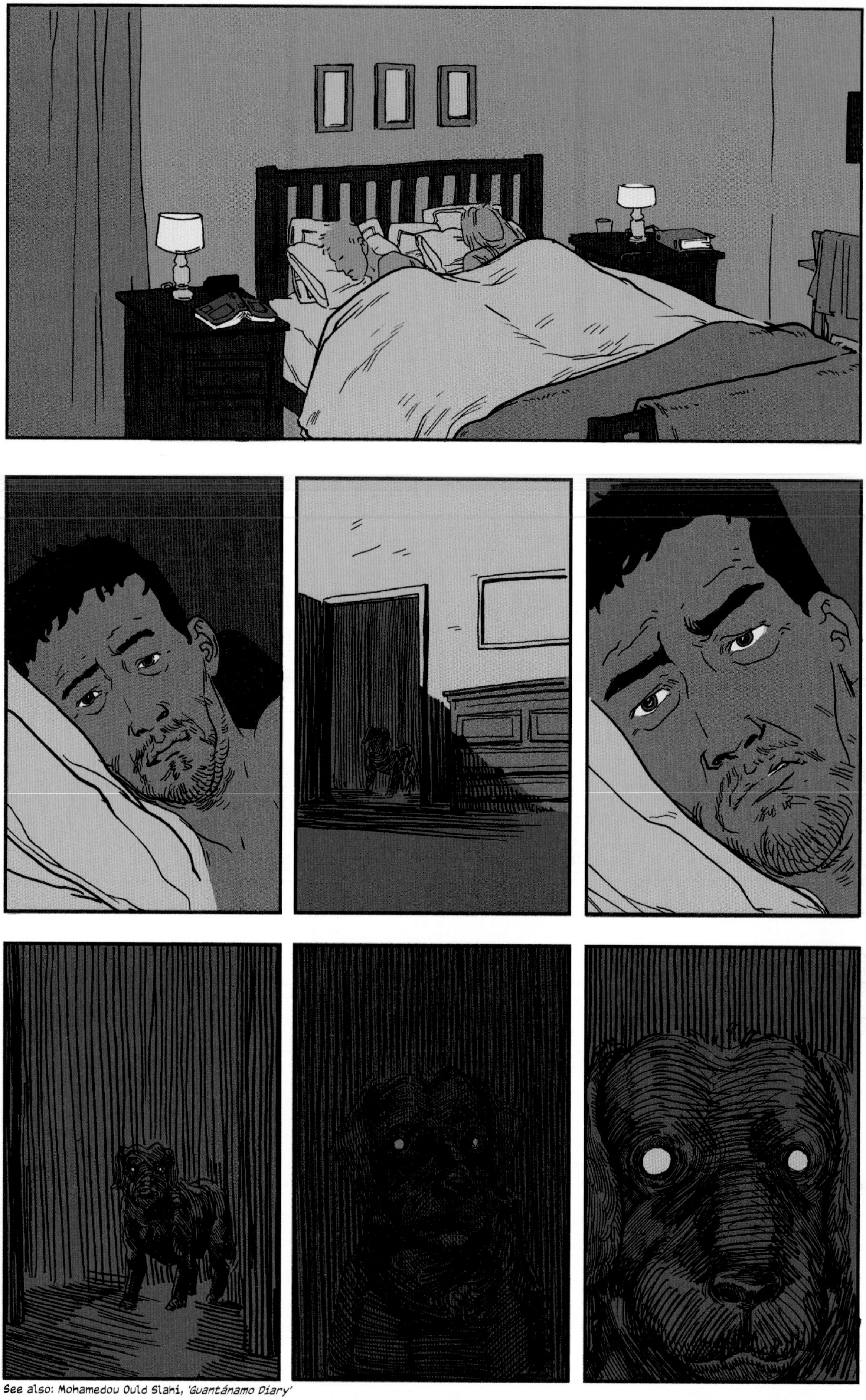

See also: Mohamedou Ould Slahi, *'Guantánamo Diary'*

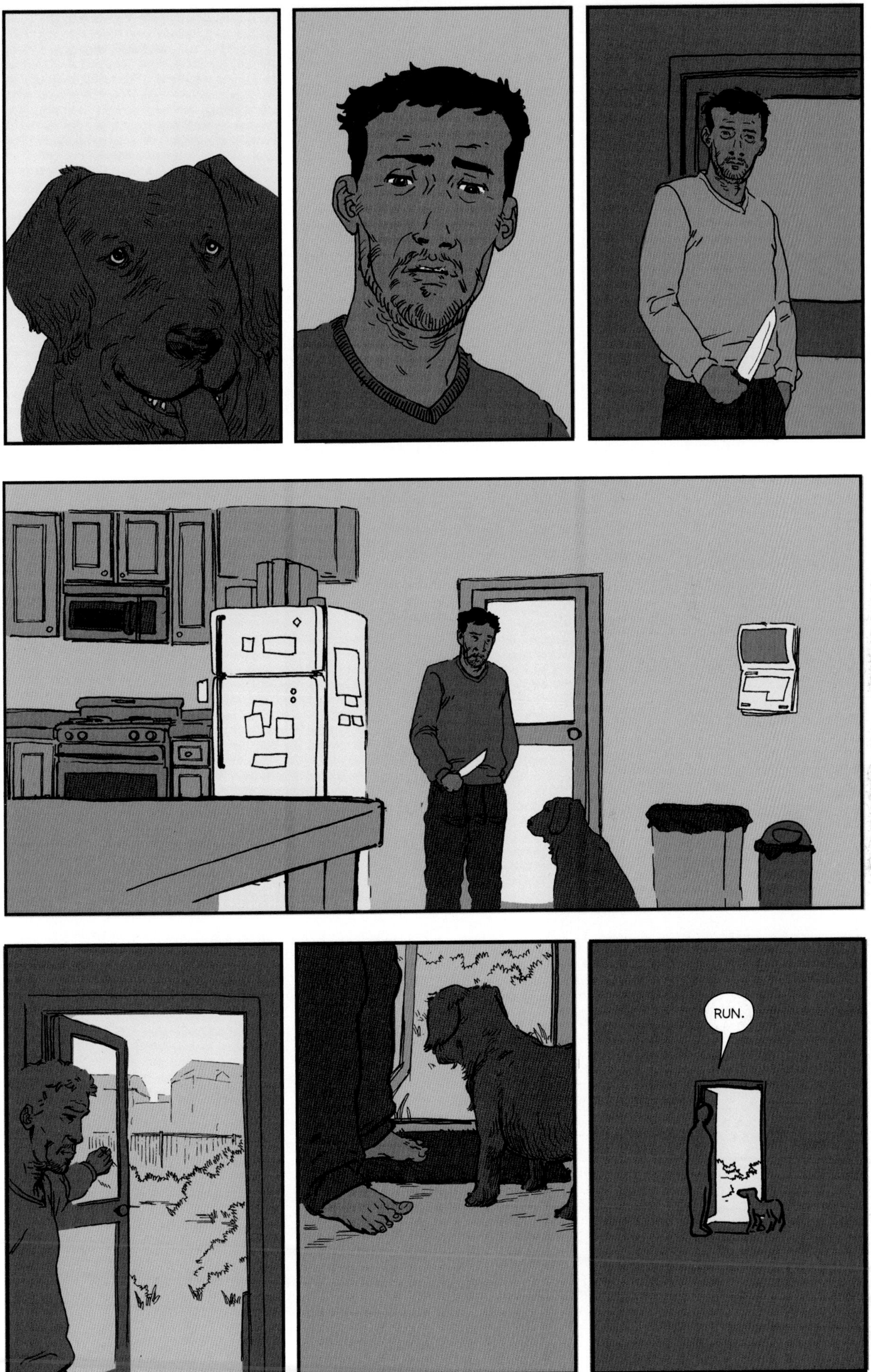
RUN.

"In our age there is no such thing as *'keeping out of politics.'* All issues are political issues, and politics itself is a mass of lies, evasions, folly, hatred and schizophrenia." -George Orwell

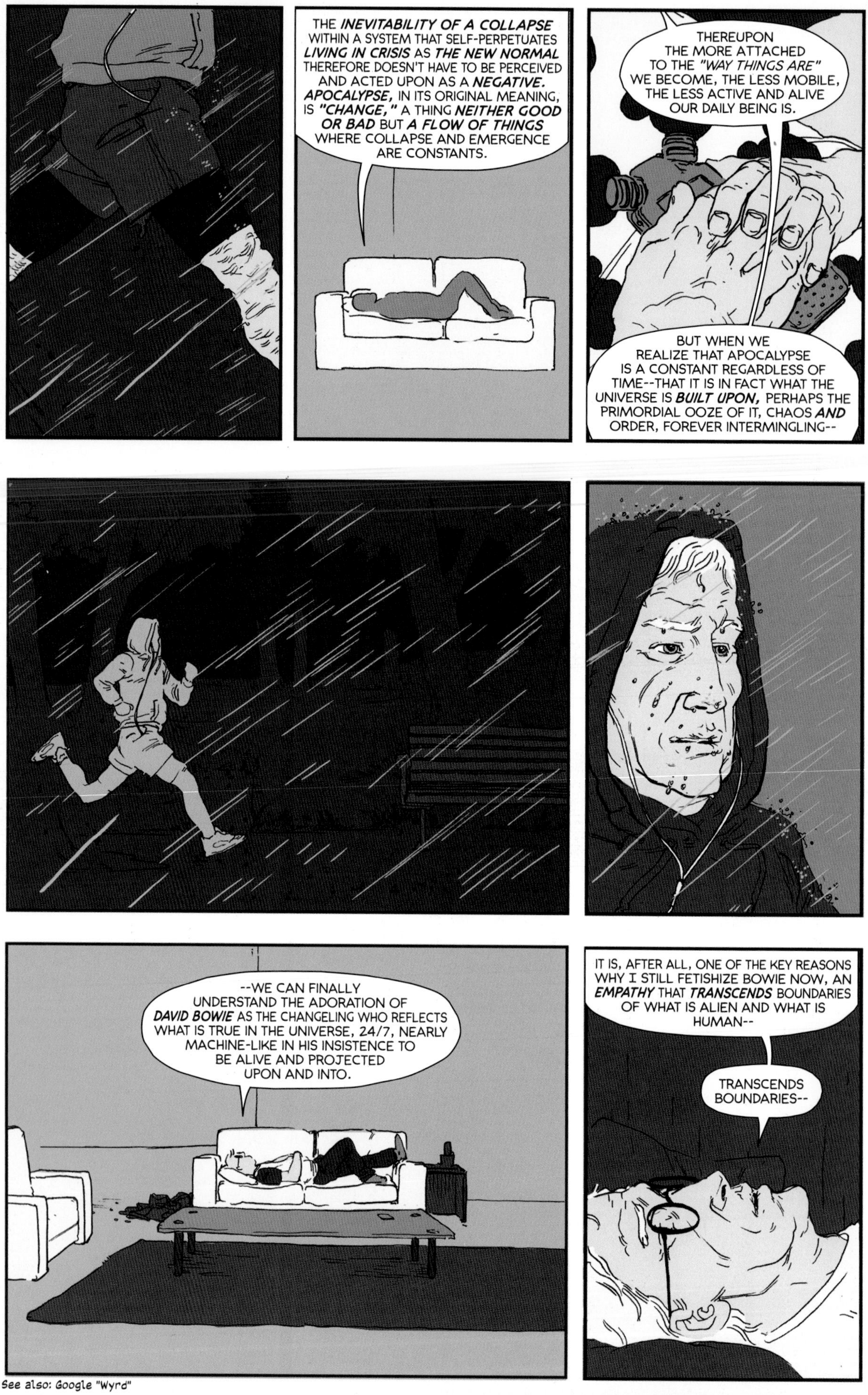
THE INEVITABILITY OF A COLLAPSE WITHIN A SYSTEM THAT SELF-PERPETUATES LIVING IN CRISIS AS THE NEW NORMAL THEREFORE DOESN'T HAVE TO BE PERCEIVED AND ACTED UPON AS A NEGATIVE. APOCALYPSE, IN ITS ORIGINAL MEANING, IS "CHANGE," A THING NEITHER GOOD OR BAD BUT A FLOW OF THINGS WHERE COLLAPSE AND EMERGENCE ARE CONSTANTS.
THEREUPON THE MORE ATTACHED TO THE "WAY THINGS ARE" WE BECOME, THE LESS MOBILE, THE LESS ACTIVE AND ALIVE OUR DAILY BEING IS.
BUT WHEN WE REALIZE THAT APOCALYPSE IS A CONSTANT REGARDLESS OF TIME--THAT IT IS IN FACT WHAT THE UNIVERSE IS BUILT UPON, PERHAPS THE PRIMORDIAL OOZE OF IT, CHAOS AND ORDER, FOREVER INTERMINGLING--
--WE CAN FINALLY UNDERSTAND THE ADORATION OF DAVID BOWIE AS THE CHANGELING WHO REFLECTS WHAT IS TRUE IN THE UNIVERSE, 24/7, NEARLY MACHINE-LIKE IN HIS INSISTENCE TO BE ALIVE AND PROJECTED UPON AND INTO.
IT IS, AFTER ALL, ONE OF THE KEY REASONS WHY I STILL FETISHIZE BOWIE NOW, AN EMPATHY THAT TRANSCENDS BOUNDARIES OF WHAT IS ALIEN AND WHAT IS HUMAN--
TRANSCENDS BOUNDARIES--

See also: Google "Wyrd"

NO...I AM SORRY.

I HAVE TO QUIT.

THE BOOK'S NOT...IT'S NOT WHAT I REALLY BELIEVE IN NOW.

I MEAN, I DO...

...BUT NOT AS MUCH AS I BELIEVE IN OTHER THINGS, YOU KNOW?

WHAT I AM SAYING IS I NEED TO MAKE SPACE SO OTHER THINGS CAN COME INTO MY LIFE.

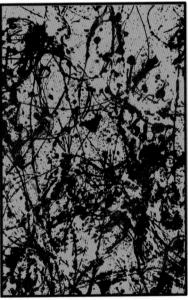

YES, I KNOW THIS CARRIES A RISK OF LOSING WHAT I HAVE AND NOT RECEIVING WHAT I WANT.

AND ENDING UP WITH *NOTHING*, YES.

I UNDERSTAND THAT YOU ARE DISAPPOINTED.

YES.

I SIMPLY...

YES.

...I HAVE TO TAKE A *LEAP OF FAITH*.

I'M AFRAID THAT IF I COLLABORATE, REALLY TRULY COLLABORATE, PEOPLE WILL TAKE ADVANTAGE OF ME! THAT THEY'LL...TWIST WHAT I HAVE TO SAY! THAT THEY'LL KILL WHAT'S TRUE IN ME!
THE BEAUTY OF REAL COLLABORATION LIES IN FINDING A WAY THAT OFFERS NO COMPROMISE!
EVERYONE GETS WHAT THEY WANT!
HOW DO YOU DO THAT?!
I GO WITH FEELING, TAKE A LEAP! OR I DON'T! I DON'T KNOW! IT'S NEW EVERY TIME, ISN'T IT, THIS LIFE?! HOW DO YOU DO THAT?!
I DON'T KNOW!
I DON'T KNOW I EVER KNOW HOW TO...
...I GUESS THAT'S THE POINT?! LOVE IS THE ACT OF NOT KNOWING, AND LOVING ANYWAY?!
WHAT WOULD HAPPEN IF PEOPLE TOOK ADVANTAGE OF YOU, NYLON?! AND HOW COULD THEY KILL WHAT'S TRUE IN YOU?!
THEY COULD KILL IT WITH... I DON'T KNOW, I'VE BEEN PRETTY GOOD ABOUT TURNING DOWN MONEY WHEN I FELT LIKE THE GIG WASN'T RIGHT! SO IT'S NOT THAT! MAYBE...I DON'T KNOW!
I THINK...
I'M AFRAID I WON'T BE SEEN!

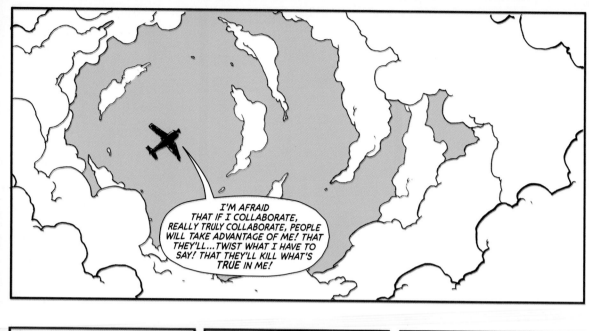

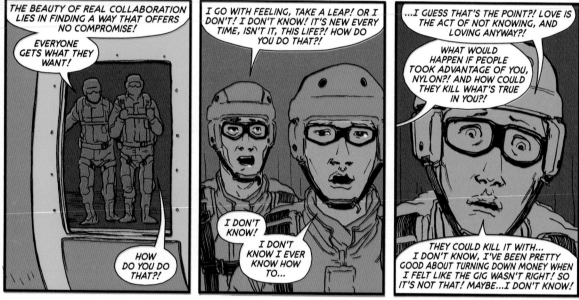

See also: John Cassavetes, *'Love Streams'*

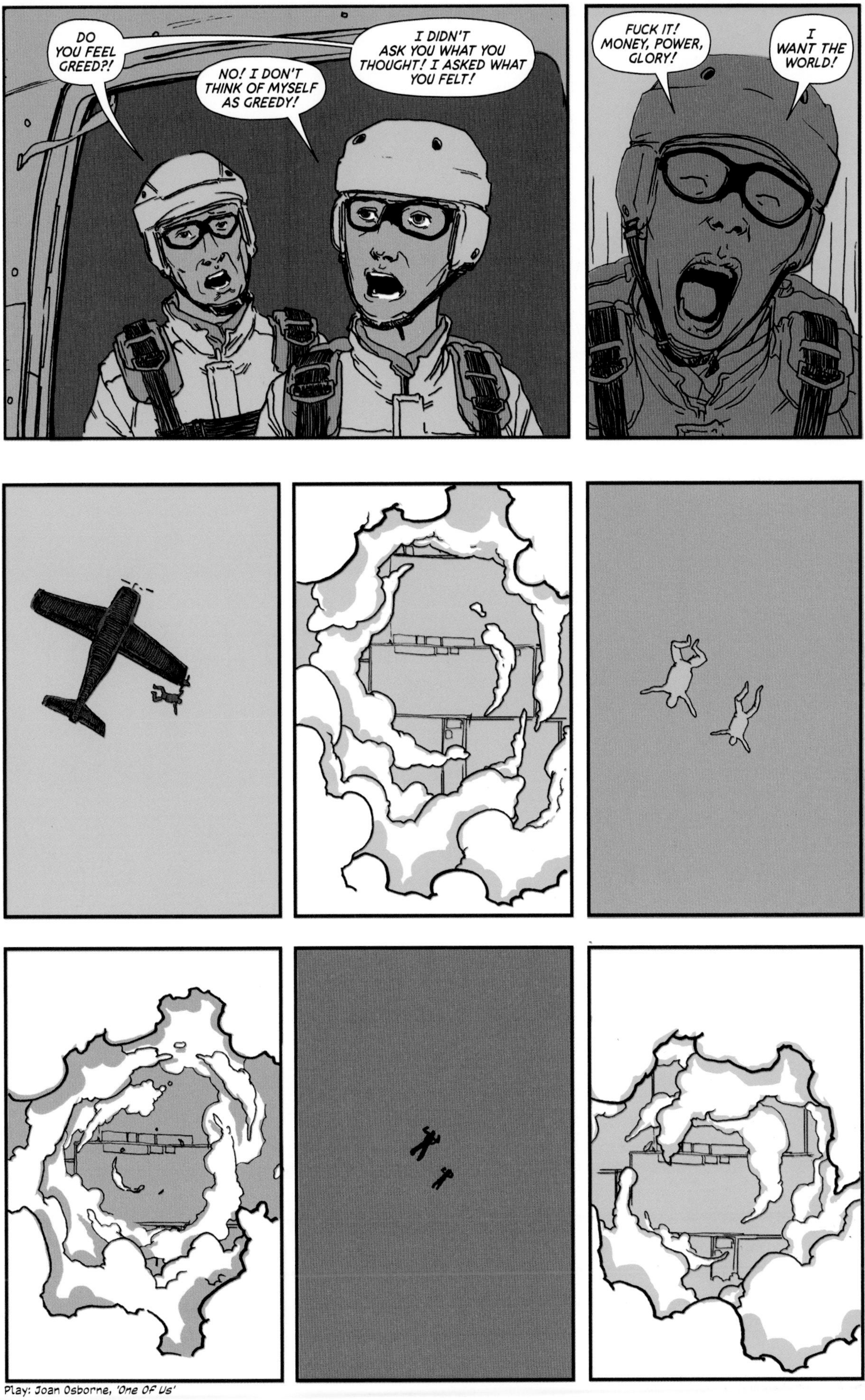
DO YOU FEEL GREED?!
NO! I DON'T THINK OF MYSELF AS GREEDY!
I DIDN'T ASK YOU WHAT YOU THOUGHT! I ASKED WHAT YOU FELT!
FUCK IT! MONEY, POWER, GLORY!
I WANT THE WORLD!

Play: Joan Osborne, *'One Of Us'*

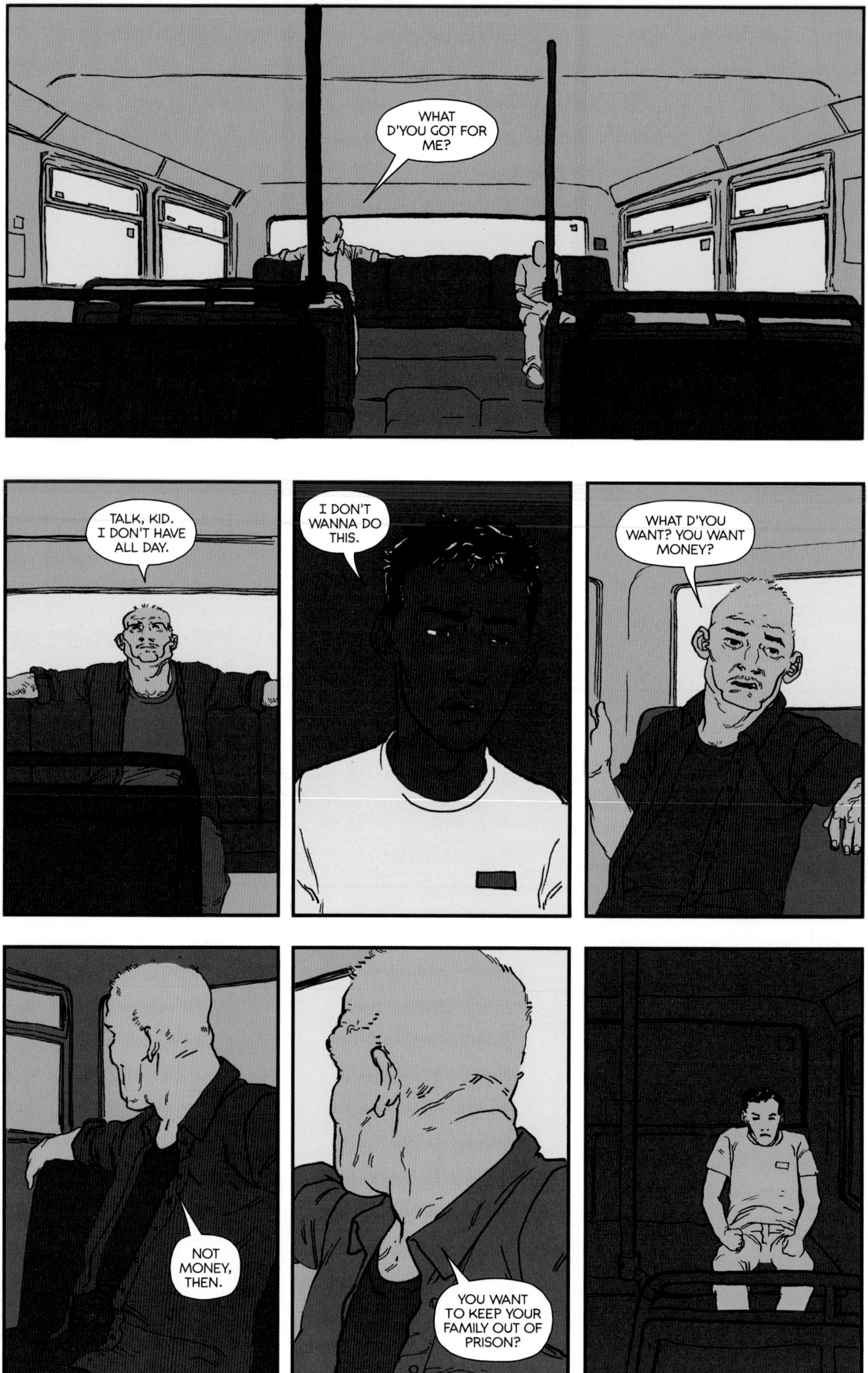
WHAT D'YOU GOT FOR ME?
TALK, KID. I DON'T HAVE ALL DAY.
I DON'T WANNA DO THIS.
WHAT D'YOU WANT? YOU WANT MONEY?
NOT MONEY, THEN.
YOU WANT TO KEEP YOUR FAMILY OUT OF PRISON?

Raheim Brown Jr.

Freddie Gray

Walter Scott

"WHAT, BOY? YOU THINK THERE'S SOMETHING EASIER THAN PLANTING DRUGS ON A NIGGER AND MAKING SURE THE WHOLE FAMILY PAYS?

"THIS IS *AMERICA.*

GENTRYFIER go HOME

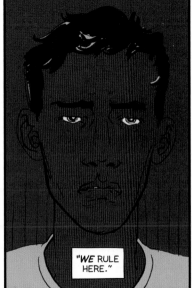

"*WE* RULE HERE."

Jordan Baker   Ramarley Graham   Tarika Wilson

WHERE IS THE DOG?!!?
ATIFEH...
I DON'T...
DON'T YOU DARE TELL ME YOU DON'T KNOW.
I AM READY TO HELP. I AM READY TO FIND HIM. BUT YOU HAVE TO TELL ME WHAT YOU DID. YOU HAVE TO.
IT'S THE ONLY WAY I CAN...
...I CAN HELP YOU.

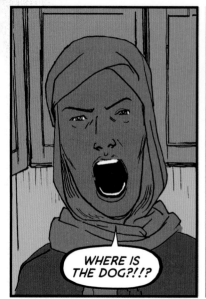

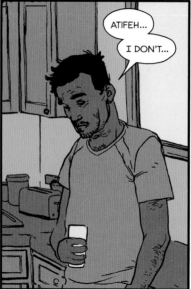

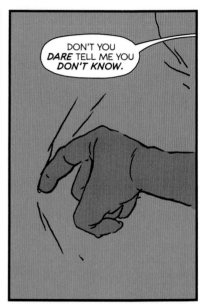

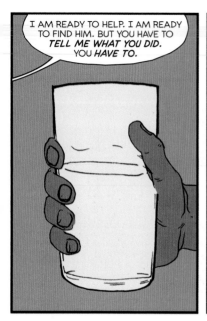

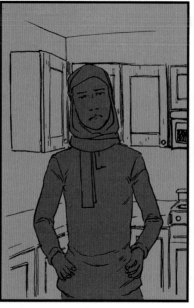

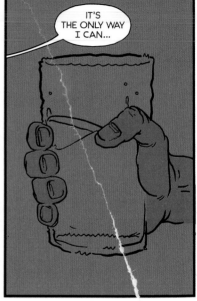

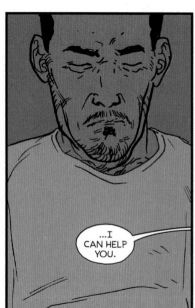

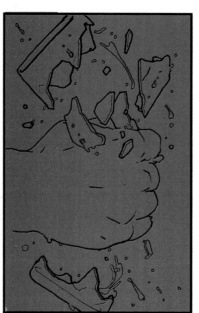

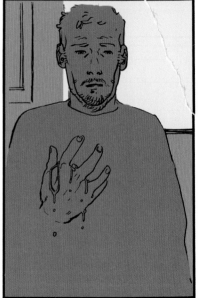

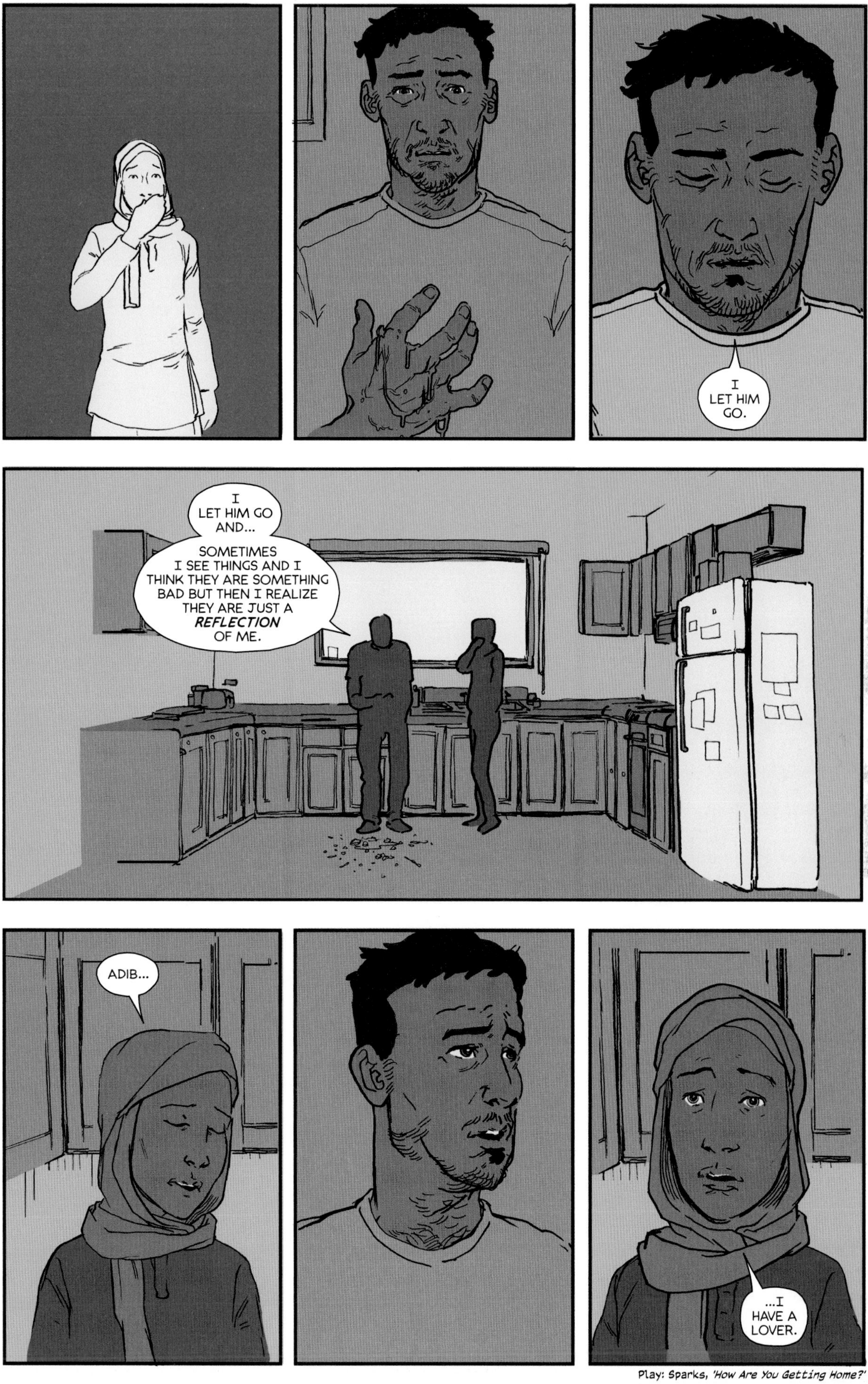
I LET HIM GO.
I LET HIM GO AND...
SOMETIMES I SEE THINGS AND I THINK THEY ARE SOMETHING BAD BUT THEN I REALIZE THEY ARE JUST A *REFLECTION* OF ME.
ADIB...
...I HAVE A LOVER.

Play: Sparks, *'How Are You Getting Home?'*

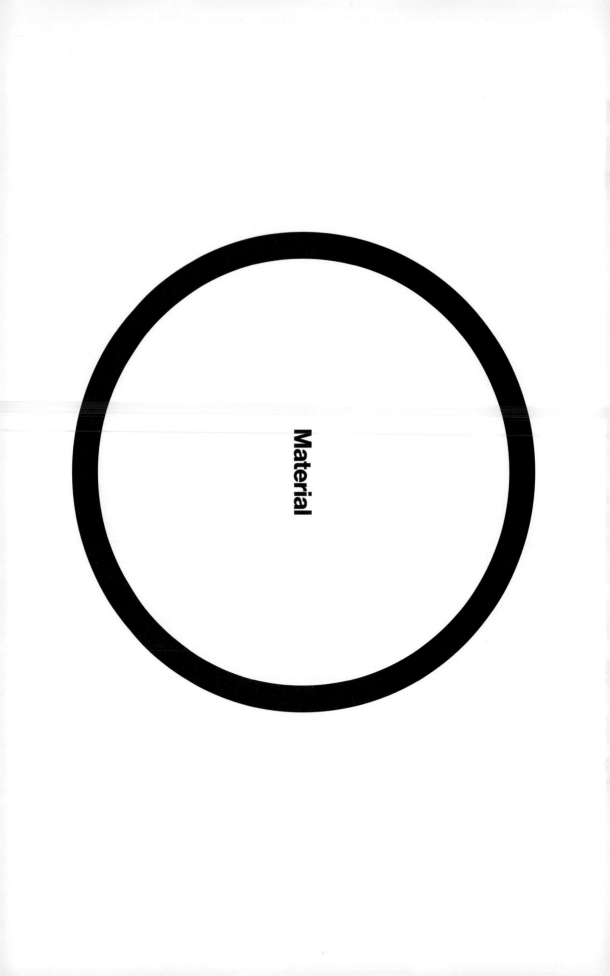

Material

Chapter 3

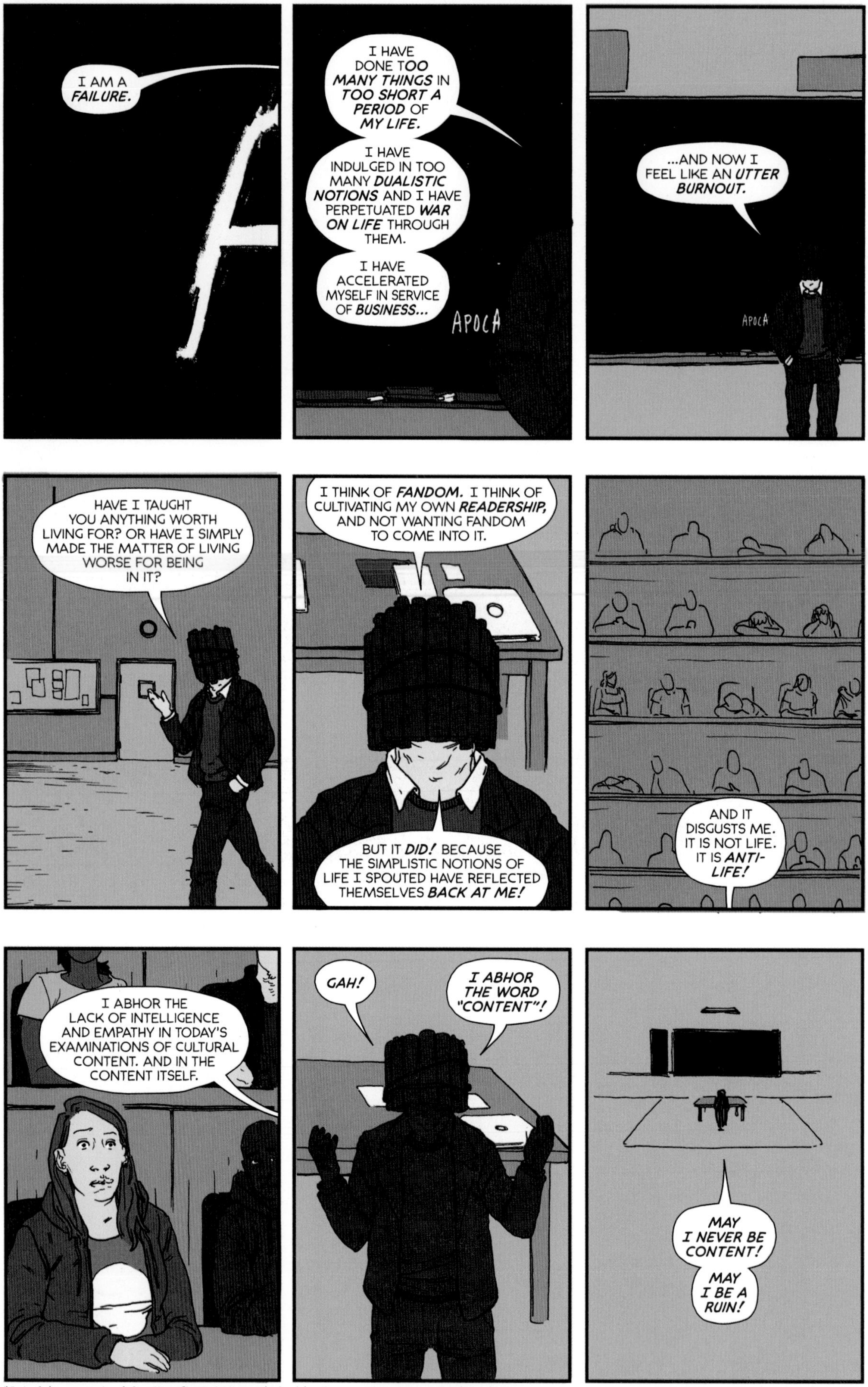
I AM A FAILURE.
I HAVE DONE TOO MANY THINGS IN TOO SHORT A PERIOD OF MY LIFE.
I HAVE INDULGED IN TOO MANY DUALISTIC NOTIONS AND I HAVE PERPETUATED WAR ON LIFE THROUGH THEM.
I HAVE ACCELERATED MYSELF IN SERVICE OF BUSINESS...
APOCA
...AND NOW I FEEL LIKE AN UTTER BURNOUT.
APOCA
HAVE I TAUGHT YOU ANYTHING WORTH LIVING FOR? OR HAVE I SIMPLY MADE THE MATTER OF LIVING WORSE FOR BEING IN IT?
I THINK OF FANDOM. I THINK OF CULTIVATING MY OWN READERSHIP, AND NOT WANTING FANDOM TO COME INTO IT.
BUT IT DID! BECAUSE THE SIMPLISTIC NOTIONS OF LIFE I SPOUTED HAVE REFLECTED THEMSELVES BACK AT ME!
AND IT DISGUSTS ME. IT IS NOT LIFE. IT IS ANTI-LIFE!
I ABHOR THE LACK OF INTELLIGENCE AND EMPATHY IN TODAY'S EXAMINATIONS OF CULTURAL CONTENT. AND IN THE CONTENT ITSELF.
GAH!
I ABHOR THE WORD "CONTENT"!
MAY I NEVER BE CONTENT!
MAY I BE A RUIN!

"I deal in raw materials. I'm after whatever is lurking beyond thought." -Clarice Lispector

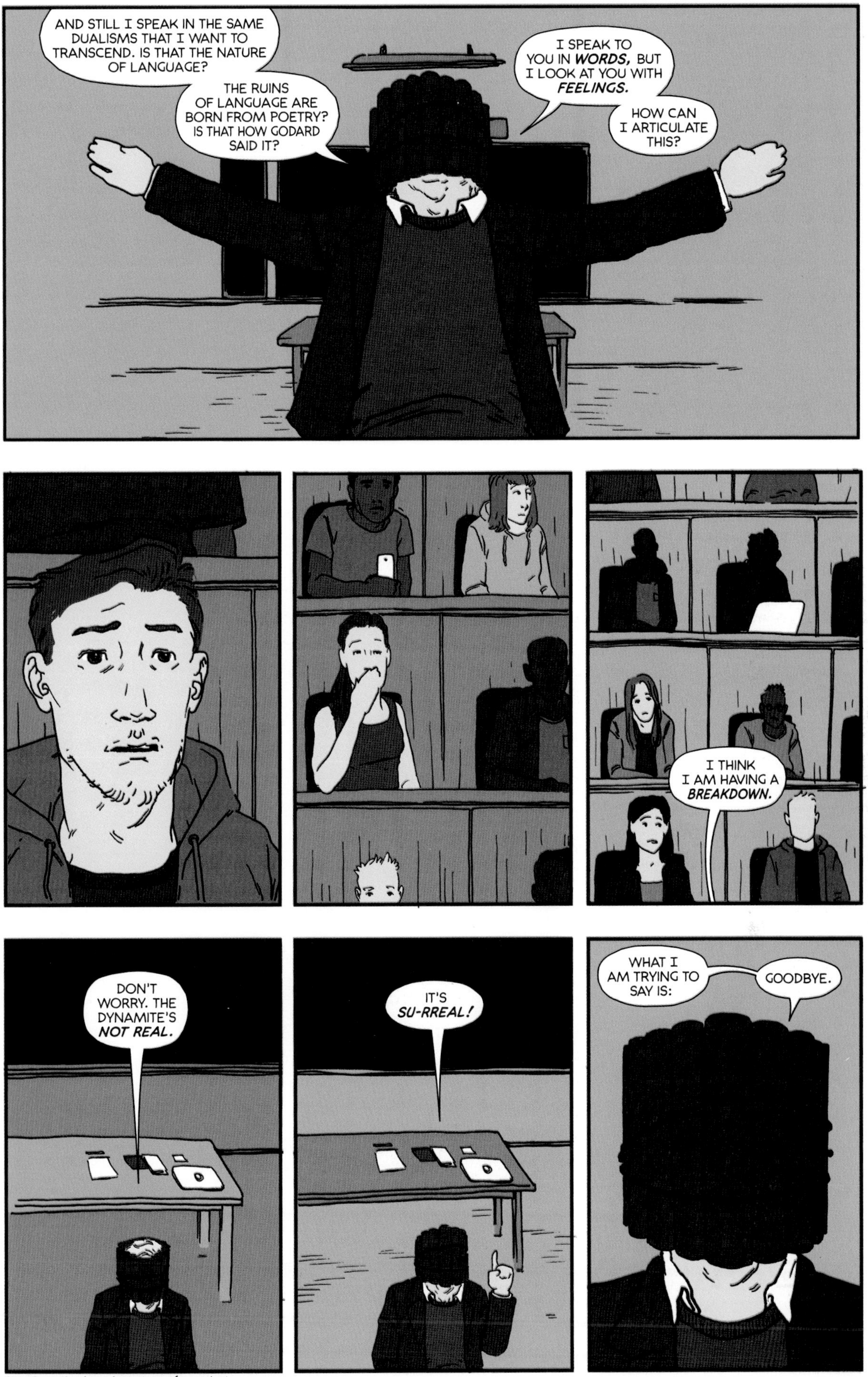
AND STILL I SPEAK IN THE SAME DUALISMS THAT I WANT TO TRANSCEND. IS THAT THE NATURE OF LANGUAGE?
THE RUINS OF LANGUAGE ARE BORN FROM POETRY? IS THAT HOW GODARD SAID IT?
I SPEAK TO YOU IN WORDS, BUT I LOOK AT YOU WITH FEELINGS.
HOW CAN I ARTICULATE THIS?
I THINK I AM HAVING A BREAKDOWN.
DON'T WORRY. THE DYNAMITE'S NOT REAL.
IT'S SU-RREAL!
WHAT I AM TRYING TO SAY IS:
GOODBYE.

See also: Clarice Lispector, *'Água Viva'*

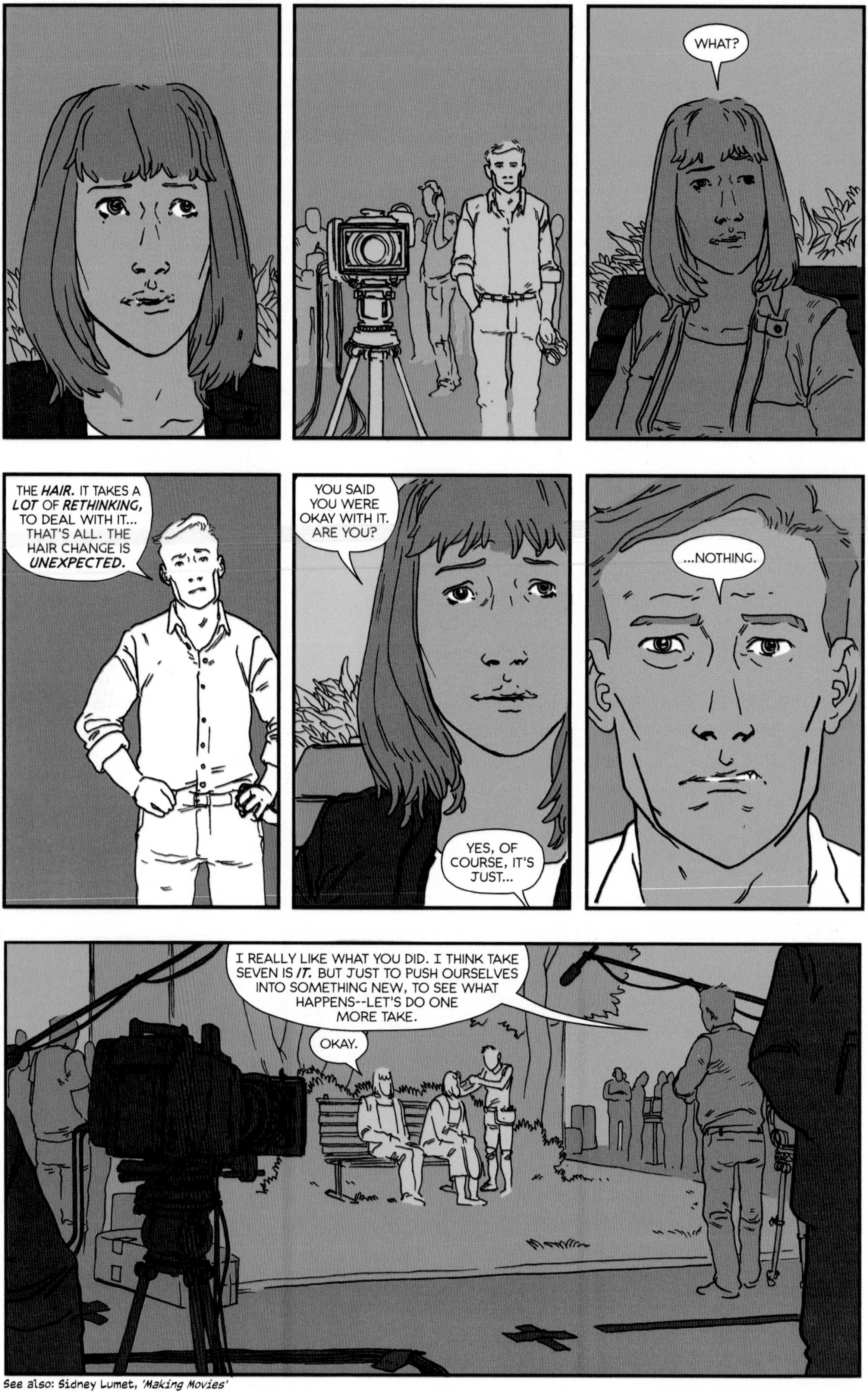
WHAT?
THE *HAIR.* IT TAKES A *LOT* OF *RETHINKING,* TO DEAL WITH IT... THAT'S ALL. THE HAIR CHANGE IS *UNEXPECTED.*
YOU SAID YOU WERE OKAY WITH IT. ARE YOU?
YES, OF COURSE, IT'S JUST...
...NOTHING.
I REALLY LIKE WHAT YOU DID. I THINK TAKE SEVEN IS *IT.* BUT JUST TO PUSH OURSELVES INTO SOMETHING NEW, TO SEE WHAT HAPPENS--LET'S DO ONE MORE TAKE.
OKAY.

See also: Sidney Lumet, *'Making Movies'*

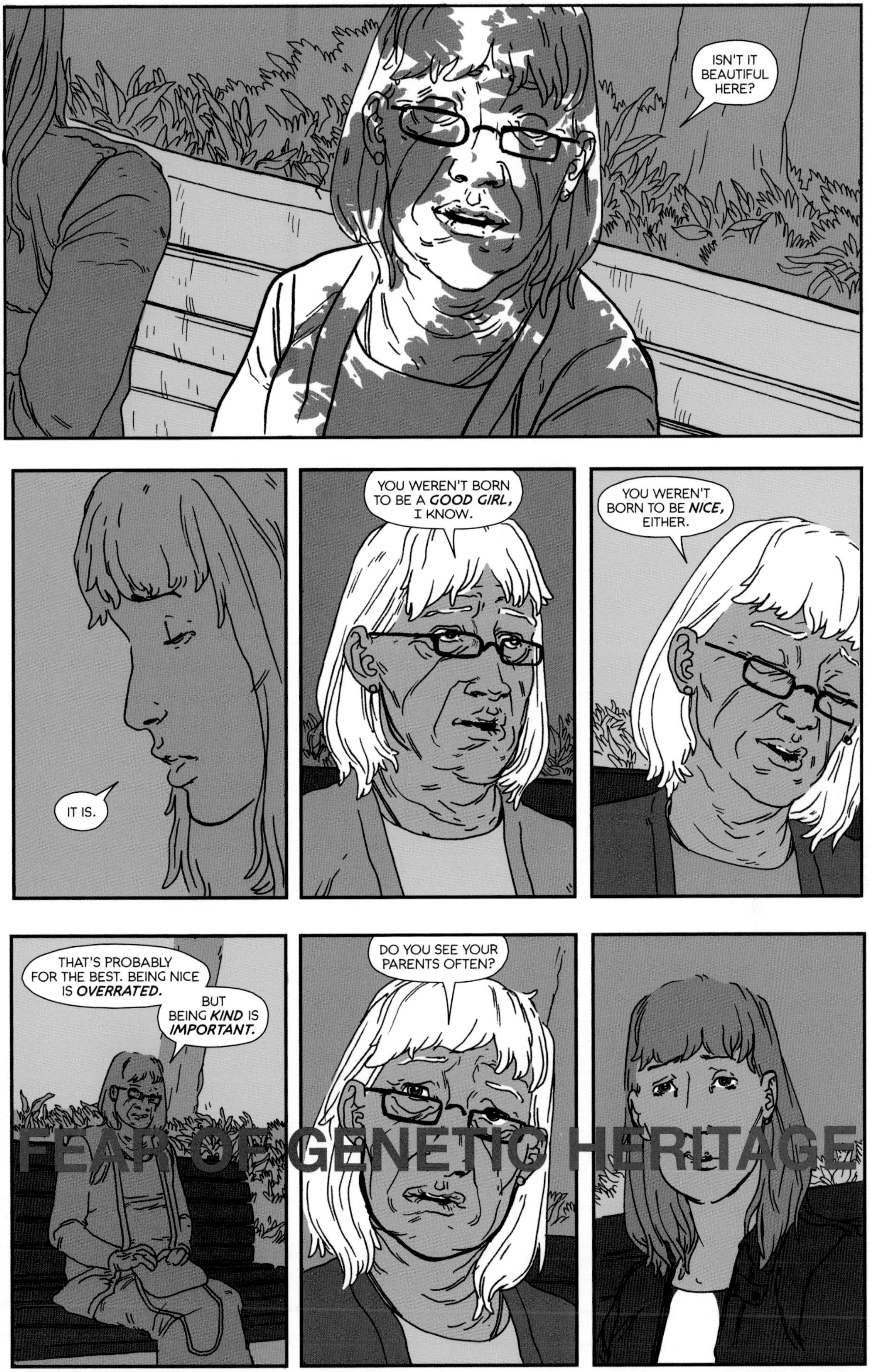
ISN'T IT BEAUTIFUL HERE?
IT IS.
YOU WEREN'T BORN TO BE A *GOOD GIRL,* I KNOW.
YOU WEREN'T BORN TO BE *NICE,* EITHER.
THAT'S PROBABLY FOR THE BEST. BEING NICE IS *OVERRATED.*
BUT BEING *KIND* IS *IMPORTANT.*
DO YOU SEE YOUR PARENTS OFTEN?

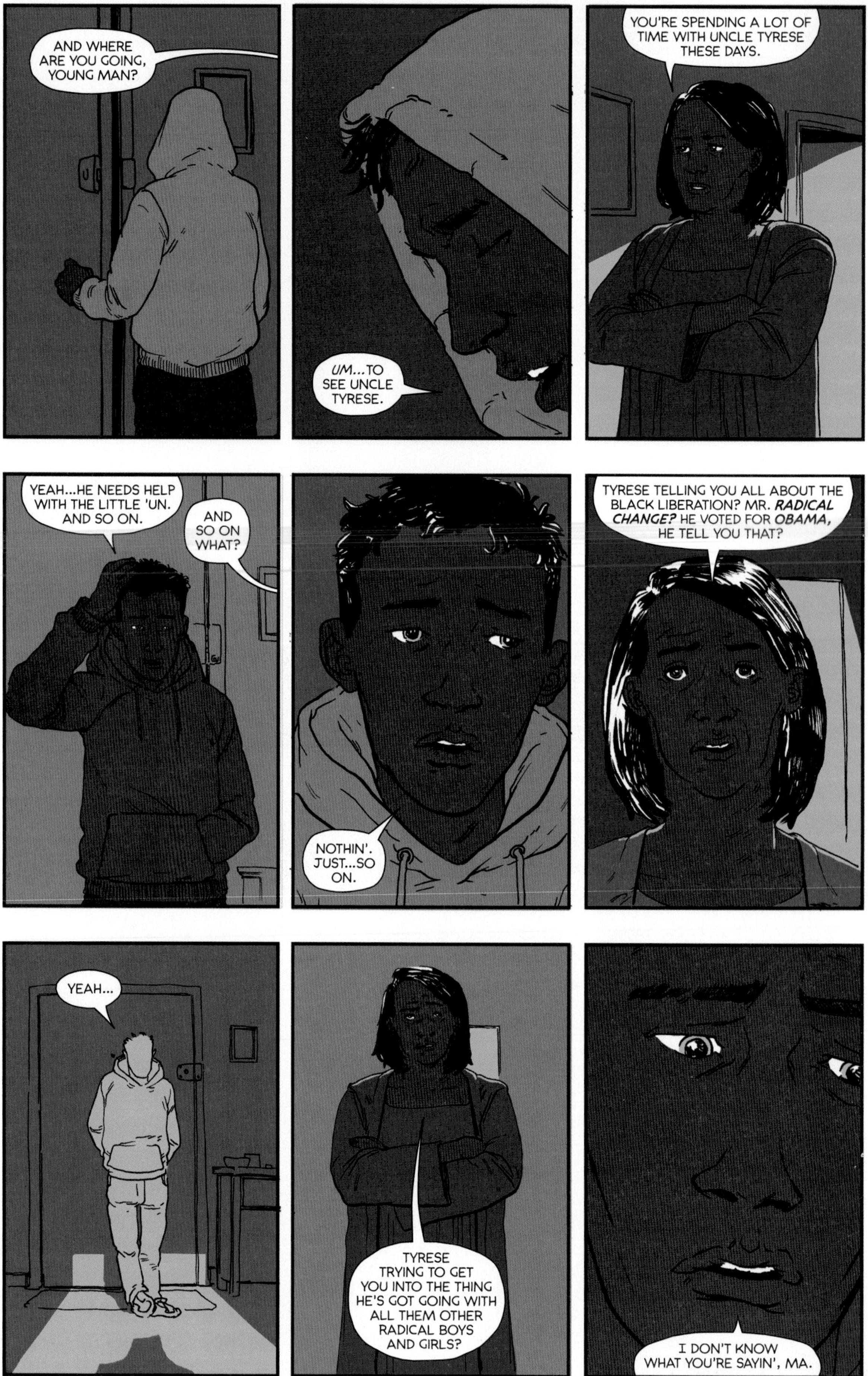
AND WHERE ARE YOU GOING, YOUNG MAN?
UM...TO SEE UNCLE TYRESE.
YOU'RE SPENDING A LOT OF TIME WITH UNCLE TYRESE THESE DAYS.
YEAH...HE NEEDS HELP WITH THE LITTLE 'UN. AND SO ON.
AND SO ON WHAT?
NOTHIN'. JUST...SO ON.
TYRESE TELLING YOU ALL ABOUT THE BLACK LIBERATION? MR. RADICAL CHANGE? HE VOTED FOR OBAMA, HE TELL YOU THAT?
YEAH...
TYRESE TRYING TO GET YOU INTO THE THING HE'S GOT GOING WITH ALL THEM OTHER RADICAL BOYS AND GIRLS?
I DON'T KNOW WHAT YOU'RE SAYIN', MA.
Steven Eugene Washington

Kiwane Carrington

Kajieme Powell

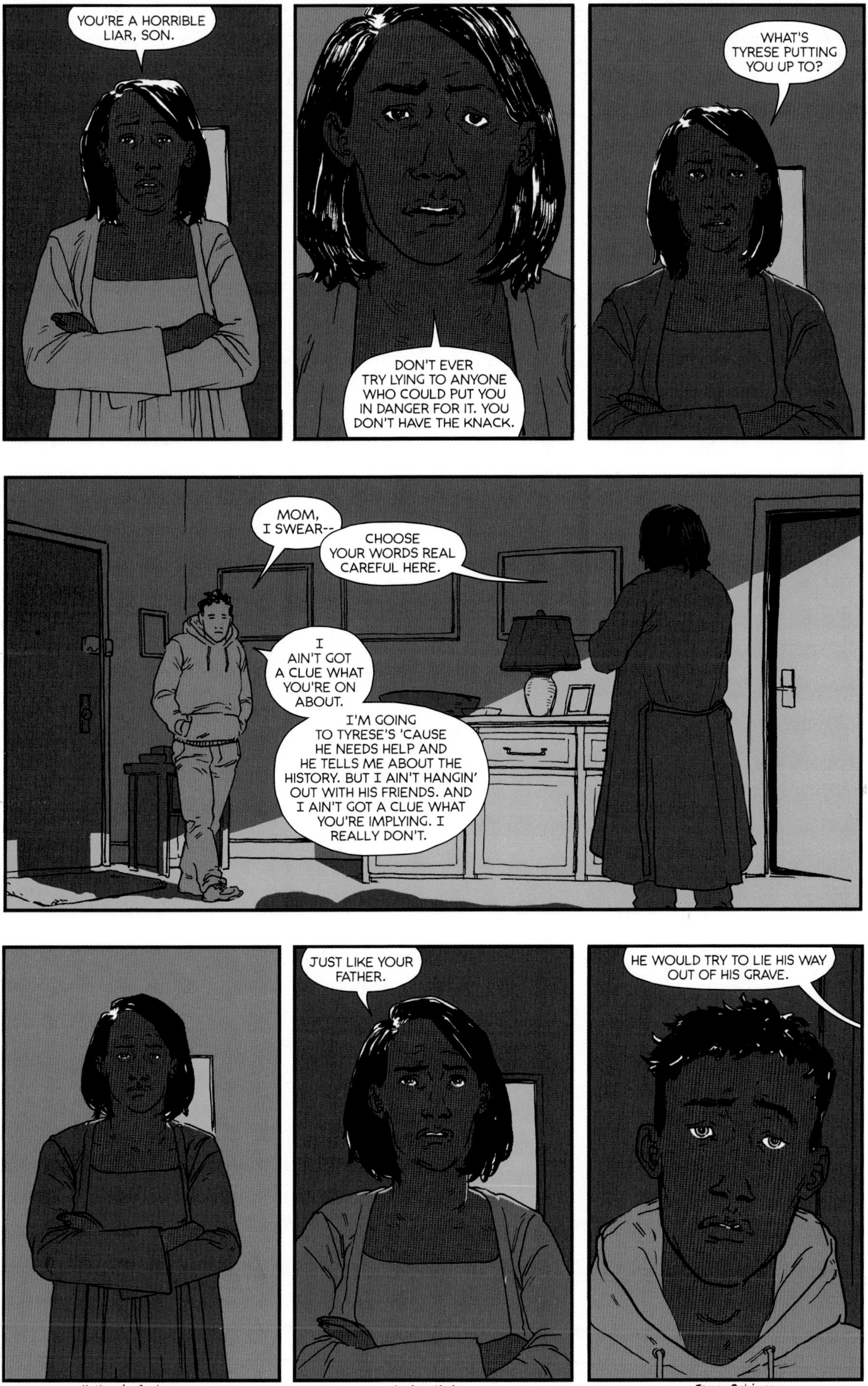
YOU'RE A HORRIBLE LIAR, SON.
DON'T EVER TRY LYING TO ANYONE WHO COULD PUT YOU IN DANGER FOR IT. YOU DON'T HAVE THE KNACK.
WHAT'S TYRESE PUTTING YOU UP TO?
MOM, I SWEAR--
CHOOSE YOUR WORDS REAL CAREFUL HERE.
I AIN'T GOT A CLUE WHAT YOU'RE ON ABOUT.
I'M GOING TO TYRESE'S 'CAUSE HE NEEDS HELP AND HE TELLS ME ABOUT THE HISTORY. BUT I AIN'T HANGIN' OUT WITH HIS FRIENDS. AND I AIN'T GOT A CLUE WHAT YOU'RE IMPLYING. I REALLY DON'T.
JUST LIKE YOUR FATHER.
HE WOULD TRY TO LIE HIS WAY OUT OF HIS GRAVE.

McKenzie Cochran Carlos Alcis Tamon Robinson

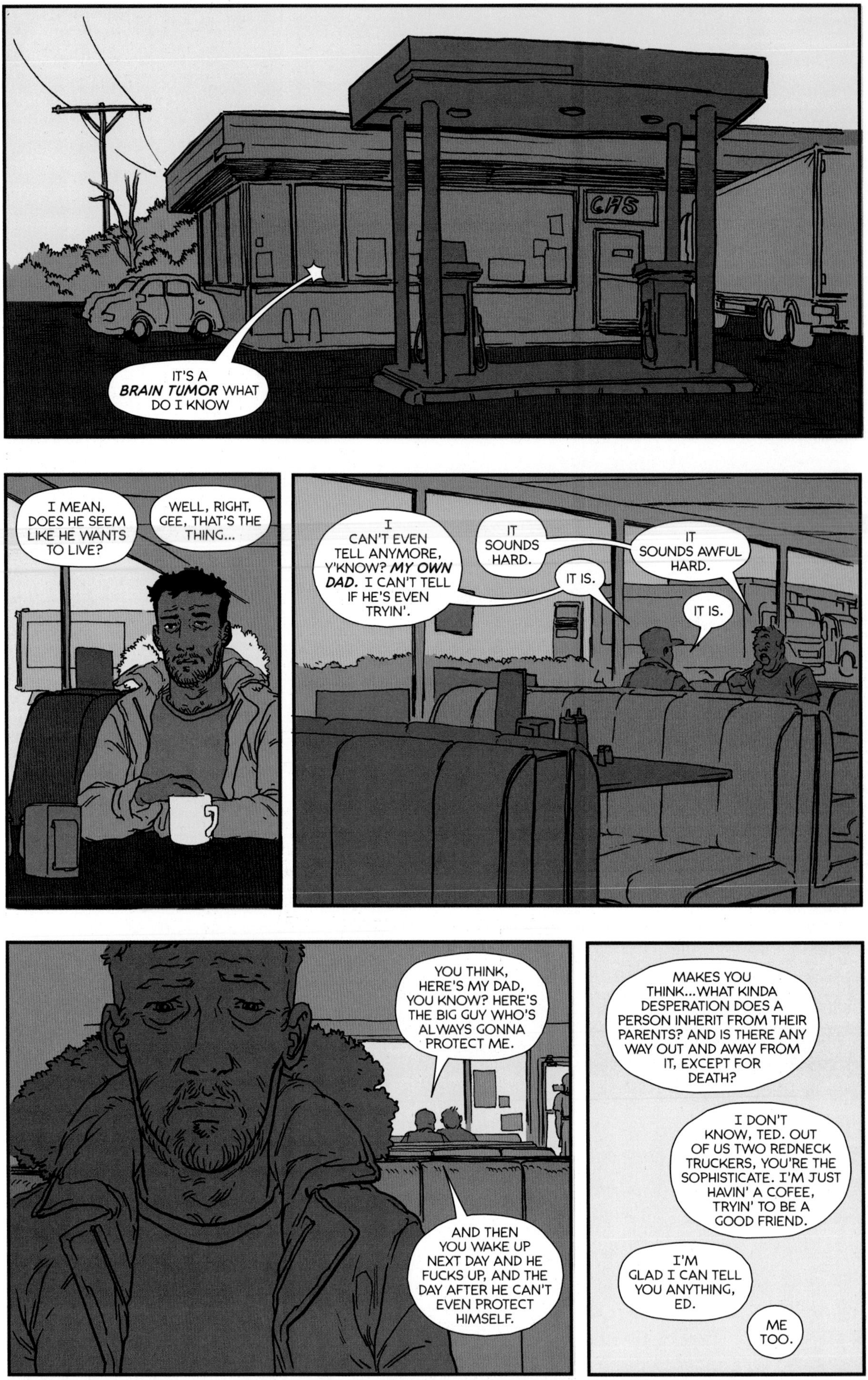
IT'S A **BRAIN TUMOR** WHAT DO I KNOW
I MEAN, DOES HE SEEM LIKE HE WANTS TO LIVE?
WELL, RIGHT, GEE, THAT'S THE THING...
I CAN'T EVEN TELL ANYMORE, Y'KNOW? **MY OWN DAD.** I CAN'T TELL IF HE'S EVEN TRYIN'.
IT SOUNDS HARD.
IT SOUNDS AWFUL HARD.
IT IS.
IT IS.
YOU THINK, HERE'S MY DAD, YOU KNOW? HERE'S THE BIG GUY WHO'S ALWAYS GONNA PROTECT ME.
AND THEN YOU WAKE UP NEXT DAY AND HE FUCKS UP, AND THE DAY AFTER HE CAN'T EVEN PROTECT HIMSELF.
MAKES YOU THINK...WHAT KINDA DESPERATION DOES A PERSON INHERIT FROM THEIR PARENTS? AND IS THERE ANY WAY OUT AND AWAY FROM IT, EXCEPT FOR DEATH?
I DON'T KNOW, TED. OUT OF US TWO REDNECK TRUCKERS, YOU'RE THE SOPHISTICATE. I'M JUST HAVIN' A COFEE, TRYIN' TO BE A GOOD FRIEND.
I'M GLAD I CAN TELL YOU ANYTHING, ED.
ME TOO.

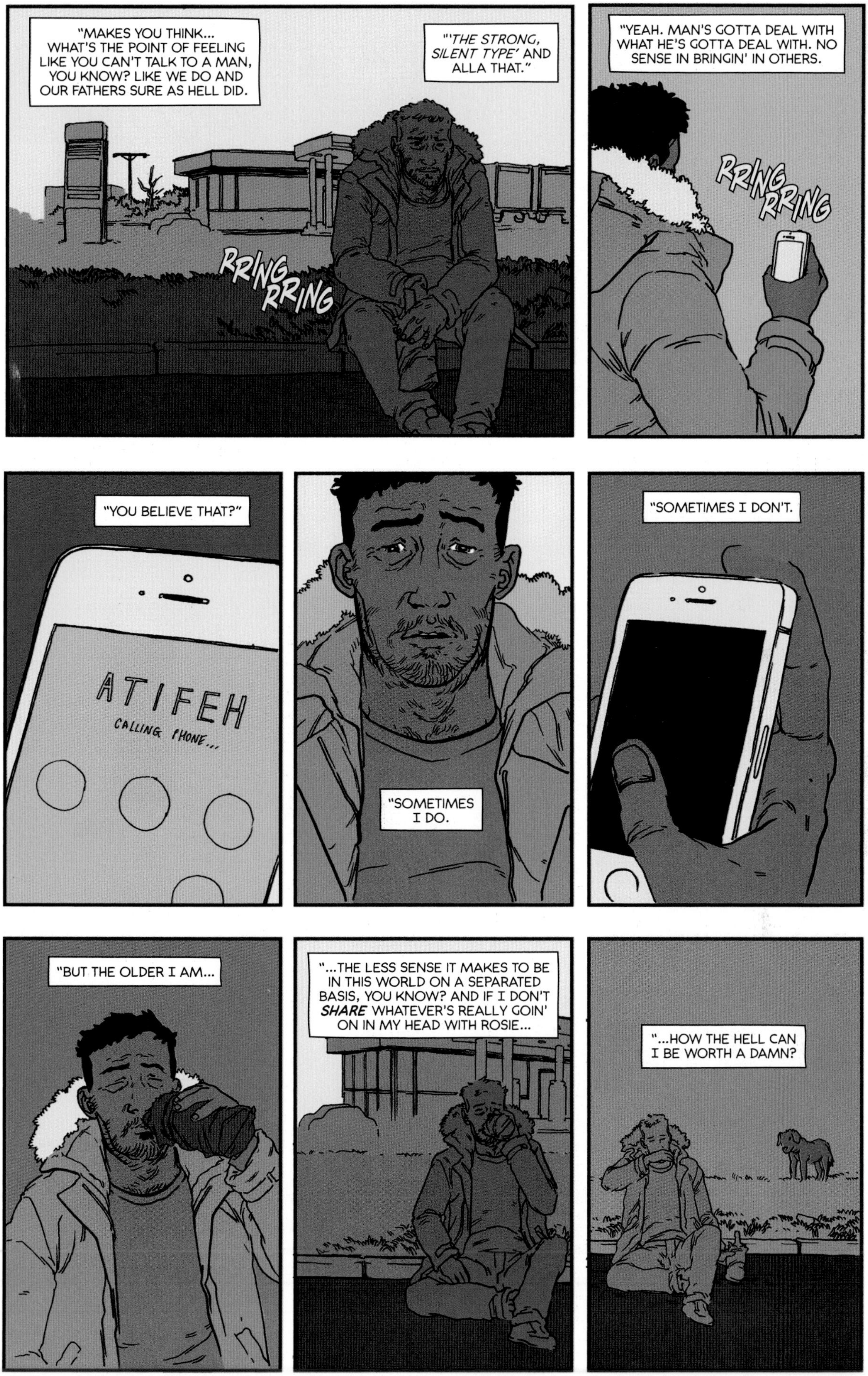
"MAKES YOU THINK... WHAT'S THE POINT OF FEELING LIKE YOU CAN'T TALK TO A MAN, YOU KNOW? LIKE WE DO AND OUR FATHERS SURE AS HELL DID.
"'THE STRONG, SILENT TYPE' AND ALLA THAT."
RRING RRING
"YEAH. MAN'S GOTTA DEAL WITH WHAT HE'S GOTTA DEAL WITH. NO SENSE IN BRINGIN' IN OTHERS.
RRING RRING
"YOU BELIEVE THAT?"
ATIFEH
CALLING PHONE...
"SOMETIMES I DO.
"SOMETIMES I DON'T.
"BUT THE OLDER I AM...
"...THE LESS SENSE IT MAKES TO BE IN THIS WORLD ON A SEPARATED BASIS, YOU KNOW? AND IF I DON'T SHARE WHATEVER'S REALLY GOIN' ON IN MY HEAD WITH ROSIE...
"...HOW THE HELL CAN I BE WORTH A DAMN?

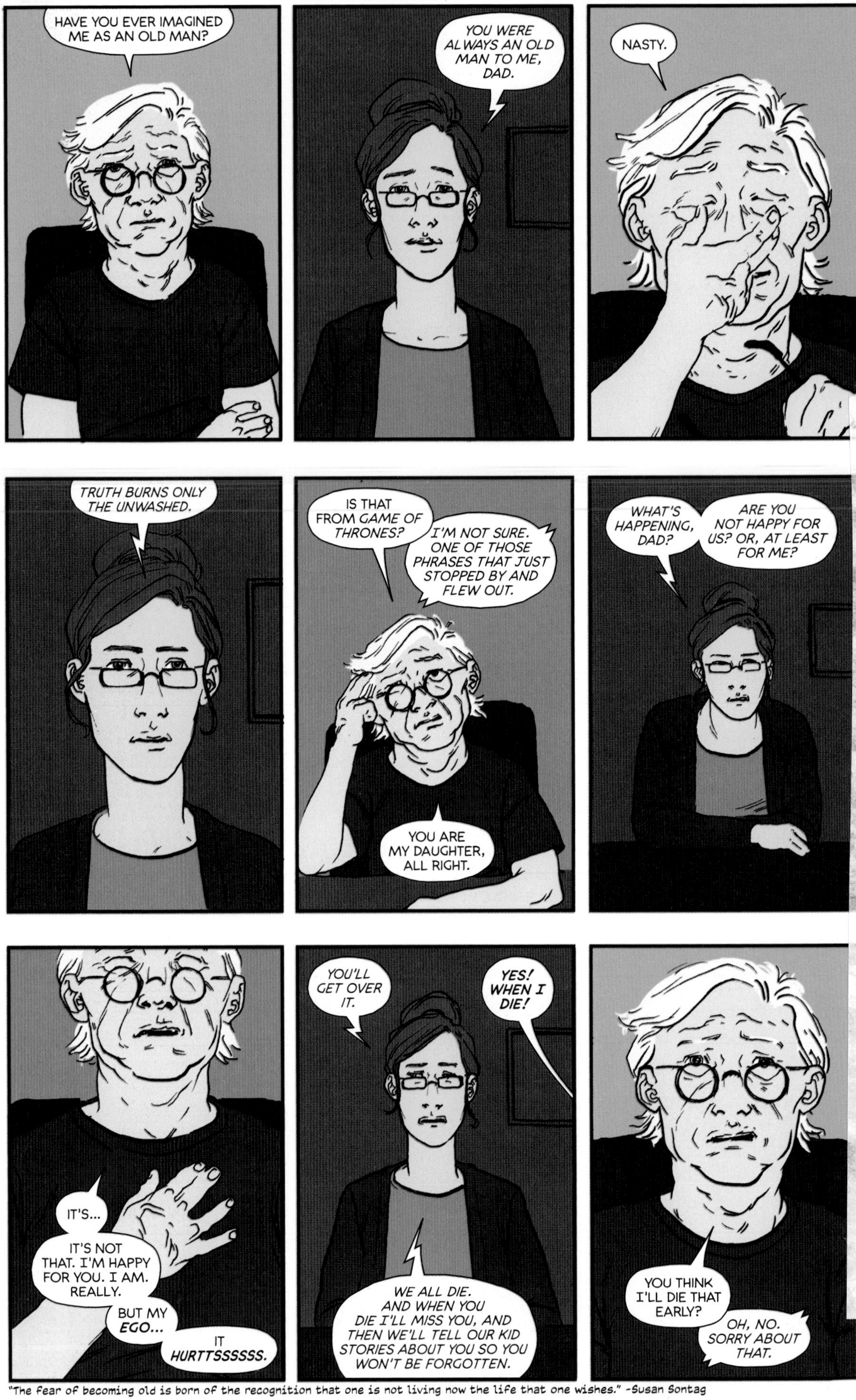
HAVE YOU EVER IMAGINED ME AS AN OLD MAN?
YOU WERE ALWAYS AN OLD MAN TO ME, DAD.
NASTY.
TRUTH BURNS ONLY THE UNWASHED.
IS THAT FROM *GAME OF THRONES*?
I'M NOT SURE. ONE OF THOSE PHRASES THAT JUST STOPPED BY AND FLEW OUT.
YOU ARE MY DAUGHTER, ALL RIGHT.
WHAT'S HAPPENING, DAD?
ARE YOU NOT HAPPY FOR US? OR, AT LEAST FOR ME?
IT'S...
IT'S NOT THAT. I'M HAPPY FOR YOU. I AM. REALLY.
BUT MY *EGO...*
IT **HURTTSSSSSS.**
YOU'LL GET OVER IT.
YES! WHEN I DIE!
WE ALL DIE. AND WHEN YOU DIE I'LL MISS YOU, AND THEN WE'LL TELL OUR KID STORIES ABOUT YOU SO YOU WON'T BE FORGOTTEN.
YOU THINK I'LL DIE THAT EARLY?
OH, NO. SORRY ABOUT THAT.

"The fear of becoming old is born of the recognition that one is not living now the life that one wishes." -Susan Sontag

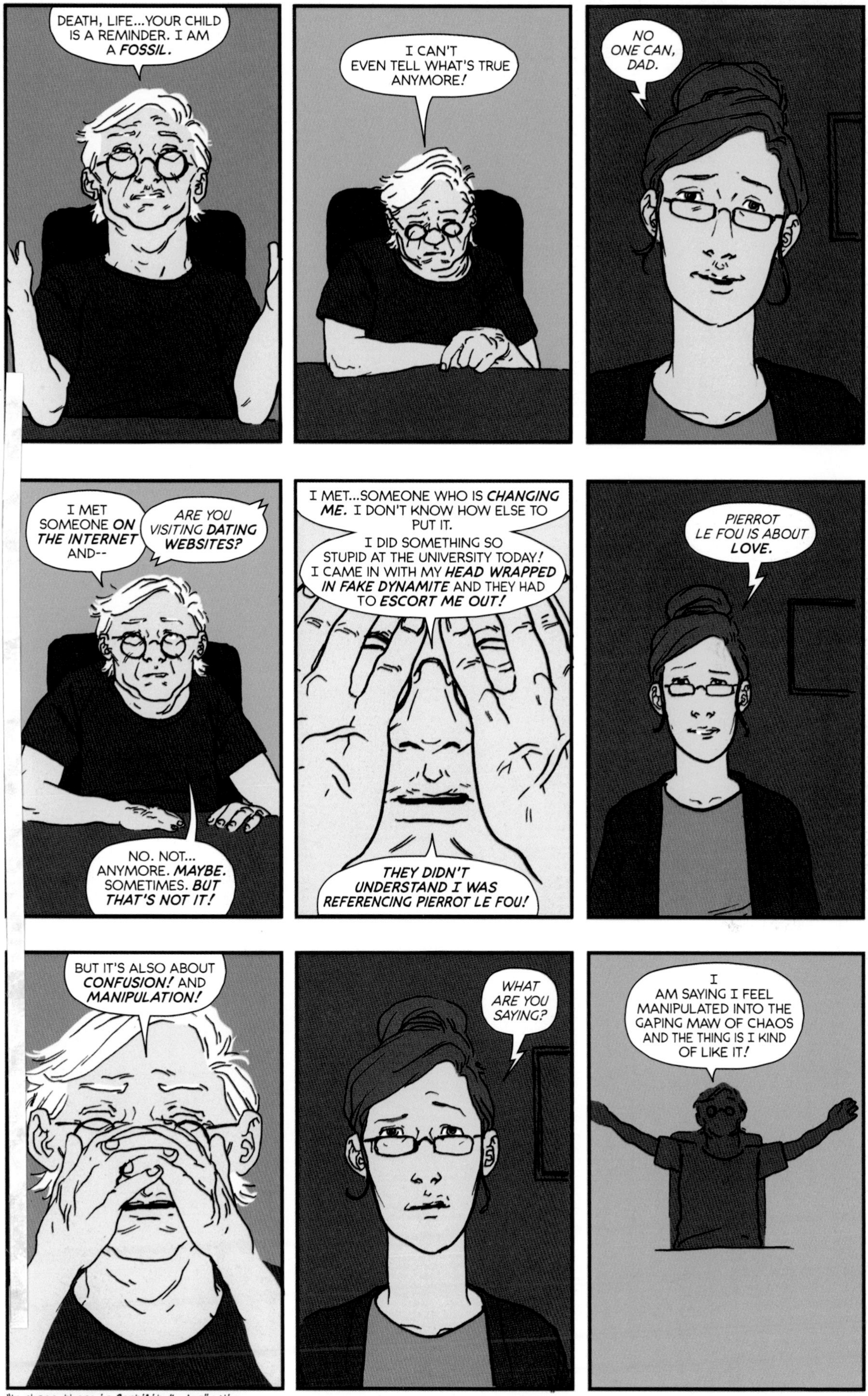
DEATH, LIFE...YOUR CHILD IS A REMINDER. I AM A *FOSSIL.*
I CAN'T EVEN TELL WHAT'S TRUE ANYMORE!
NO ONE CAN, DAD.
I MET SOMEONE **ON THE INTERNET** AND--
ARE YOU VISITING **DATING WEBSITES?**
NO. NOT... ANYMORE. **MAYBE.** SOMETIMES. **BUT THAT'S NOT IT!**
I MET...SOMEONE WHO IS **CHANGING ME.** I DON'T KNOW HOW ELSE TO PUT IT.
I DID SOMETHING SO STUPID AT THE UNIVERSITY TODAY! I CAME IN WITH MY **HEAD WRAPPED IN FAKE DYNAMITE** AND THEY HAD TO **ESCORT ME OUT!**
THEY DIDN'T UNDERSTAND I WAS REFERENCING PIERROT LE FOU!
PIERROT LE FOU IS ABOUT **LOVE.**
BUT IT'S ALSO ABOUT **CONFUSION!** AND **MANIPULATION!**
WHAT ARE YOU SAYING?
I AM SAYING I FEEL MANIPULATED INTO THE GAPING MAW OF CHAOS AND THE THING IS I KIND OF LIKE IT!

"In chaos, there is fertility" -Anaïs Nin

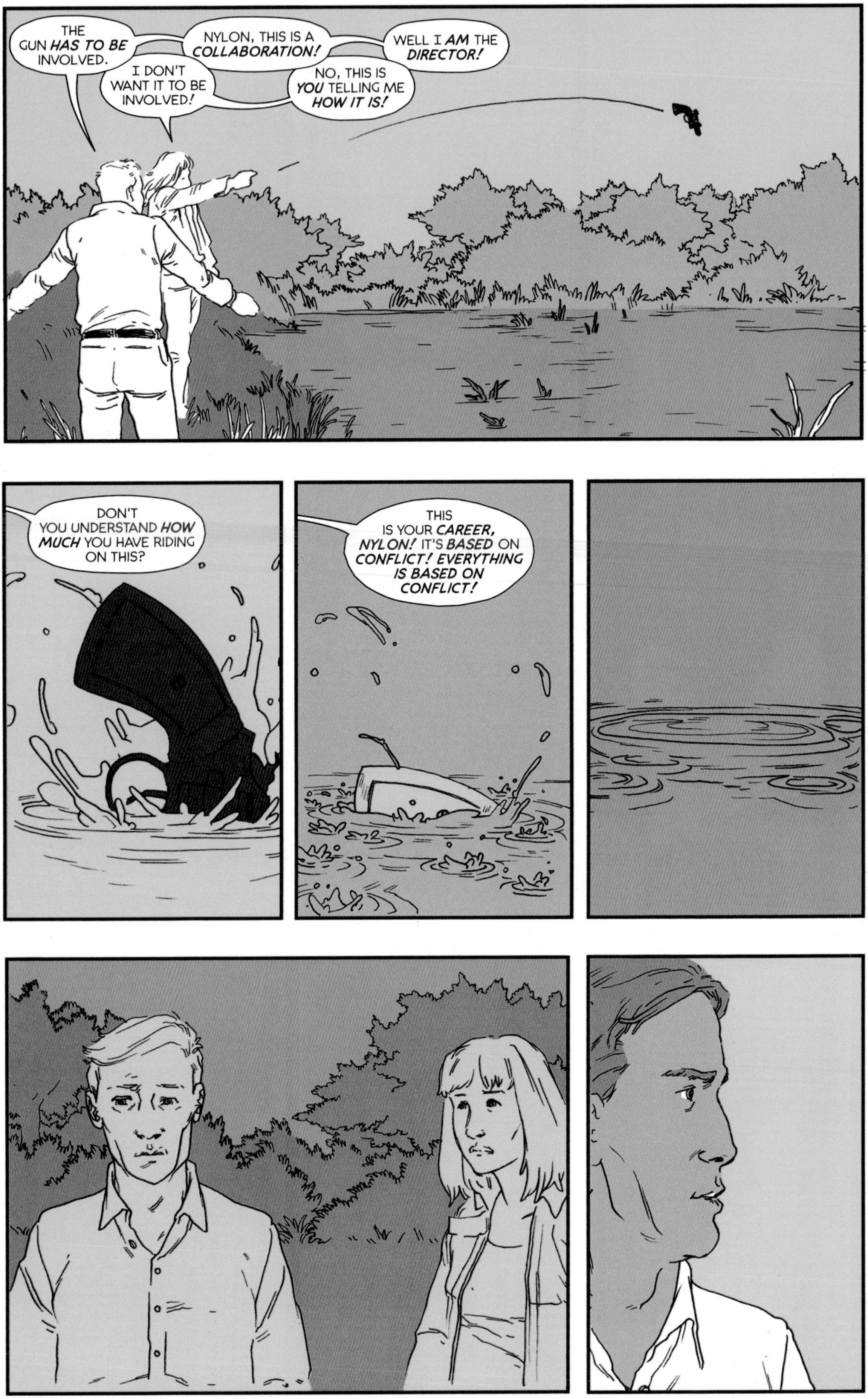
THE GUN HAS TO BE INVOLVED.
NYLON, THIS IS A COLLABORATION!
WELL I AM THE DIRECTOR!
I DON'T WANT IT TO BE INVOLVED!
NO, THIS IS YOU TELLING ME HOW IT IS!
DON'T YOU UNDERSTAND HOW MUCH YOU HAVE RIDING ON THIS?
THIS IS YOUR CAREER, NYLON! IT'S BASED ON CONFLICT! EVERYTHING IS BASED ON CONFLICT!

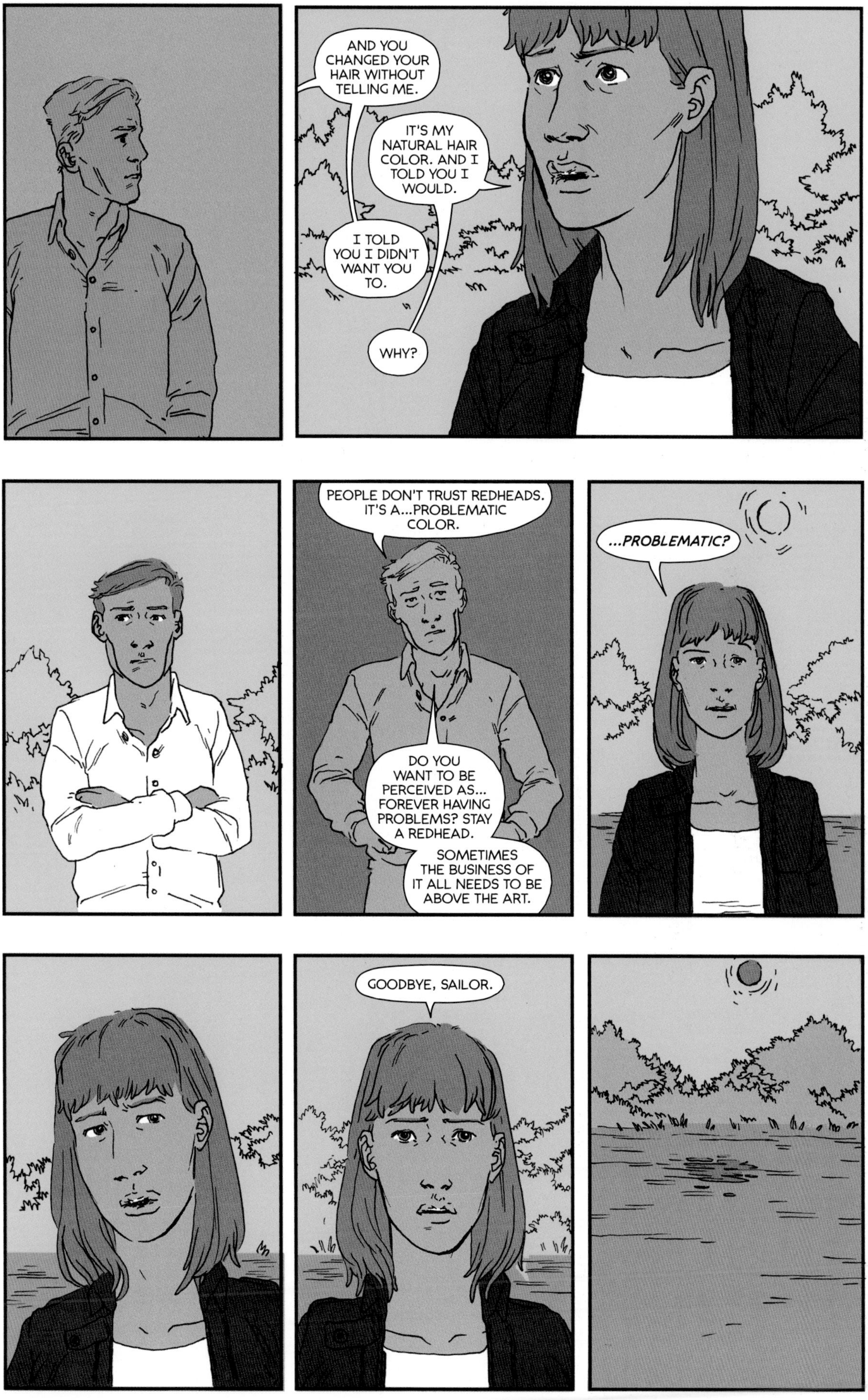
AND YOU CHANGED YOUR HAIR WITHOUT TELLING ME.
IT'S MY NATURAL HAIR COLOR. AND I TOLD YOU I WOULD.
I TOLD YOU I DIDN'T WANT YOU TO.
WHY?
PEOPLE DON'T TRUST REDHEADS. IT'S A...PROBLEMATIC COLOR.
DO YOU WANT TO BE PERCEIVED AS... FOREVER HAVING PROBLEMS? STAY A REDHEAD.
SOMETIMES THE BUSINESS OF IT ALL NEEDS TO BE ABOVE THE ART.
...PROBLEMATIC?
GOODBYE, SAILOR.

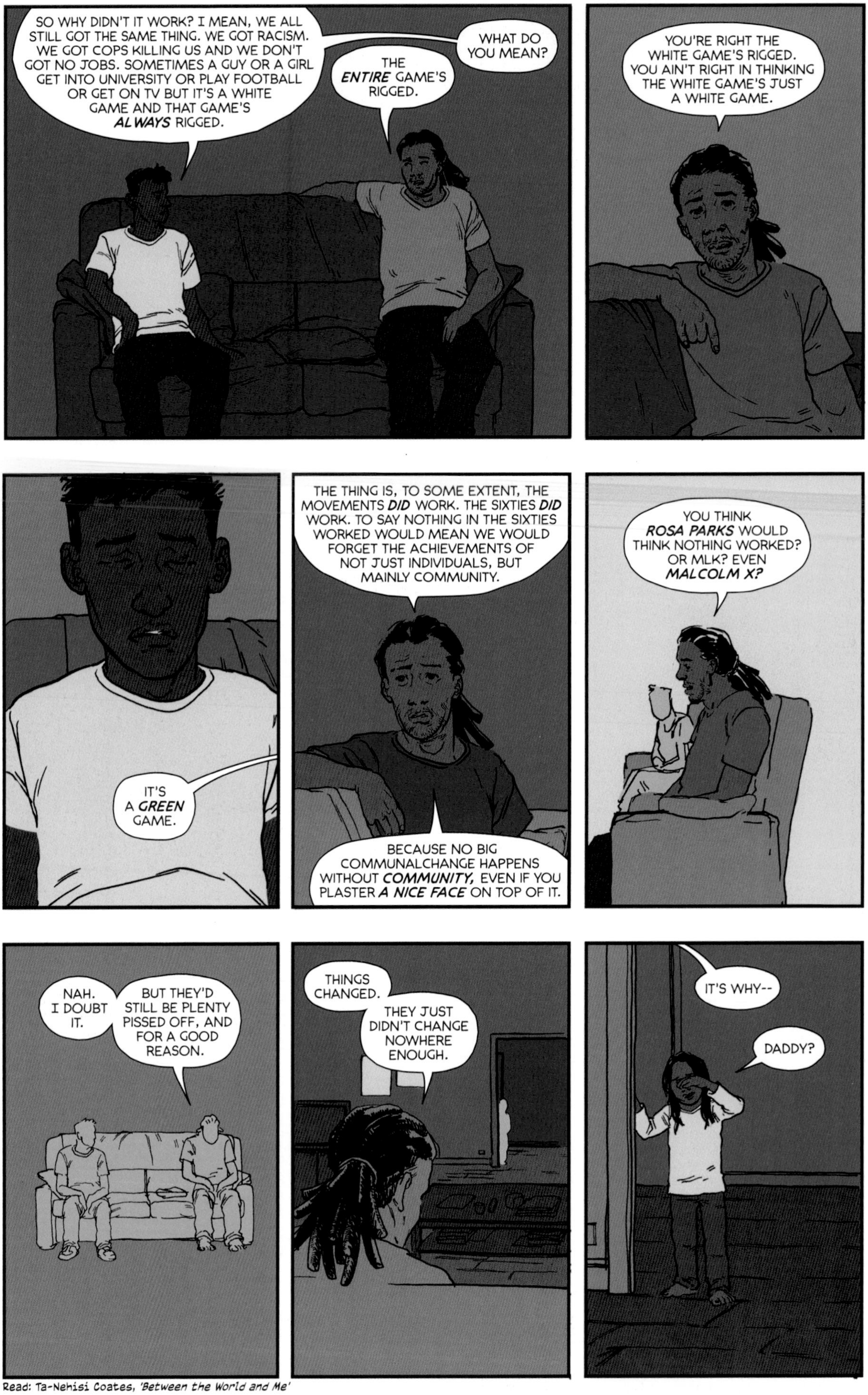
SO WHY DIDN'T IT WORK? I MEAN, WE ALL STILL GOT THE SAME THING. WE GOT RACISM. WE GOT COPS KILLING US AND WE DON'T GOT NO JOBS. SOMETIMES A GUY OR A GIRL GET INTO UNIVERSITY OR PLAY FOOTBALL OR GET ON TV BUT IT'S A WHITE GAME AND THAT GAME'S ALWAYS RIGGED.
WHAT DO YOU MEAN?
THE ENTIRE GAME'S RIGGED.
YOU'RE RIGHT THE WHITE GAME'S RIGGED. YOU AIN'T RIGHT IN THINKING THE WHITE GAME'S JUST A WHITE GAME.
IT'S A GREEN GAME.
THE THING IS, TO SOME EXTENT, THE MOVEMENTS DID WORK. THE SIXTIES DID WORK. TO SAY NOTHING IN THE SIXTIES WORKED WOULD MEAN WE WOULD FORGET THE ACHIEVEMENTS OF NOT JUST INDIVIDUALS, BUT MAINLY COMMUNITY.
BECAUSE NO BIG COMMUNALCHANGE HAPPENS WITHOUT COMMUNITY, EVEN IF YOU PLASTER A NICE FACE ON TOP OF IT.
YOU THINK ROSA PARKS WOULD THINK NOTHING WORKED? OR MLK? EVEN MALCOLM X?
NAH. I DOUBT IT.
BUT THEY'D STILL BE PLENTY PISSED OFF, AND FOR A GOOD REASON.
THINGS CHANGED.
THEY JUST DIDN'T CHANGE NOWHERE ENOUGH.
IT'S WHY--
DADDY?

Read: Ta-Nehisi Coates, *'Between the World and Me'*

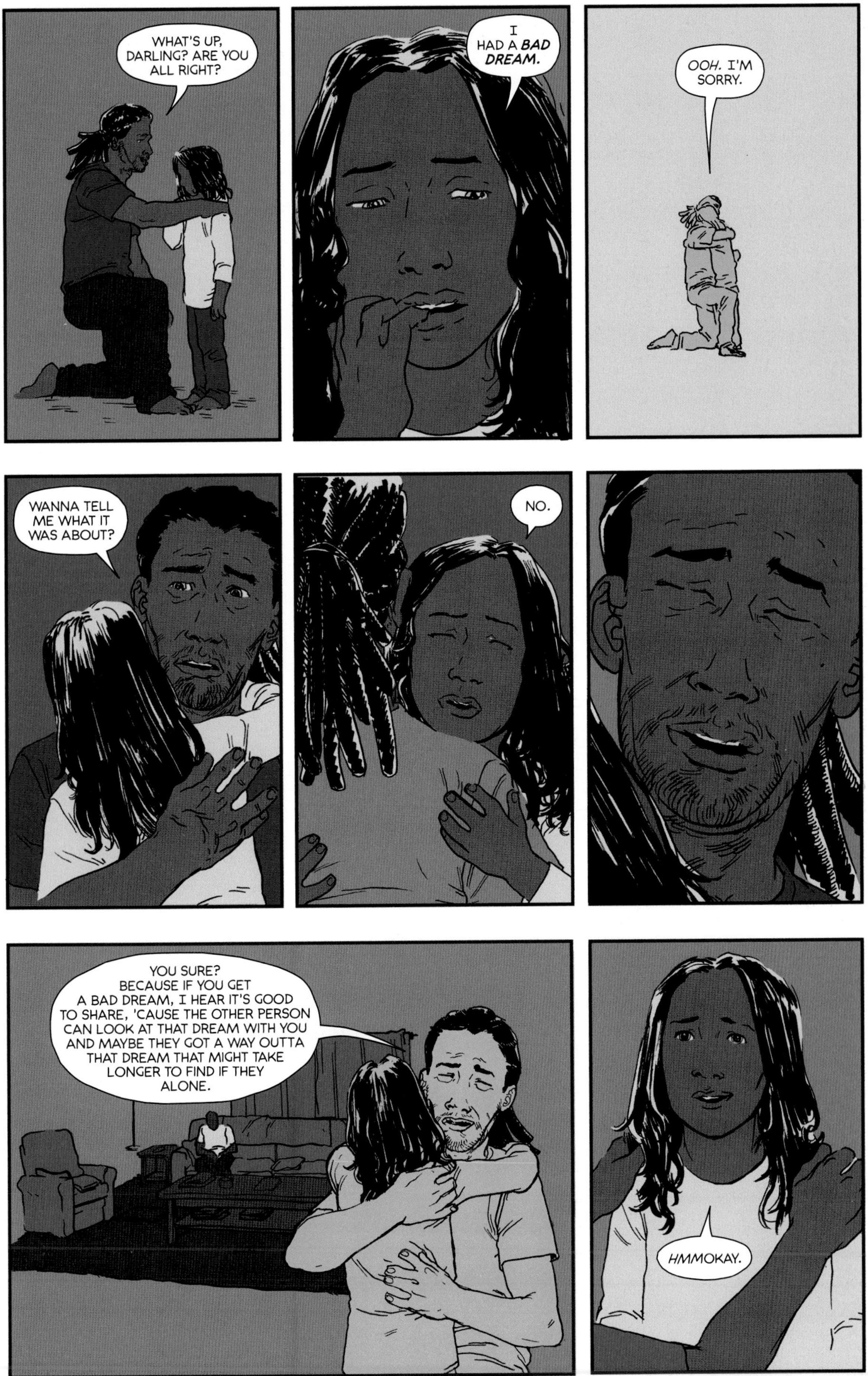
WHAT'S UP, DARLING? ARE YOU ALL RIGHT?
I HAD A *BAD DREAM.*
OOH. I'M SORRY.
WANNA TELL ME WHAT IT WAS ABOUT?
NO.
YOU SURE? BECAUSE IF YOU GET A BAD DREAM, I HEAR IT'S GOOD TO SHARE, 'CAUSE THE OTHER PERSON CAN LOOK AT THAT DREAM WITH YOU AND MAYBE THEY GOT A WAY OUTTA THAT DREAM THAT MIGHT TAKE LONGER TO FIND IF THEY ALONE.
HMMOKAY.

"Numbers alone can't convey what the justice system does to the individual black body." -Ta-Nehisi Coates

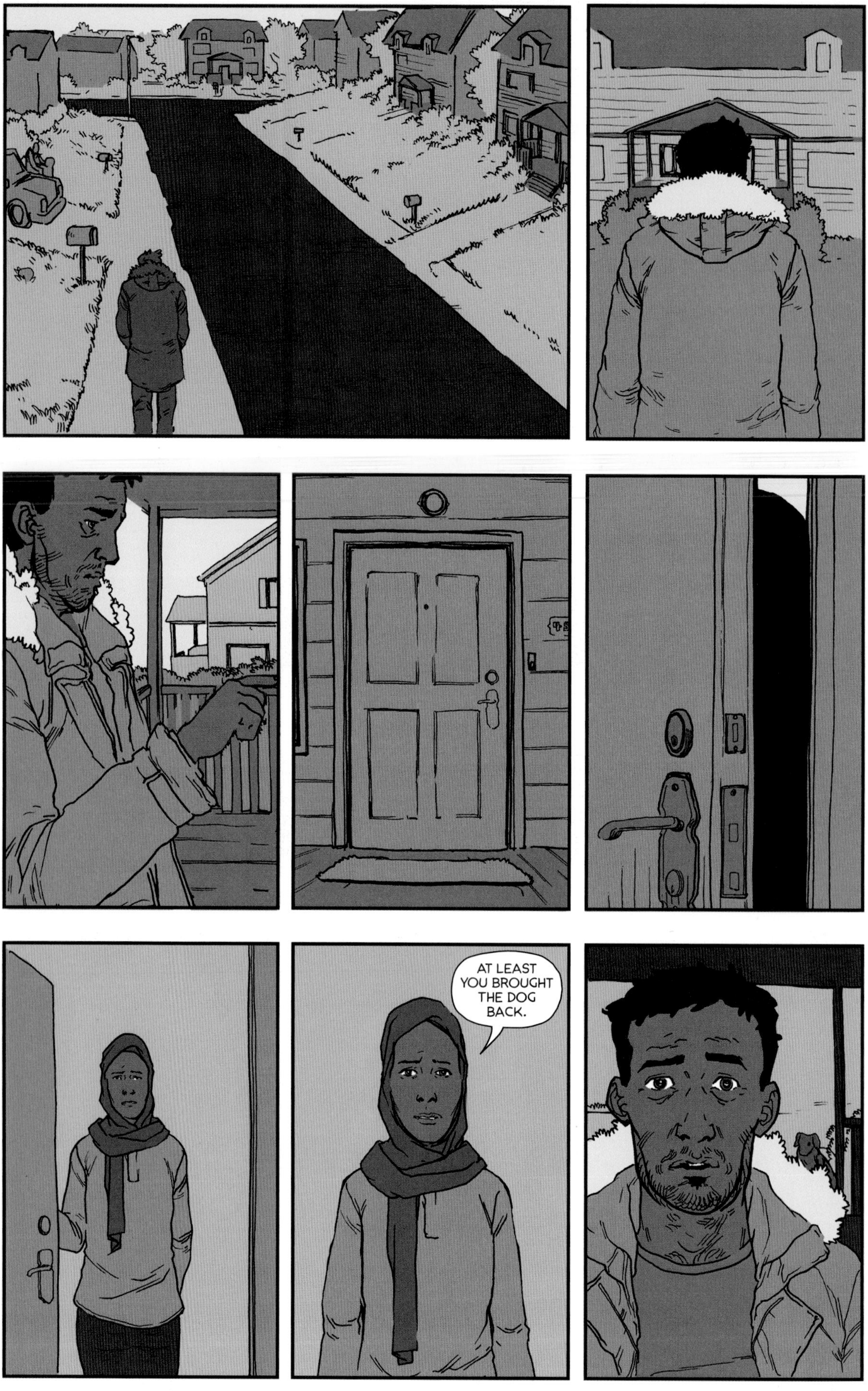
AT LEAST YOU BROUGHT THE DOG BACK.

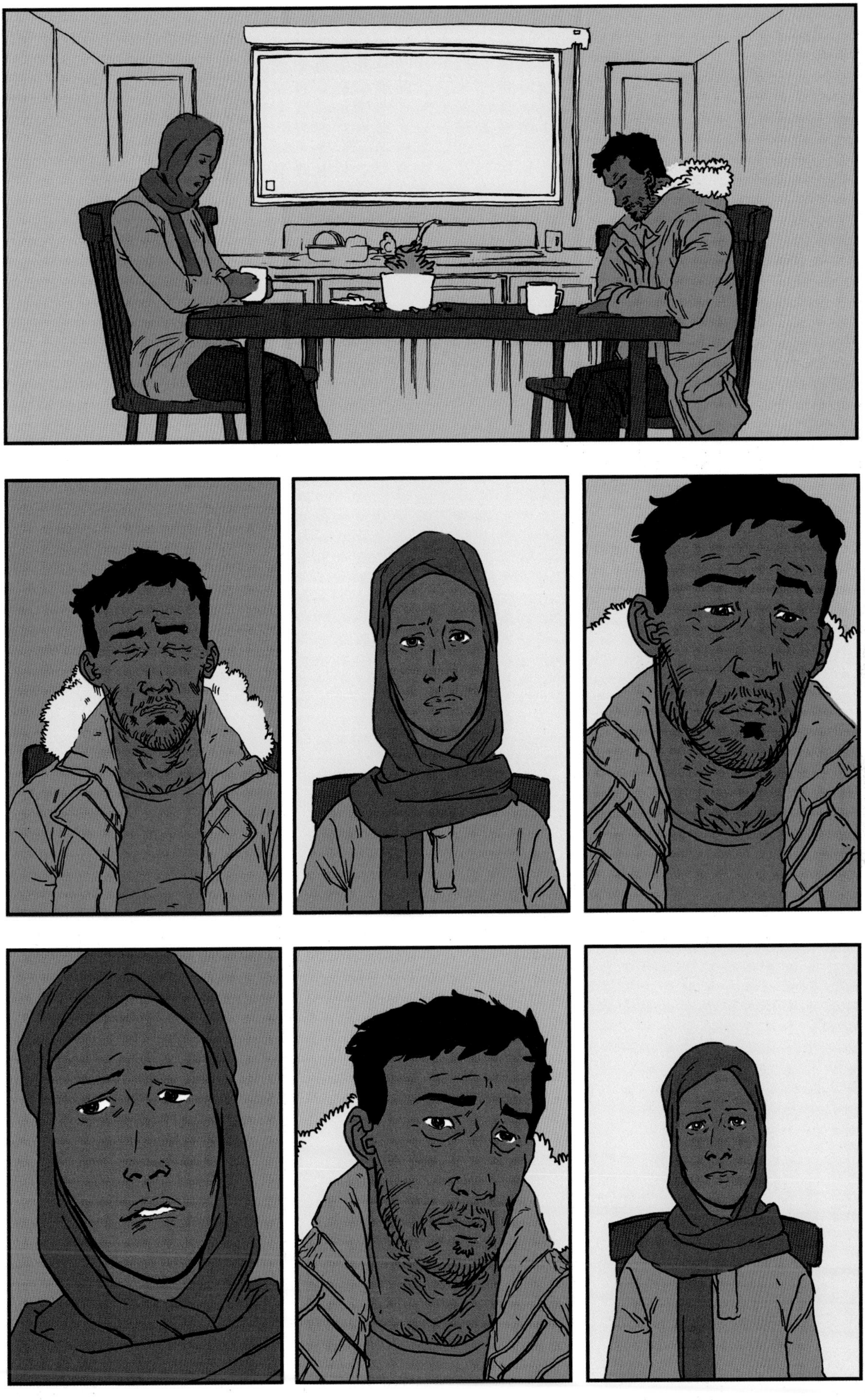

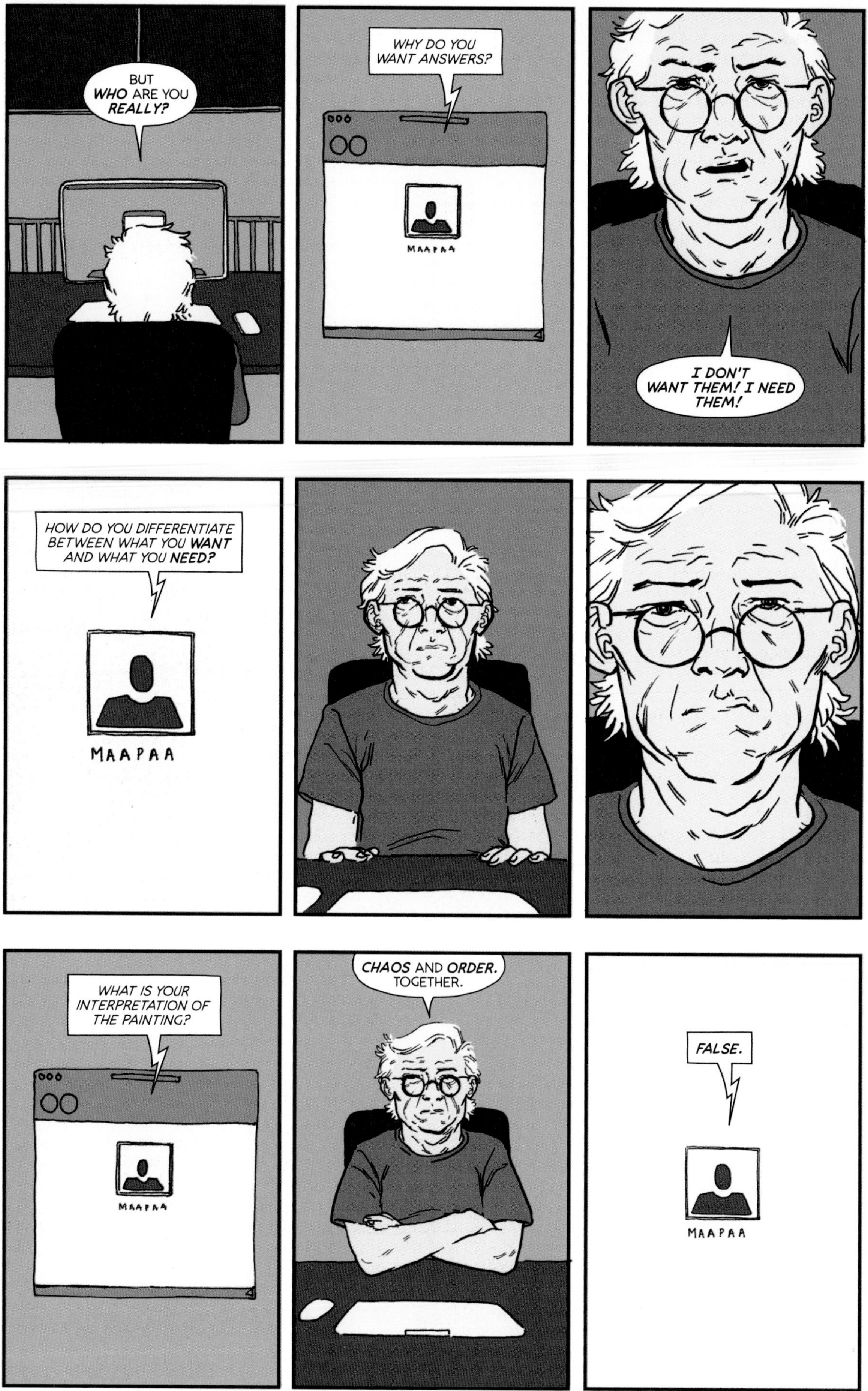
BUT WHO ARE YOU REALLY?
WHY DO YOU WANT ANSWERS?
MAAPAA
I DON'T WANT THEM! I NEED THEM!
HOW DO YOU DIFFERENTIATE BETWEEN WHAT YOU WANT AND WHAT YOU NEED?
MAAPAA
WHAT IS YOUR INTERPRETATION OF THE PAINTING?
MAAPAA
CHAOS AND ORDER. TOGETHER.
FALSE.
MAAPAA

"Laughter on American television has taken the place of the chorus in Greek tragedy." -Jean Baudrillard, *'Americana'*

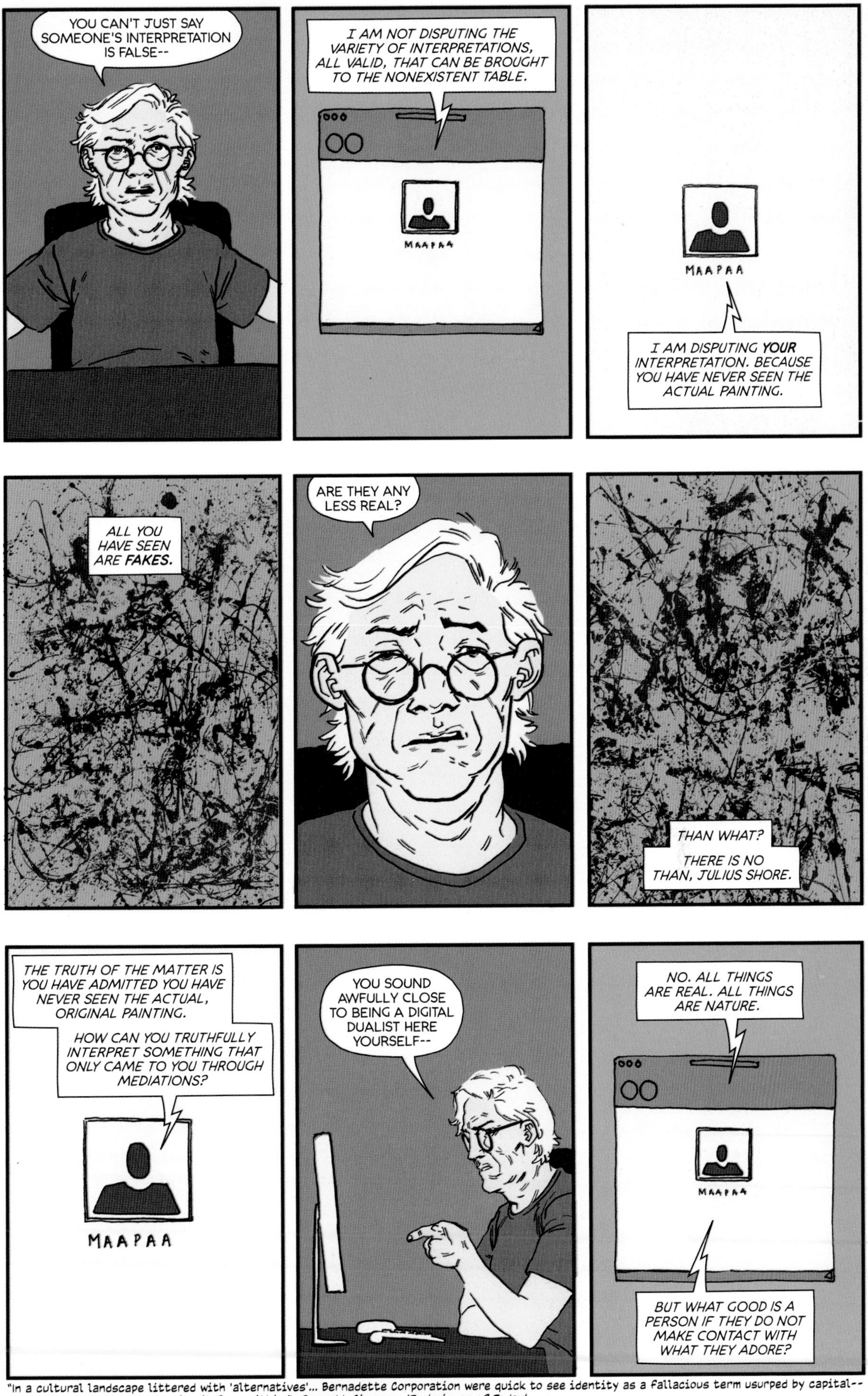
YOU CAN'T JUST SAY SOMEONE'S INTERPRETATION IS FALSE--
I AM NOT DISPUTING THE VARIETY OF INTERPRETATIONS, ALL VALID, THAT CAN BE BROUGHT TO THE NONEXISTENT TABLE.
MAAPAA
MAAPAA
I AM DISPUTING **YOUR** INTERPRETATION. BECAUSE YOU HAVE NEVER SEEN THE ACTUAL PAINTING.
ALL YOU HAVE SEEN ARE **FAKES.**
ARE THEY ANY LESS REAL?
THAN WHAT?
THERE IS NO THAN, JULIUS SHORE.
THE TRUTH OF THE MATTER IS YOU HAVE ADMITTED YOU HAVE NEVER SEEN THE ACTUAL, ORIGINAL PAINTING.
HOW CAN YOU TRUTHFULLY INTERPRET SOMETHING THAT ONLY CAME TO YOU THROUGH MEDIATIONS?
MAAPAA
YOU SOUND AWFULLY CLOSE TO BEING A DIGITAL DUALIST HERE YOURSELF--
NO. ALL THINGS ARE REAL. ALL THINGS ARE NATURE.
MAAPAA
BUT WHAT GOOD IS A PERSON IF THEY DO NOT MAKE CONTACT WITH WHAT THEY ADORE?

"In a cultural landscape littered with 'alternatives'... Bernadette Corporation were quick to see identity as a fallacious term usurped by capital--and so they sought to undermine it from within." -Bennett Simpson, *'Techniques of Today'*

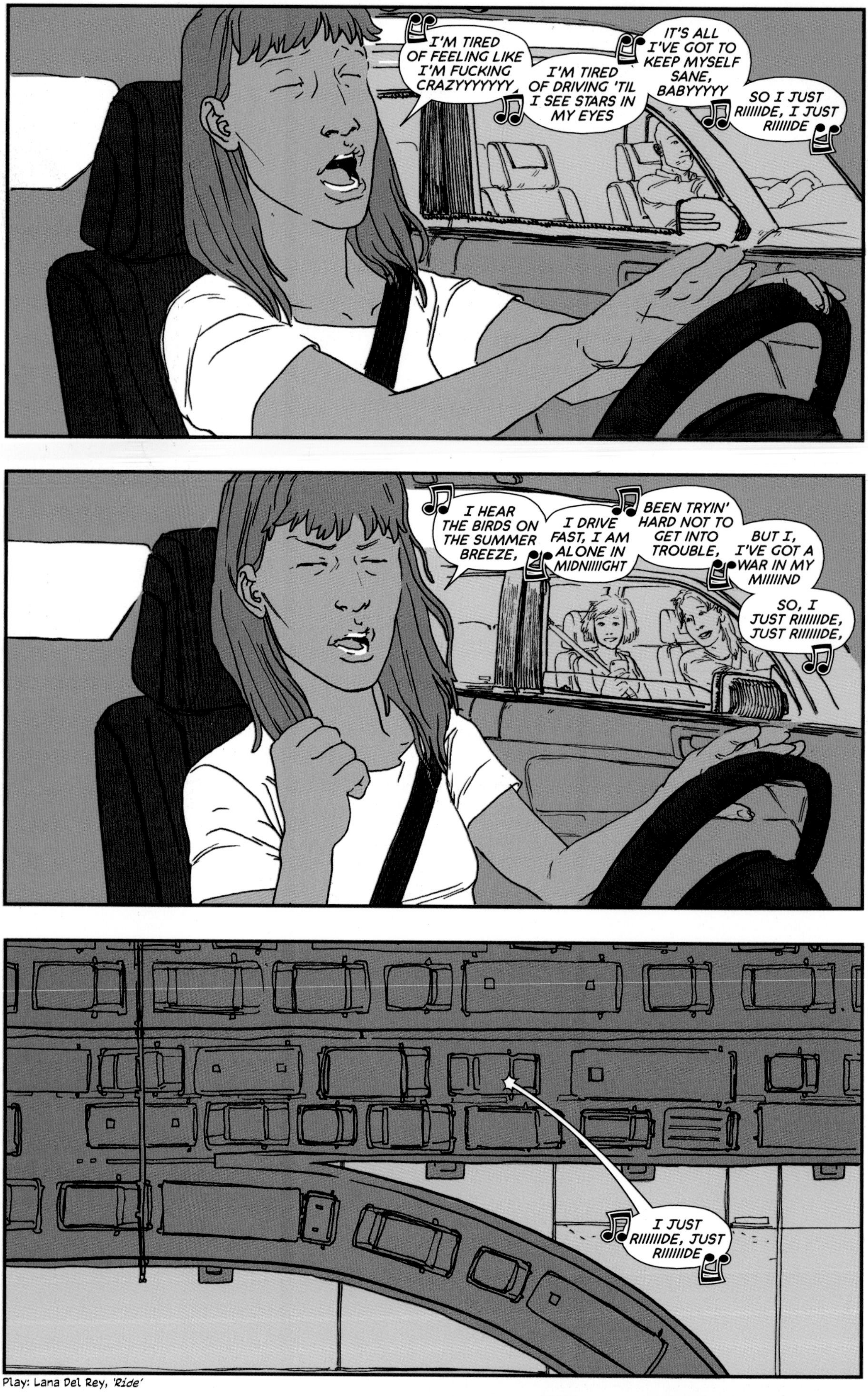
I'M TIRED OF FEELING LIKE I'M FUCKING CRAZYYYYYYY
I'M TIRED OF DRIVING 'TIL I SEE STARS IN MY EYES
IT'S ALL I'VE GOT TO KEEP MYSELF SANE, BABYYYYY
SO I JUST RIIIIIDE, I JUST RIIIIIDE
I HEAR THE BIRDS ON THE SUMMER BREEZE,
I DRIVE FAST, I AM ALONE IN MIDNIIIIGHT
BEEN TRYIN' HARD NOT TO GET INTO TROUBLE,
BUT I, I'VE GOT A WAR IN MY MIIIIIND
SO, I JUST RIIIIIDE, JUST RIIIIIDE,
I JUST RIIIIIDE, JUST RIIIIIDE

Play: Lana Del Rey, *'Ride'*

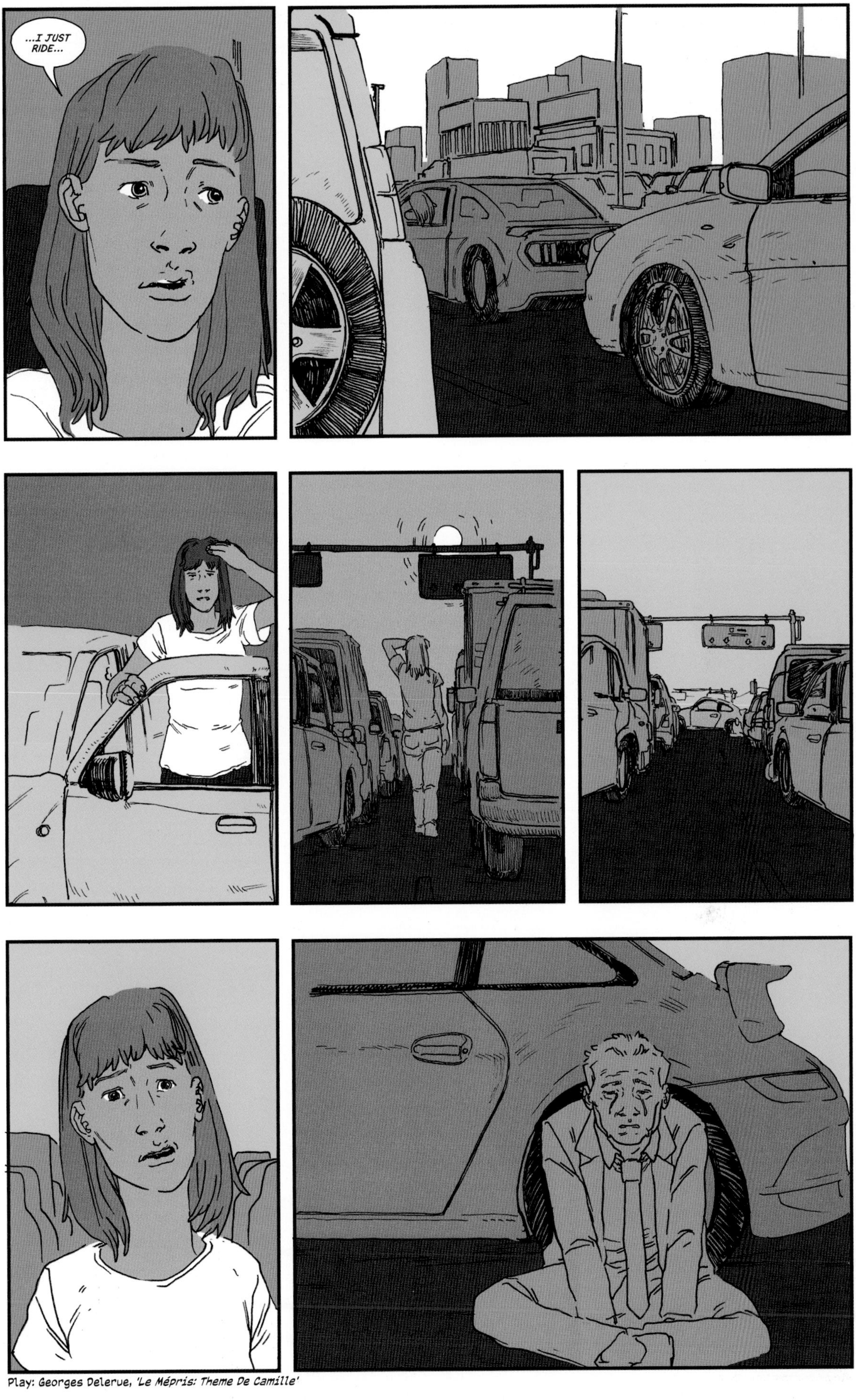
...I JUST RIDE...

Play: Georges Delerue, *'Le Mépris: Theme De Camille'*

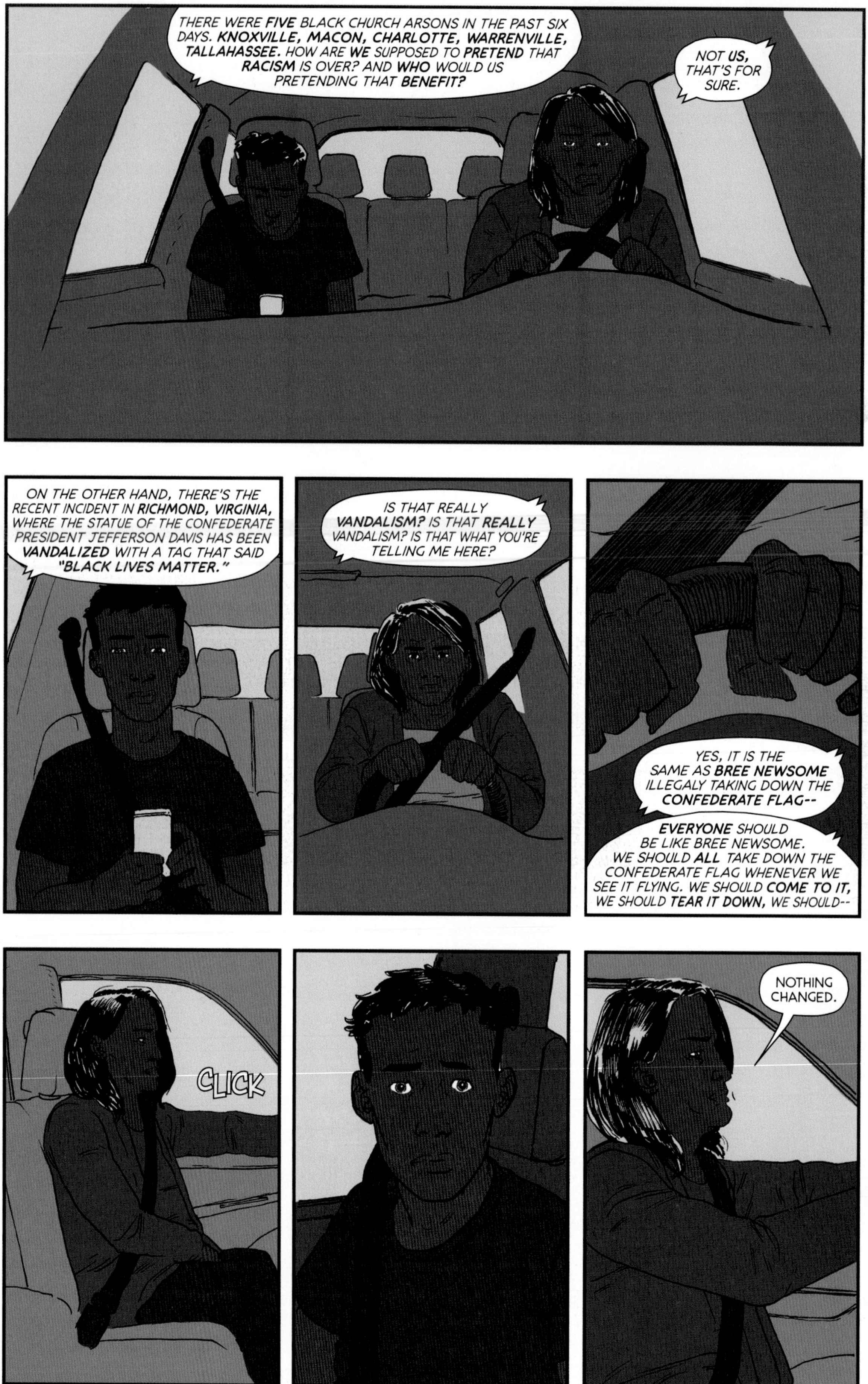
THERE WERE FIVE BLACK CHURCH ARSONS IN THE PAST SIX DAYS. KNOXVILLE, MACON, CHARLOTTE, WARRENVILLE, TALLAHASSEE. HOW ARE WE SUPPOSED TO PRETEND THAT RACISM IS OVER? AND WHO WOULD US PRETENDING THAT BENEFIT?
NOT US, THAT'S FOR SURE.
ON THE OTHER HAND, THERE'S THE RECENT INCIDENT IN RICHMOND, VIRGINIA, WHERE THE STATUE OF THE CONFEDERATE PRESIDENT JEFFERSON DAVIS HAS BEEN VANDALIZED WITH A TAG THAT SAID "BLACK LIVES MATTER."
IS THAT REALLY VANDALISM? IS THAT REALLY VANDALISM? IS THAT WHAT YOU'RE TELLING ME HERE?
YES, IT IS THE SAME AS BREE NEWSOME ILLEGALY TAKING DOWN THE CONFEDERATE FLAG--
EVERYONE SHOULD BE LIKE BREE NEWSOME. WE SHOULD ALL TAKE DOWN THE CONFEDERATE FLAG WHENEVER WE SEE IT FLYING. WE SHOULD COME TO IT, WE SHOULD TEAR IT DOWN, WE SHOULD--
CLICK
NOTHING CHANGED.

http://twitter.com/breenewsome

Read: Claudia Rankine, *'Citizen: An American Lyric'*

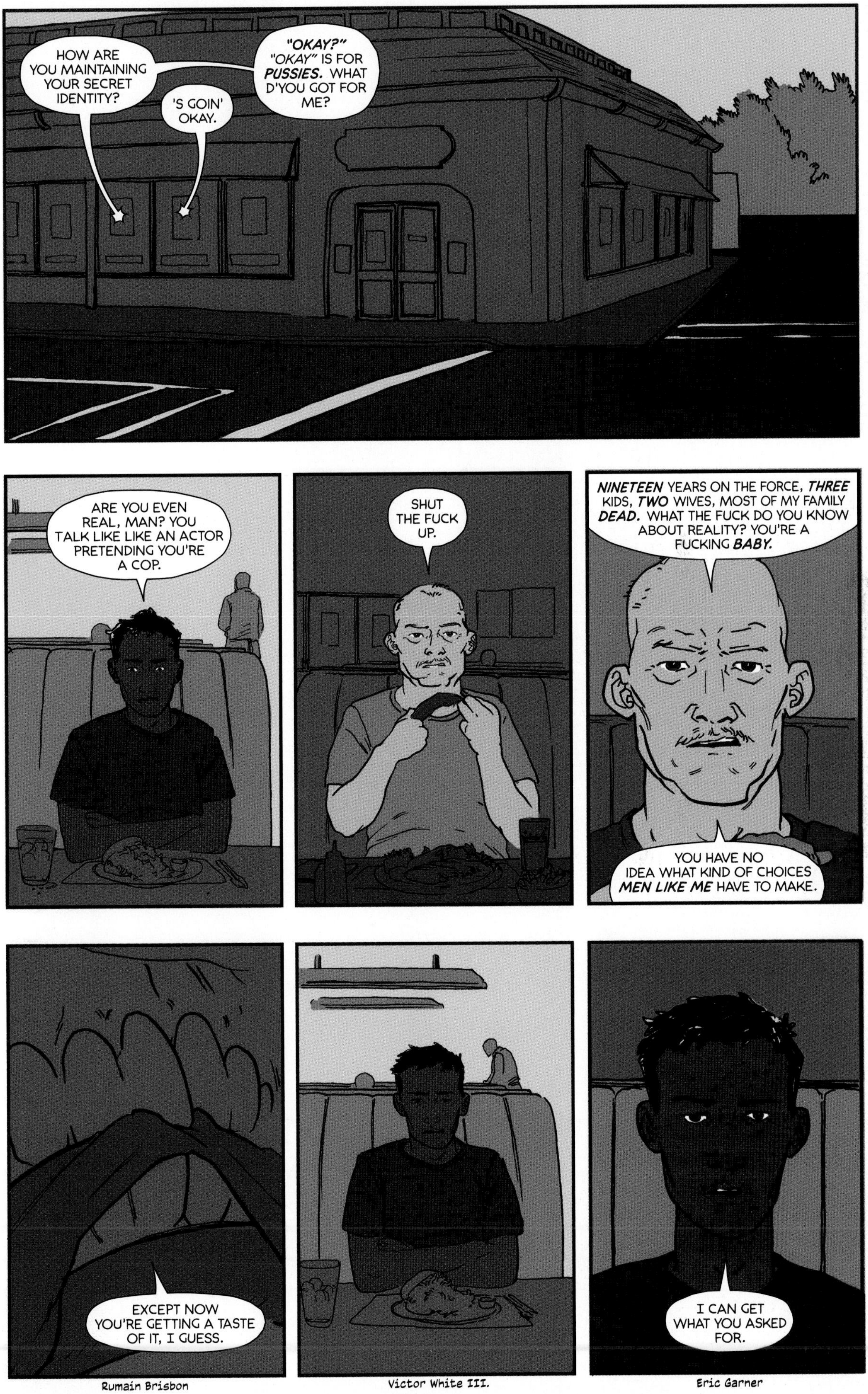
HOW ARE YOU MAINTAINING YOUR SECRET IDENTITY?
'S GOIN' OKAY.
"OKAY?" "OKAY" IS FOR PUSSIES. WHAT D'YOU GOT FOR ME?
ARE YOU EVEN REAL, MAN? YOU TALK LIKE LIKE AN ACTOR PRETENDING YOU'RE A COP.
SHUT THE FUCK UP.
NINETEEN YEARS ON THE FORCE, THREE KIDS, TWO WIVES, MOST OF MY FAMILY DEAD. WHAT THE FUCK DO YOU KNOW ABOUT REALITY? YOU'RE A FUCKING BABY.
YOU HAVE NO IDEA WHAT KIND OF CHOICES MEN LIKE ME HAVE TO MAKE.
EXCEPT NOW YOU'RE GETTING A TASTE OF IT, I GUESS.
I CAN GET WHAT YOU ASKED FOR.

Rumain Brisbon

Victor White III.

Eric Garner

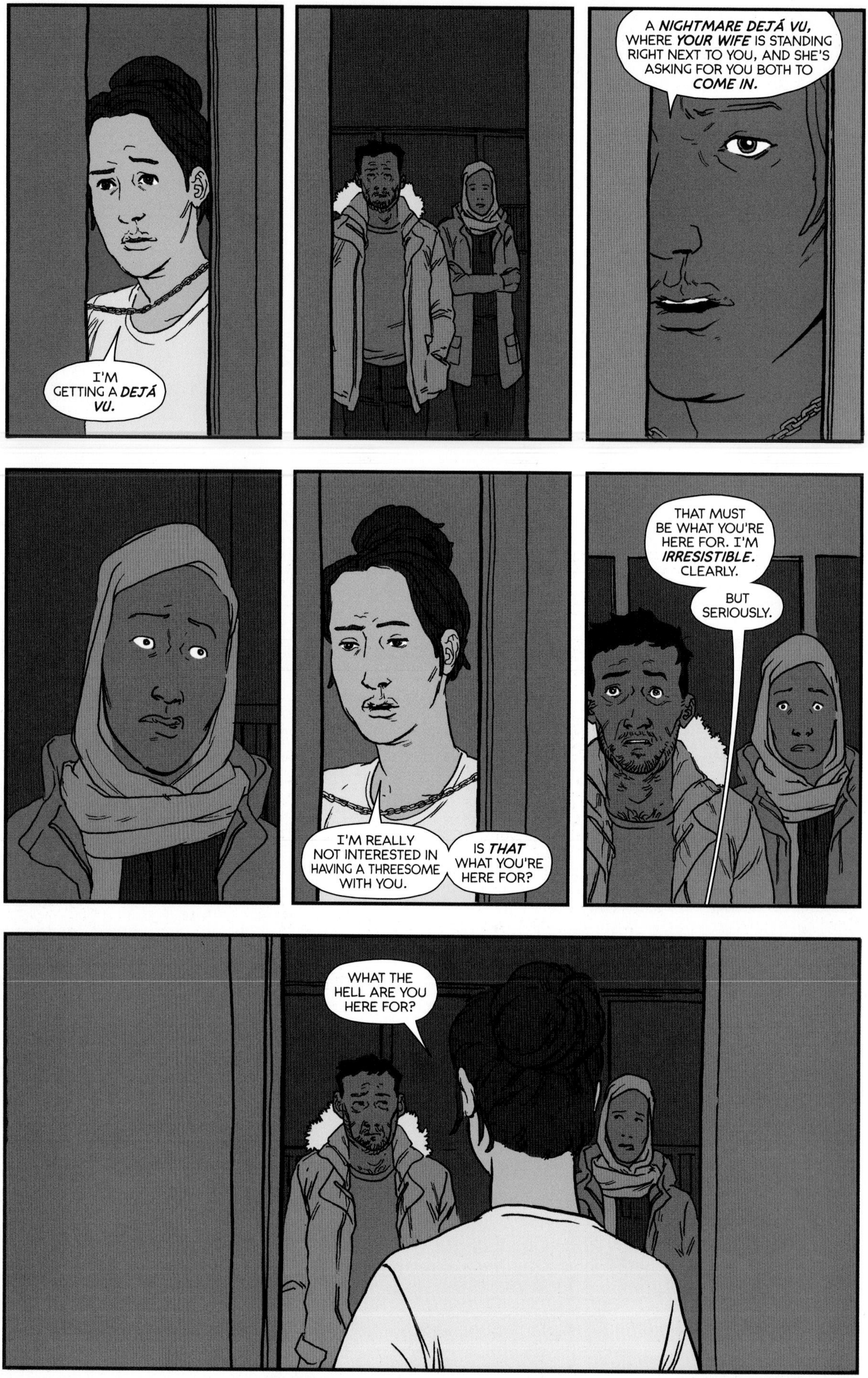
I'M GETTING A *DEJÁ VU.*
A *NIGHTMARE DEJÁ VU,* WHERE *YOUR WIFE* IS STANDING RIGHT NEXT TO YOU, AND SHE'S ASKING FOR YOU BOTH TO *COME IN.*
I'M REALLY NOT INTERESTED IN HAVING A THREESOME WITH YOU.
IS *THAT* WHAT YOU'RE HERE FOR?
THAT MUST BE WHAT YOU'RE HERE FOR. I'M *IRRESISTIBLE.* CLEARLY.
BUT SERIOUSLY.
WHAT THE HELL ARE YOU HERE FOR?

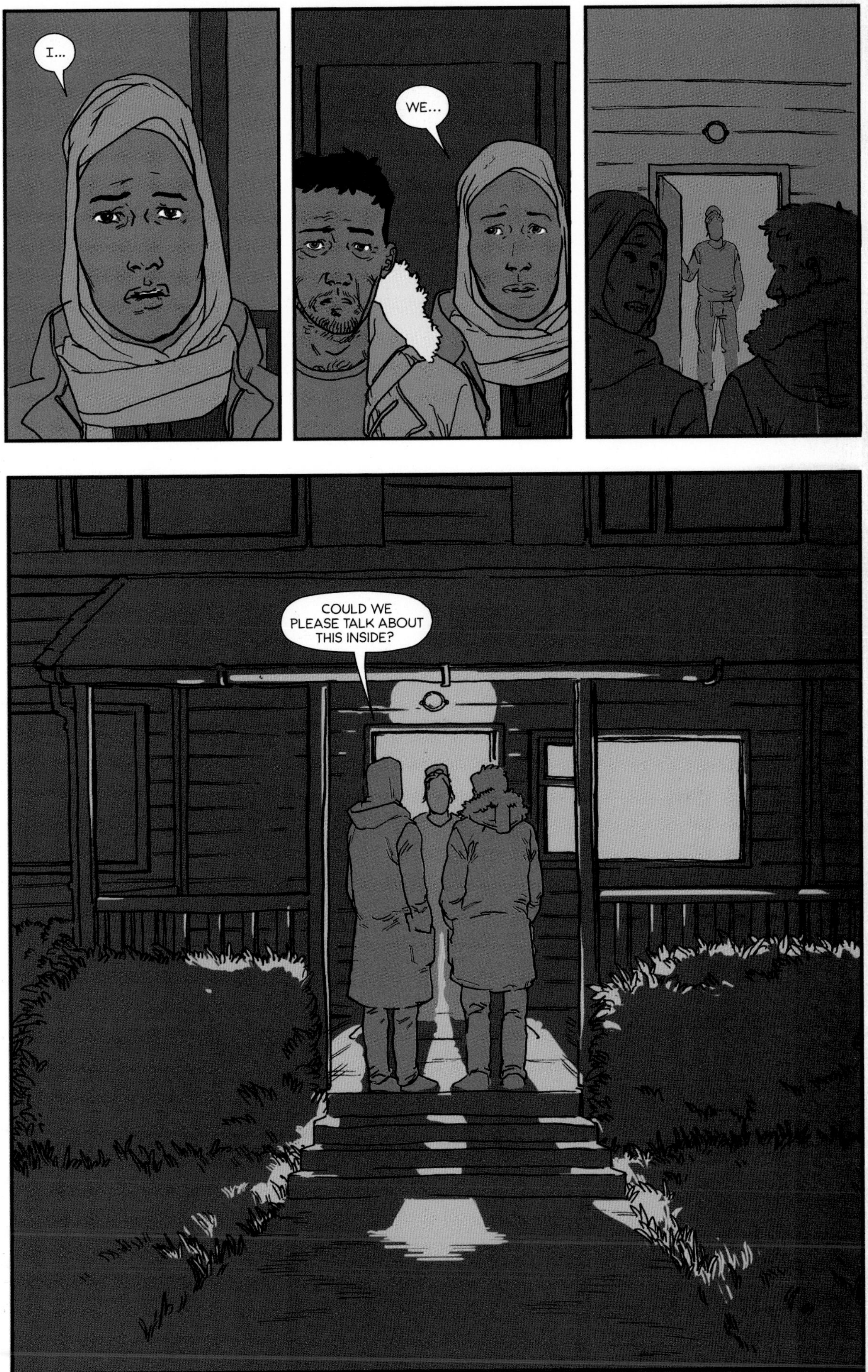
I...
WE...
COULD WE PLEASE TALK ABOUT THIS INSIDE?

"If you could say, That is the future. Up that road where you are walking now. That is the actual future and I will meet you there. Then I could say, Now I am safe." -Fanny Howe, *'The Winter Sun: Notes on a Vocation'*

Material

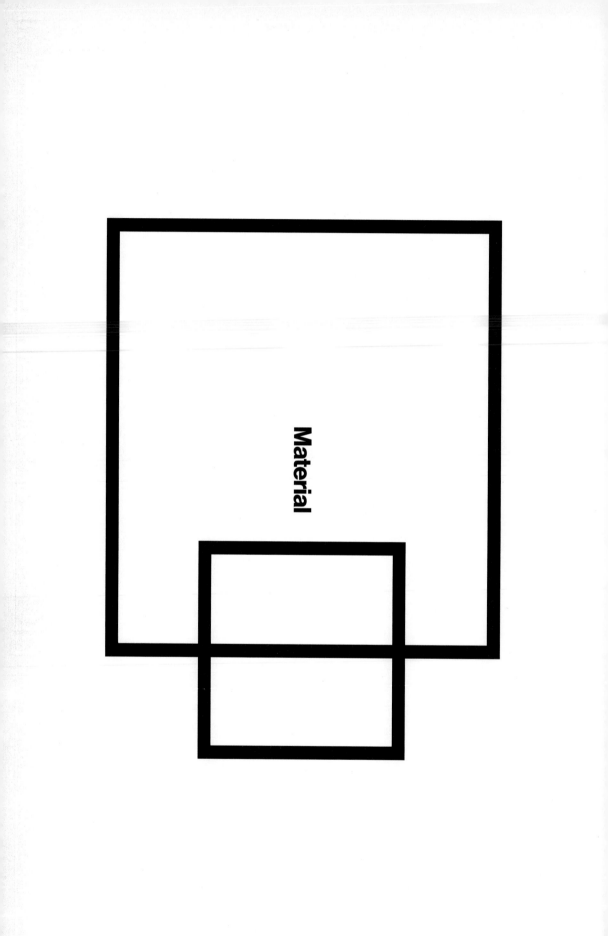

Chapter 4

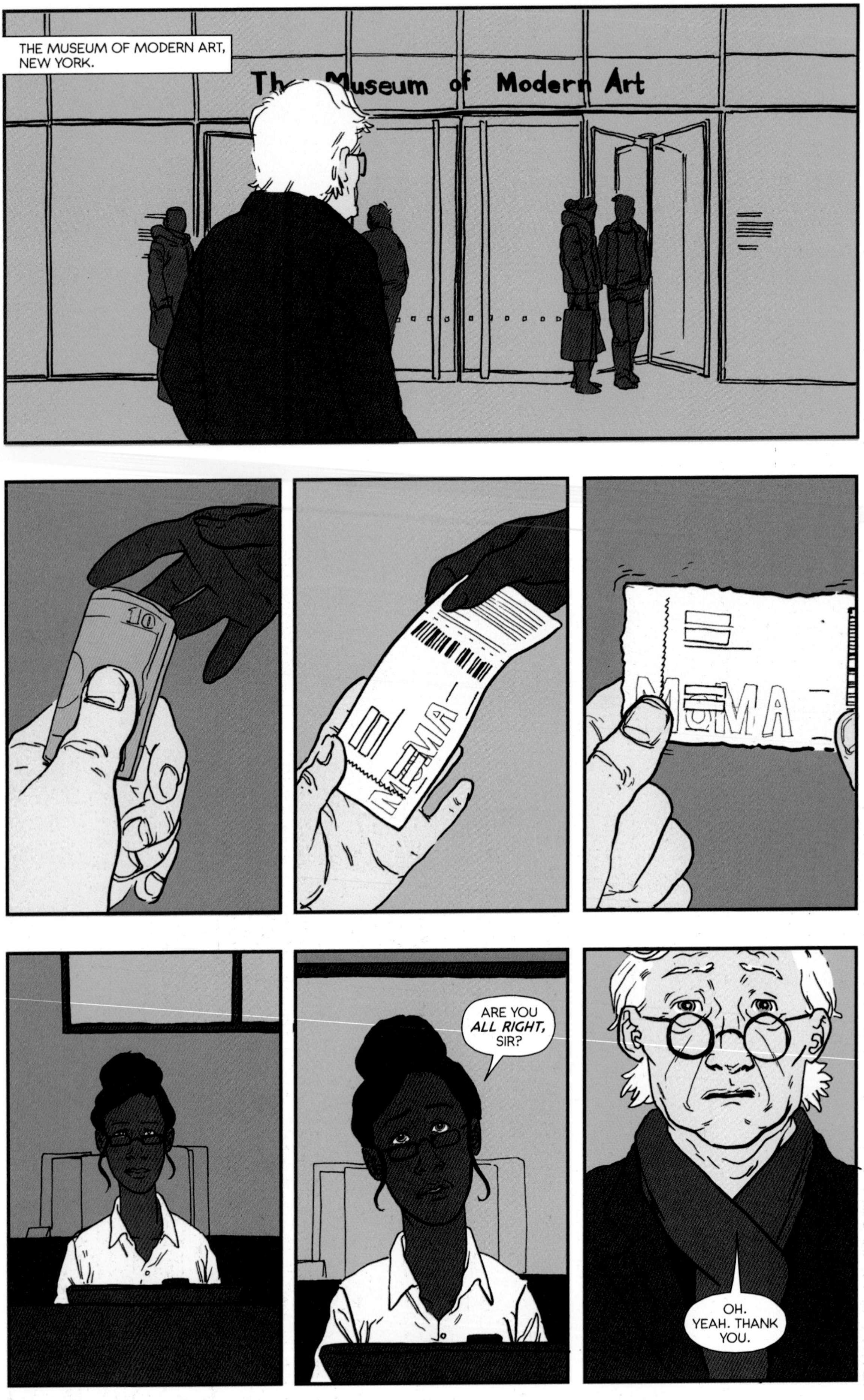
THE MUSEUM OF MODERN ART, NEW YORK.
The Museum of Modern Art
ARE YOU ALL RIGHT, SIR?
OH. YEAH. THANK YOU.

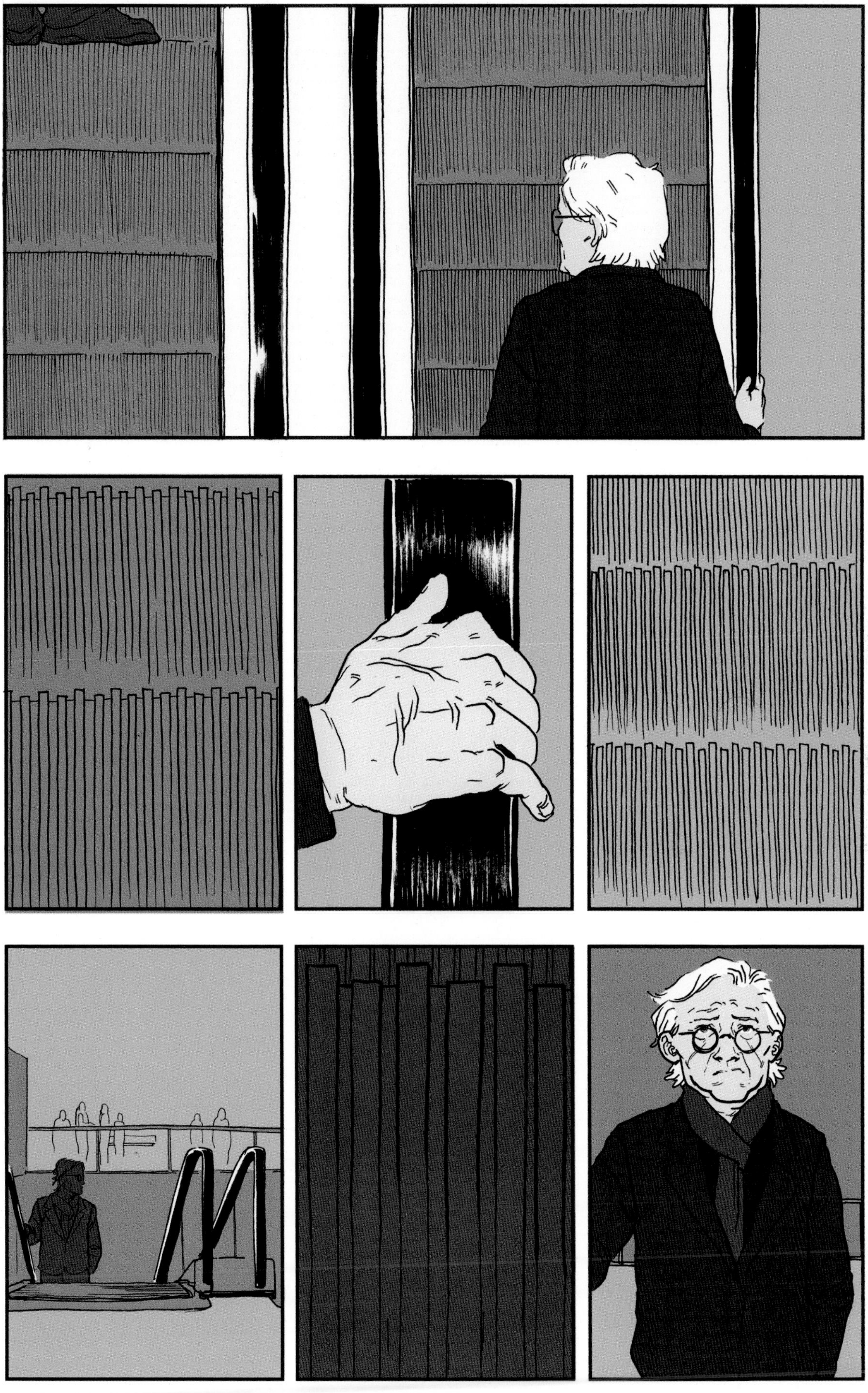

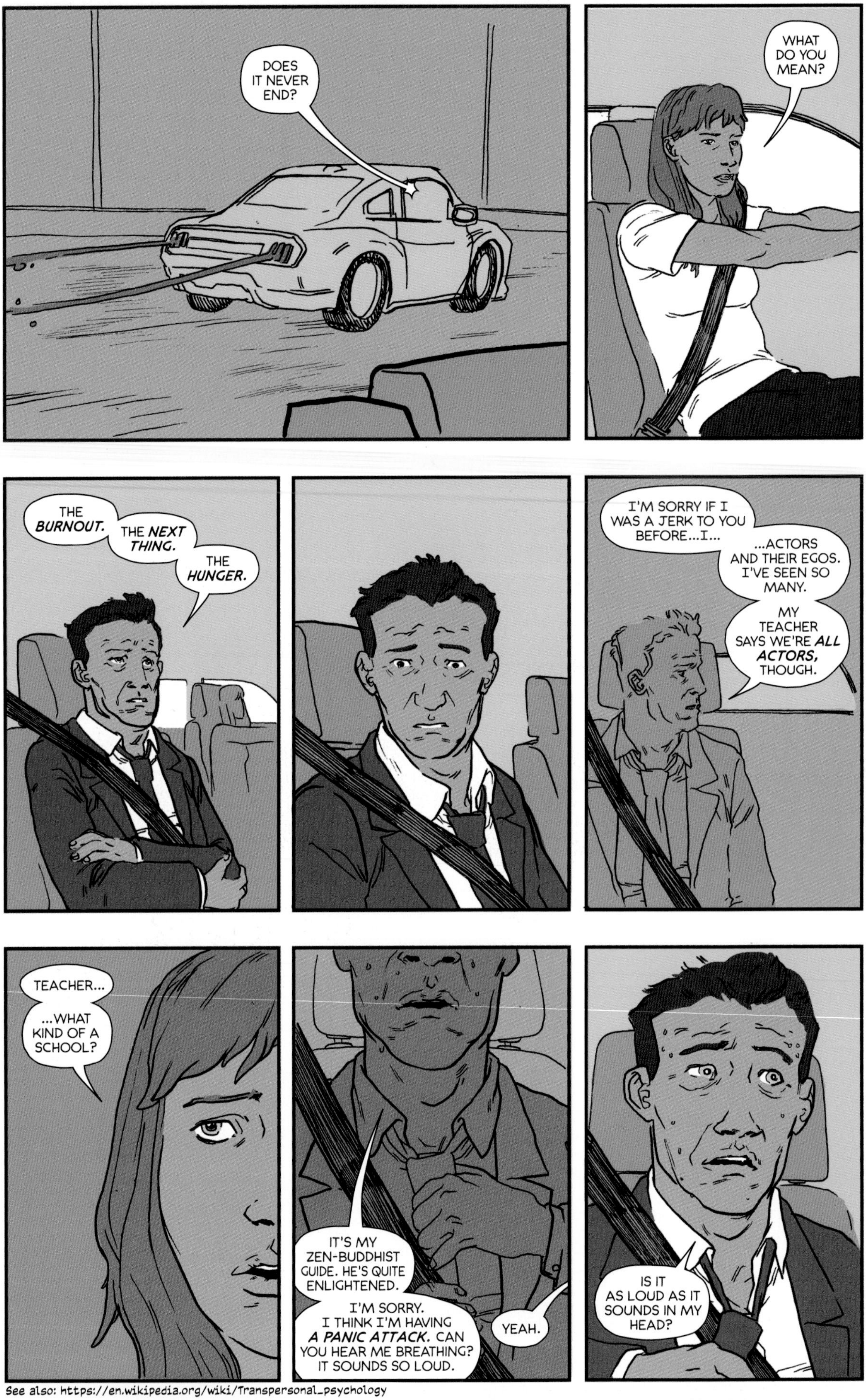
DOES IT NEVER END?
WHAT DO YOU MEAN?
THE *BURNOUT.*
THE *NEXT THING.*
THE *HUNGER.*
I'M SORRY IF I WAS A JERK TO YOU BEFORE...I...
...ACTORS AND THEIR EGOS. I'VE SEEN SO MANY.
MY TEACHER SAYS WE'RE *ALL ACTORS,* THOUGH.
TEACHER...
...WHAT KIND OF A SCHOOL?
IT'S MY ZEN-BUDDHIST GUIDE. HE'S QUITE ENLIGHTENED.
I'M SORRY. I THINK I'M HAVING *A PANIC ATTACK.* CAN YOU HEAR ME BREATHING? IT SOUNDS SO LOUD.
YEAH.
IS IT AS LOUD AS IT SOUNDS IN MY HEAD?

See also: https://en.wikipedia.org/wiki/Transpersonal_psychology

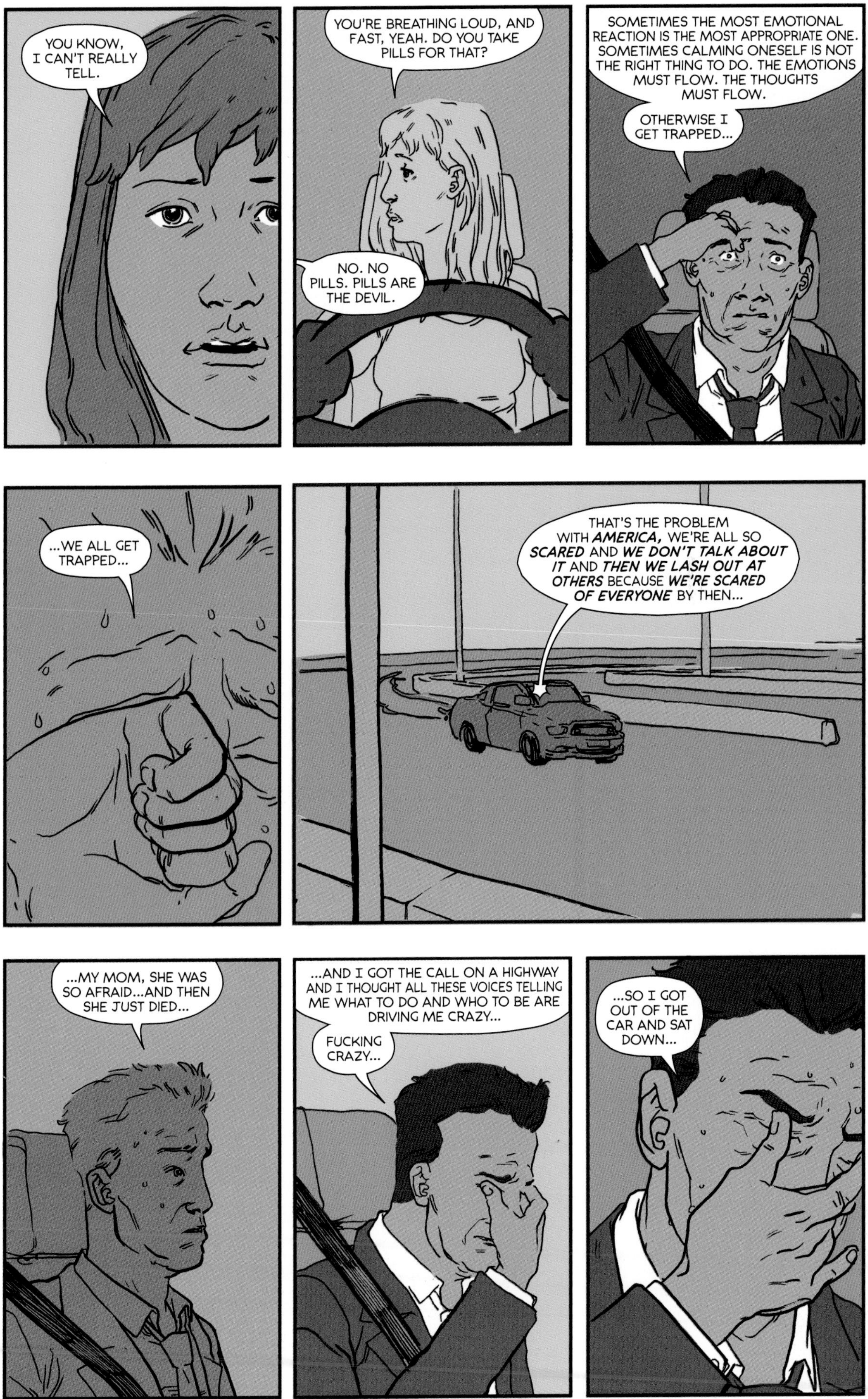
YOU KNOW, I CAN'T REALLY TELL.
YOU'RE BREATHING LOUD, AND FAST, YEAH. DO YOU TAKE PILLS FOR THAT?
NO. NO PILLS. PILLS ARE THE DEVIL.
SOMETIMES THE MOST EMOTIONAL REACTION IS THE MOST APPROPRIATE ONE. SOMETIMES CALMING ONESELF IS NOT THE RIGHT THING TO DO. THE EMOTIONS MUST FLOW. THE THOUGHTS MUST FLOW.
OTHERWISE I GET TRAPPED...
...WE ALL GET TRAPPED...
THAT'S THE PROBLEM WITH AMERICA, WE'RE ALL SO SCARED AND WE DON'T TALK ABOUT IT AND THEN WE LASH OUT AT OTHERS BECAUSE WE'RE SCARED OF EVERYONE BY THEN...
...MY MOM, SHE WAS SO AFRAID...AND THEN SHE JUST DIED...
...AND I GOT THE CALL ON A HIGHWAY AND I THOUGHT ALL THESE VOICES TELLING ME WHAT TO DO AND WHO TO BE ARE DRIVING ME CRAZY...
FUCKING CRAZY...
...SO I GOT OUT OF THE CAR AND SAT DOWN...

See also: https://en.wikipedia.org/wiki/Eye_movement_desensitization_and_reprocessing

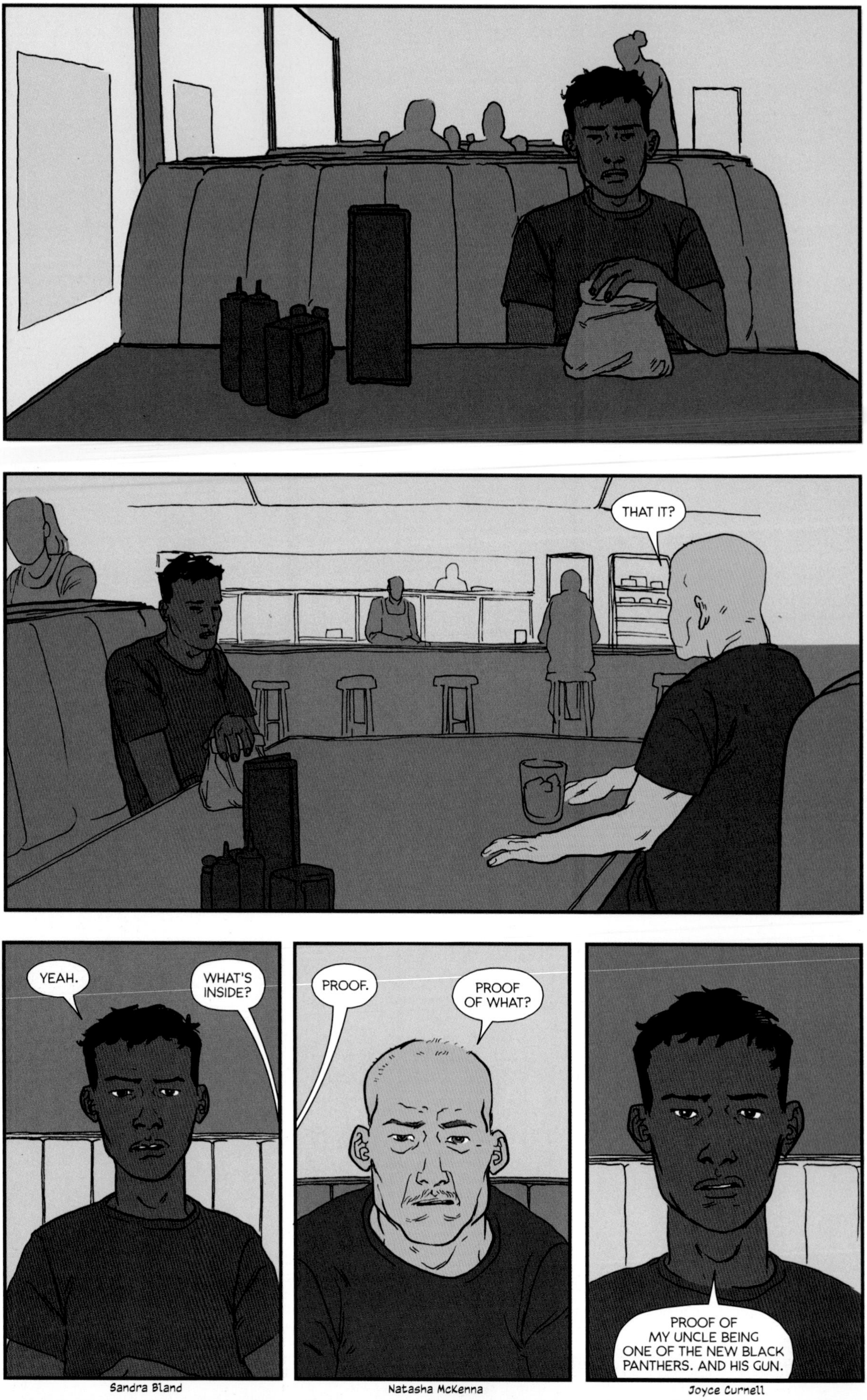
THAT IT?
YEAH.
WHAT'S INSIDE?
PROOF.
PROOF OF WHAT?
PROOF OF MY UNCLE BEING ONE OF THE NEW BLACK PANTHERS. AND HIS GUN.

Sandra Bland

Natasha McKenna

Joyce Curnell

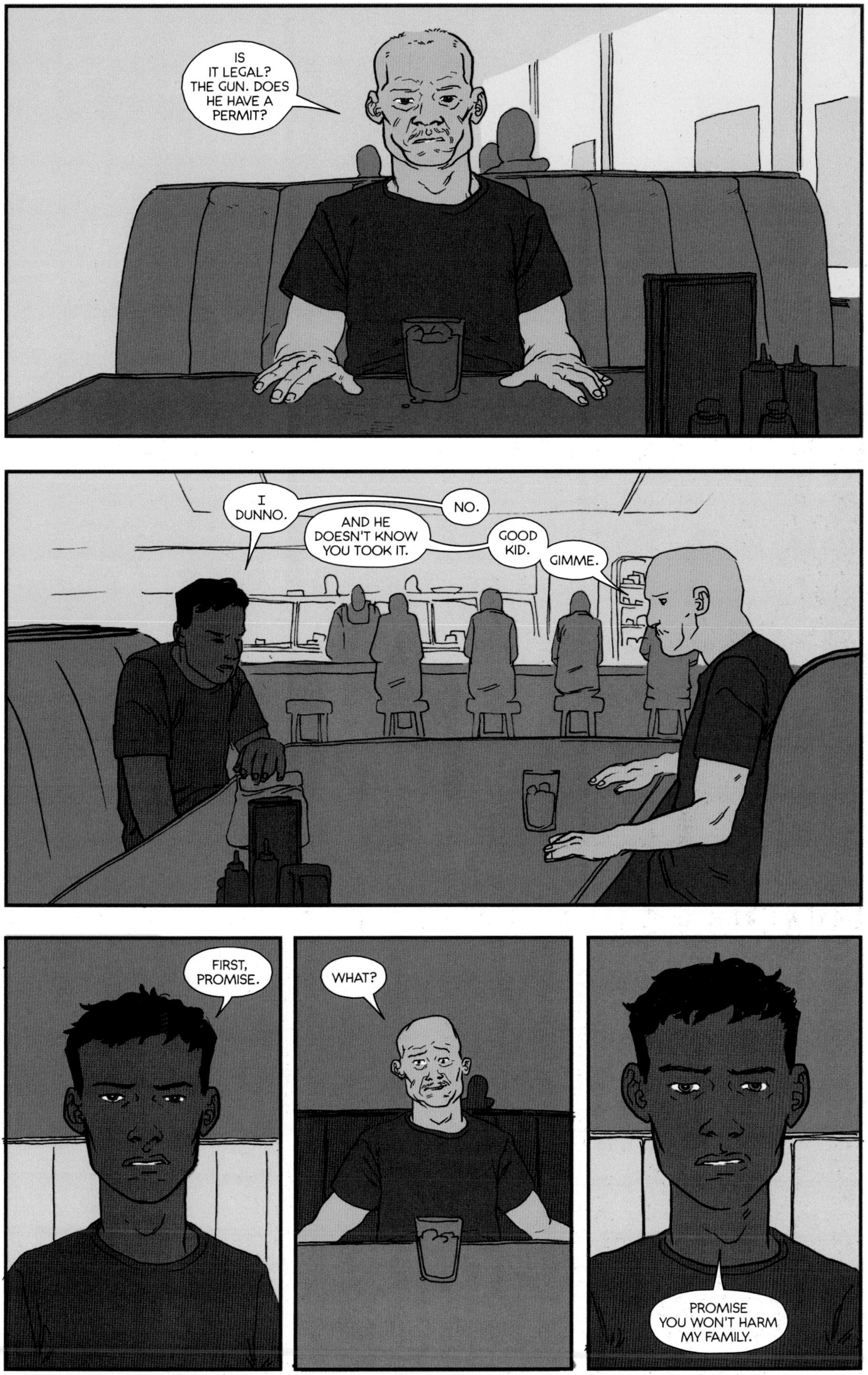
IS IT LEGAL? THE GUN. DOES HE HAVE A PERMIT?
I DUNNO.
NO.
AND HE DOESN'T KNOW YOU TOOK IT.
GOOD KID.
GIMME.
FIRST, PROMISE.
WHAT?
PROMISE YOU WON'T HARM MY FAMILY.

Ernest Satterwhite

Tanisha Anderson

Oscar Grant

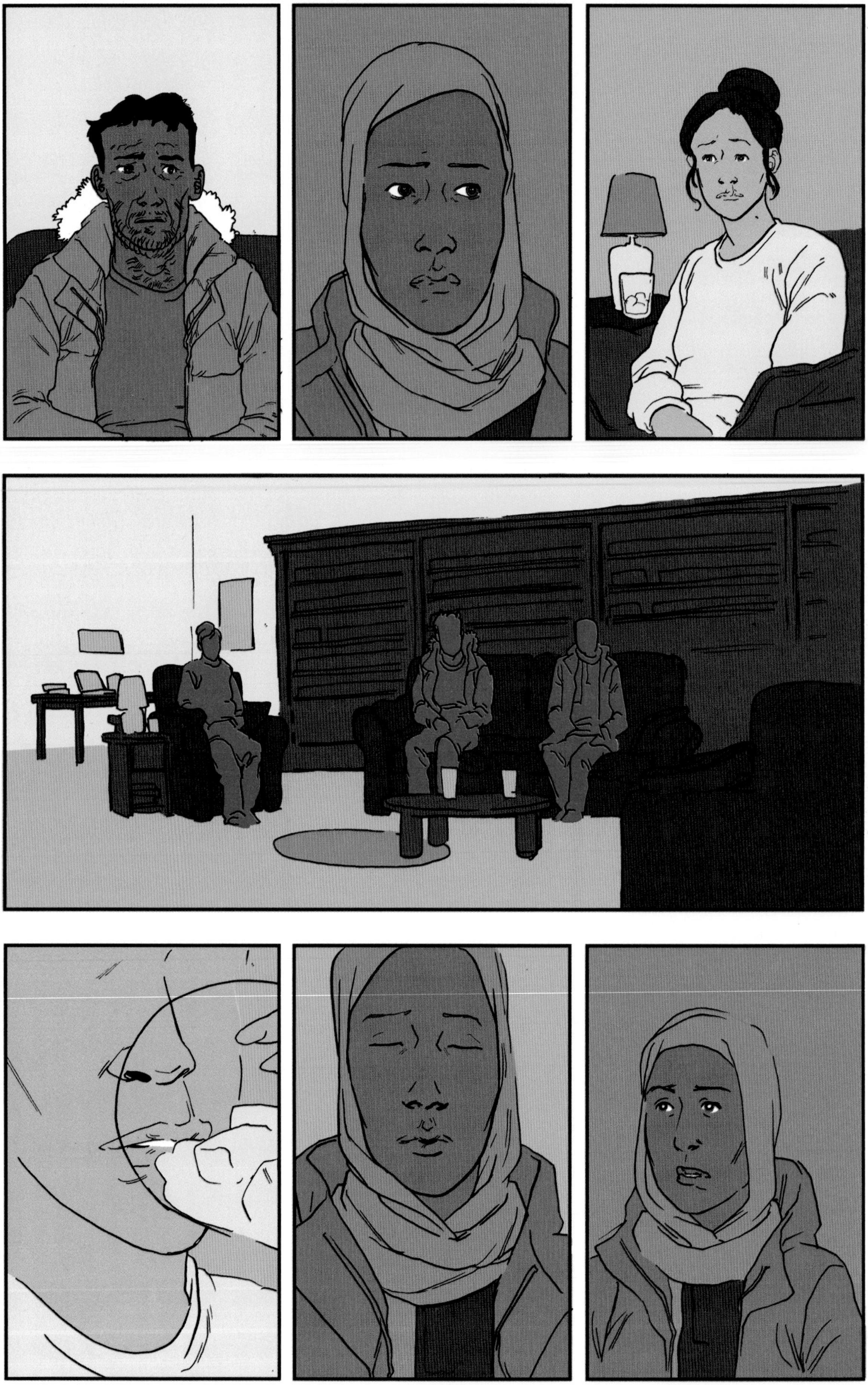

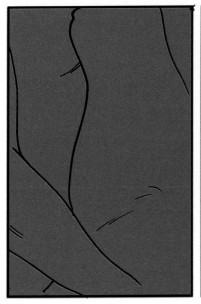

THAT WOULD BE... ACCURATE.

WHY ARE WE HERE?

THAT'S A GREAT QUESTION, ACTUALLY.

WE ARE HERE BECAUSE WE BOTH *STRUGGLED* AND *LIED,* AND BECAUSE I WANTED TO MEET MY HUSBAND'S *NEW LOVER.*

LOOK, IT WAS A *ONE-TIME THING,* I DON'T REALLY KNOW--

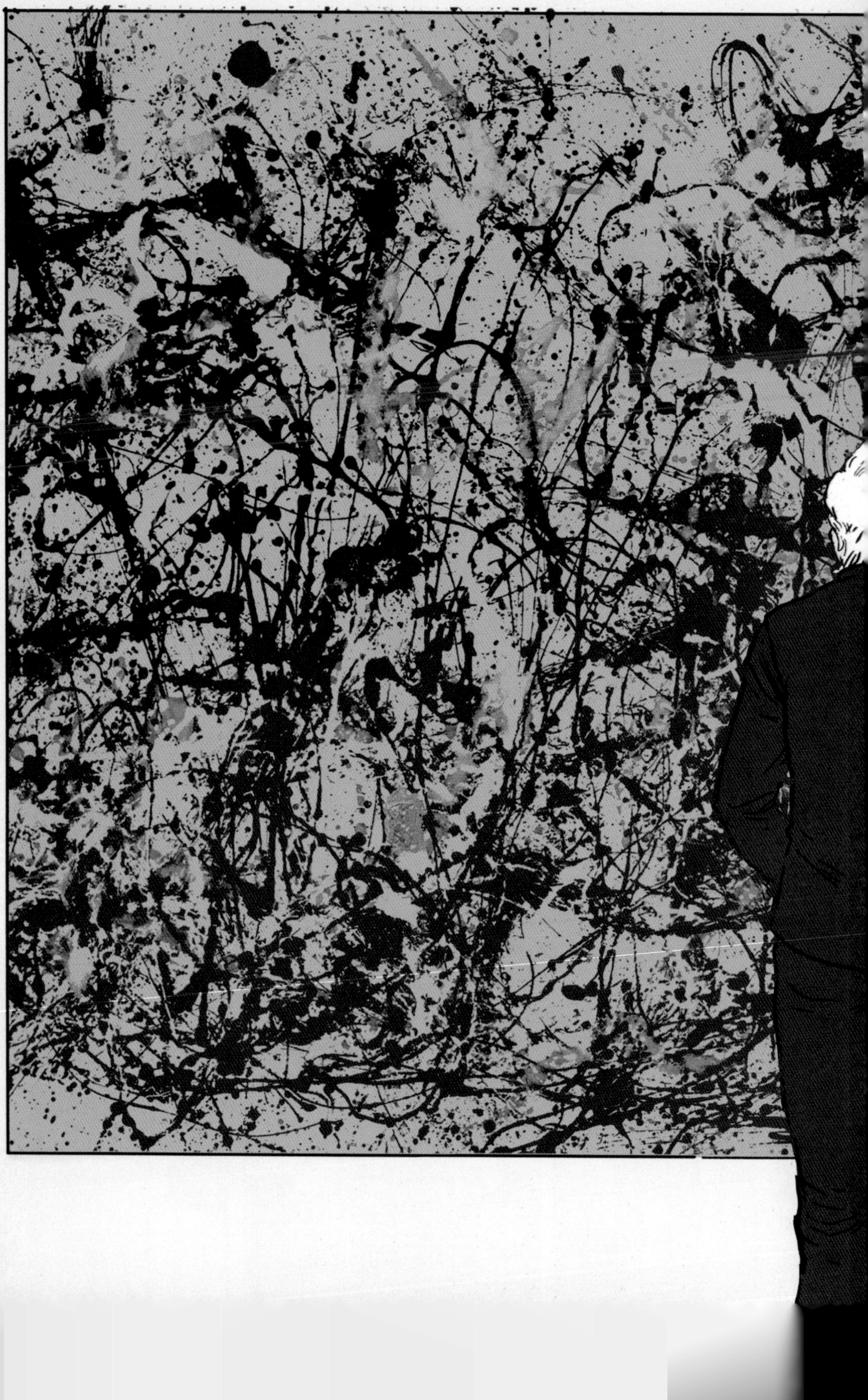

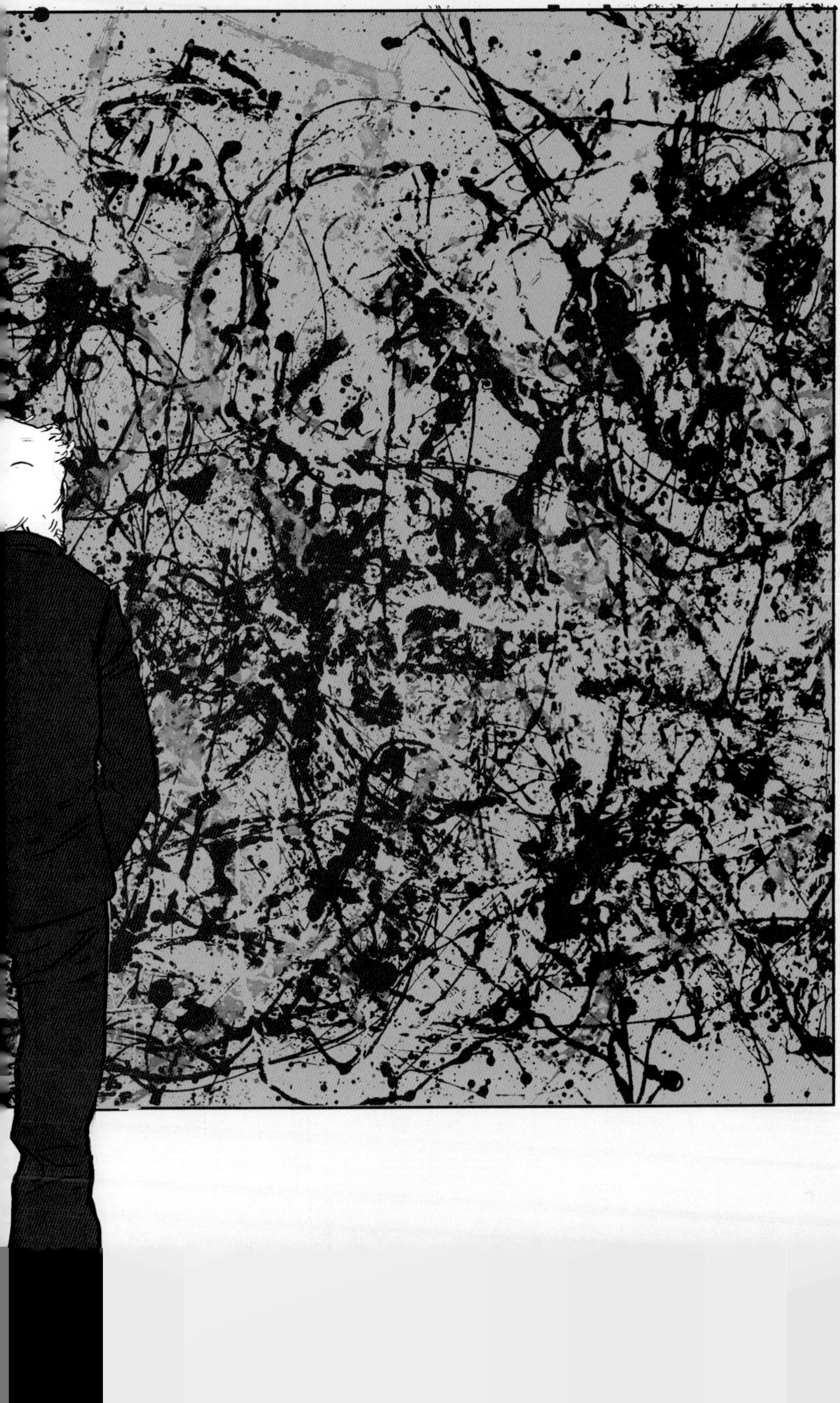

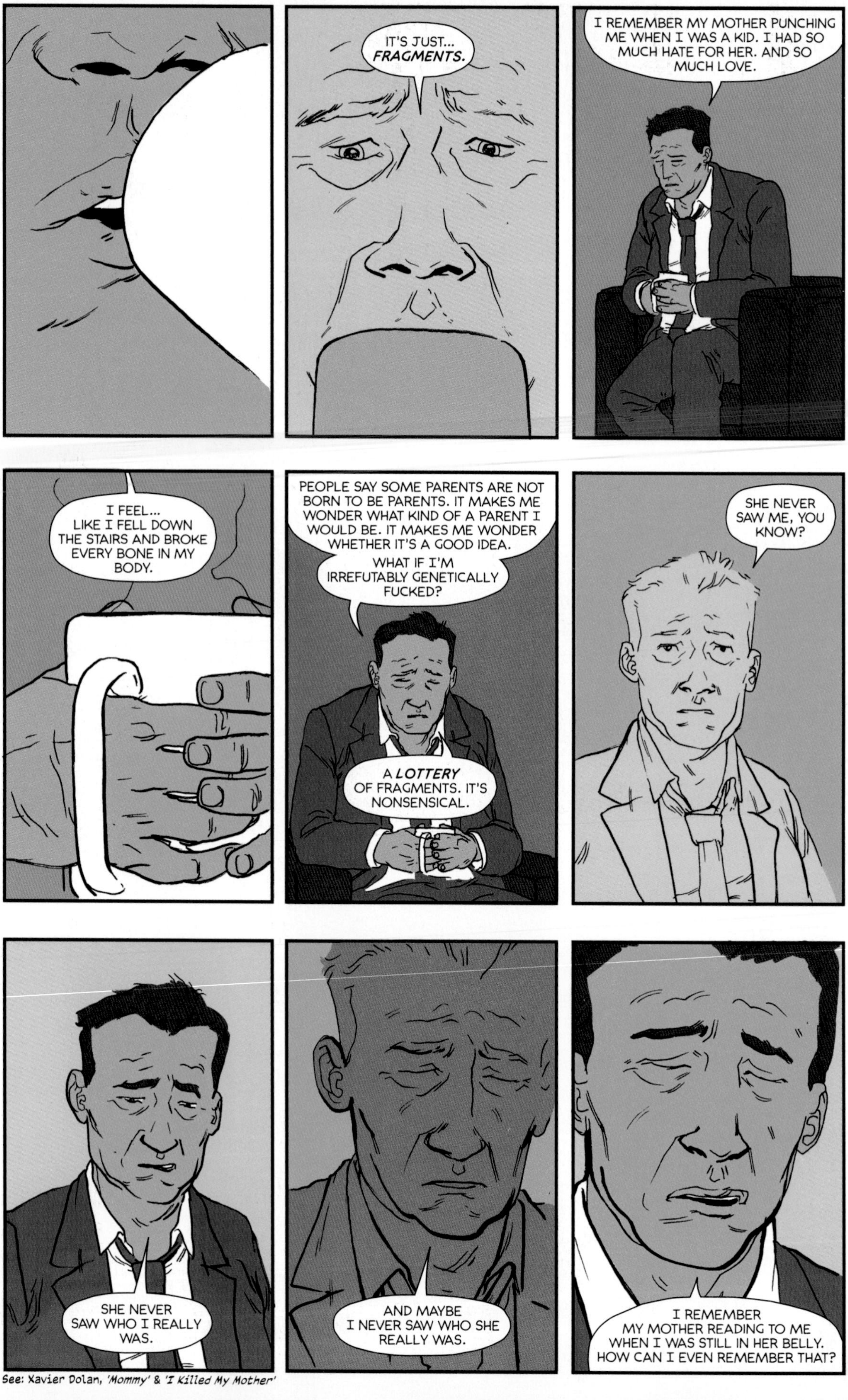
IT'S JUST... FRAGMENTS.
I REMEMBER MY MOTHER PUNCHING ME WHEN I WAS A KID. I HAD SO MUCH HATE FOR HER. AND SO MUCH LOVE.
I FEEL... LIKE I FELL DOWN THE STAIRS AND BROKE EVERY BONE IN MY BODY.
PEOPLE SAY SOME PARENTS ARE NOT BORN TO BE PARENTS. IT MAKES ME WONDER WHAT KIND OF A PARENT I WOULD BE. IT MAKES ME WONDER WHETHER IT'S A GOOD IDEA.
WHAT IF I'M IRREFUTABLY GENETICALLY FUCKED?
A LOTTERY OF FRAGMENTS. IT'S NONSENSICAL.
SHE NEVER SAW ME, YOU KNOW?
SHE NEVER SAW WHO I REALLY WAS.
AND MAYBE I NEVER SAW WHO SHE REALLY WAS.
I REMEMBER MY MOTHER READING TO ME WHEN I WAS STILL IN HER BELLY. HOW CAN I EVEN REMEMBER THAT?

See: Xavier Dolan, *'Mommy'* & *'I Killed My Mother'*

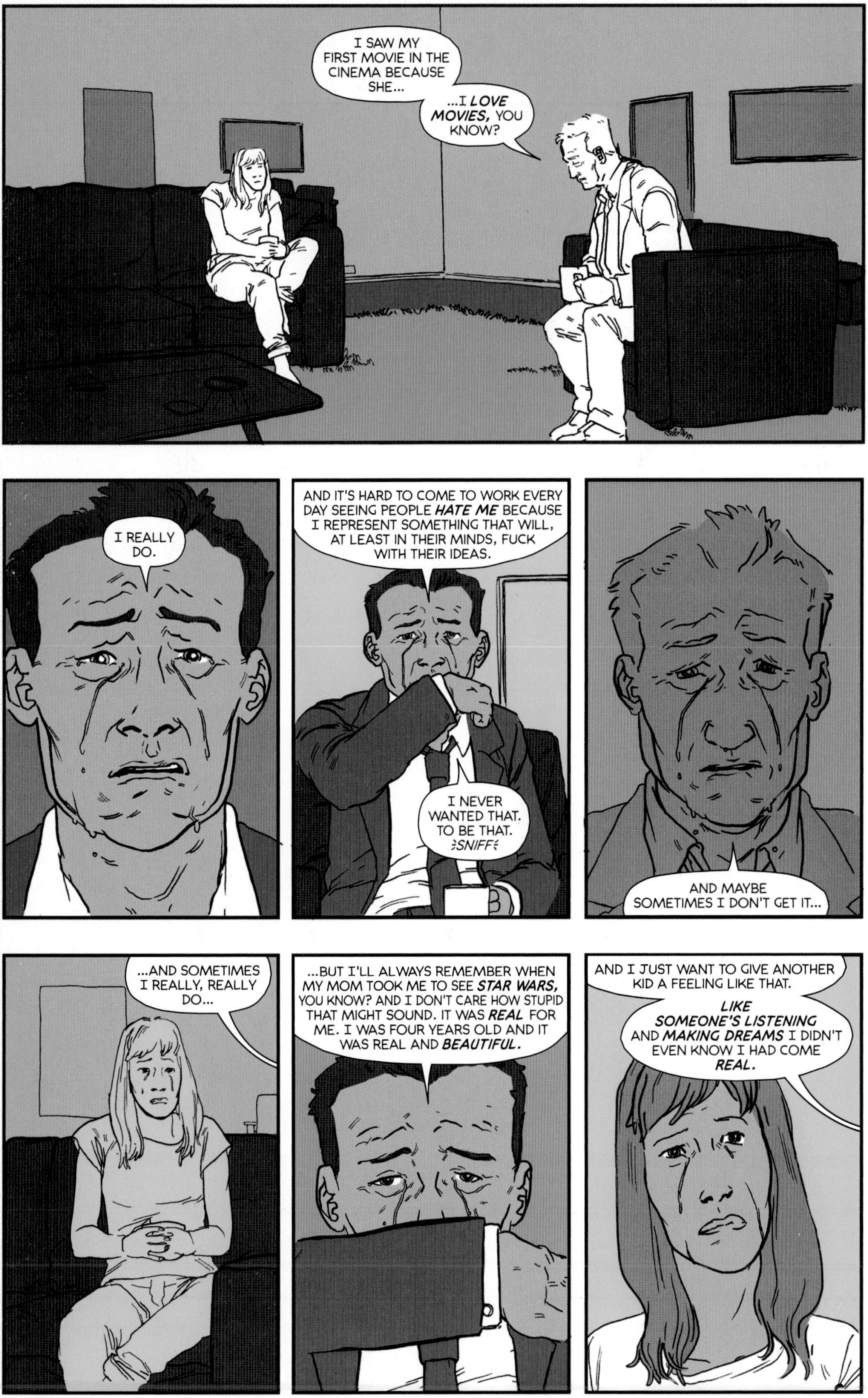

I SAW MY FIRST MOVIE IN THE CINEMA BECAUSE SHE...
...I LOVE MOVIES, YOU KNOW?
I REALLY DO.
AND IT'S HARD TO COME TO WORK EVERY DAY SEEING PEOPLE HATE ME BECAUSE I REPRESENT SOMETHING THAT WILL, AT LEAST IN THEIR MINDS, FUCK WITH THEIR IDEAS.
I NEVER WANTED THAT. TO BE THAT. SNIFF
AND MAYBE SOMETIMES I DON'T GET IT...
...AND SOMETIMES I REALLY, REALLY DO...
...BUT I'LL ALWAYS REMEMBER WHEN MY MOM TOOK ME TO SEE STAR WARS, YOU KNOW? AND I DON'T CARE HOW STUPID THAT MIGHT SOUND. IT WAS REAL FOR ME. I WAS FOUR YEARS OLD AND IT WAS REAL AND BEAUTIFUL.
AND I JUST WANT TO GIVE ANOTHER KID A FEELING LIKE THAT.
LIKE SOMEONE'S LISTENING AND MAKING DREAMS I DIDN'T EVEN KNOW I HAD COME REAL.

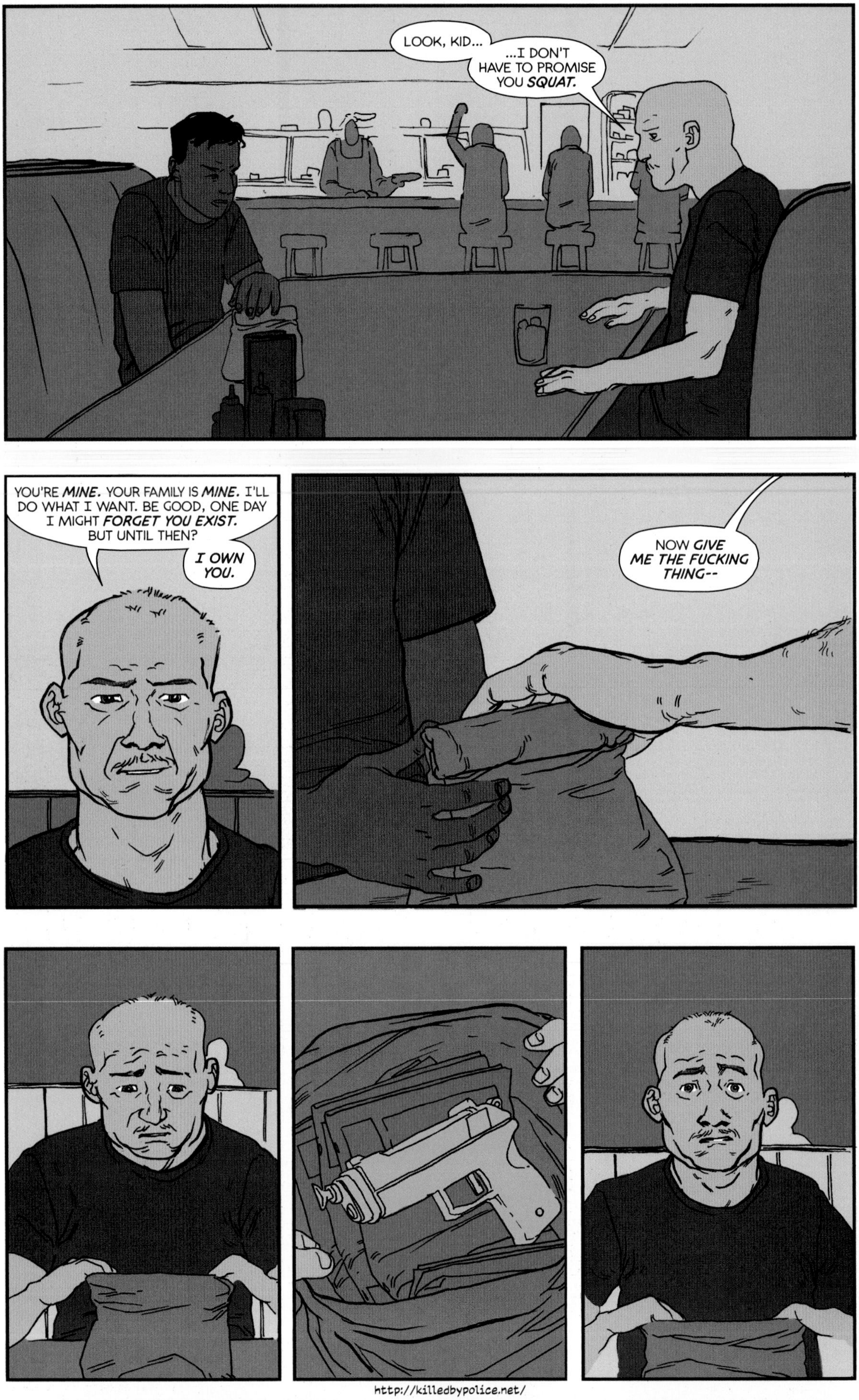

LOOK, KID...
...I DON'T HAVE TO PROMISE YOU *SQUAT.*
YOU'RE *MINE.* YOUR FAMILY IS *MINE.* I'LL DO WHAT I WANT. BE GOOD, ONE DAY I MIGHT *FORGET YOU EXIST.* BUT UNTIL THEN?
I OWN YOU.
NOW *GIVE ME THE FUCKING THING--*

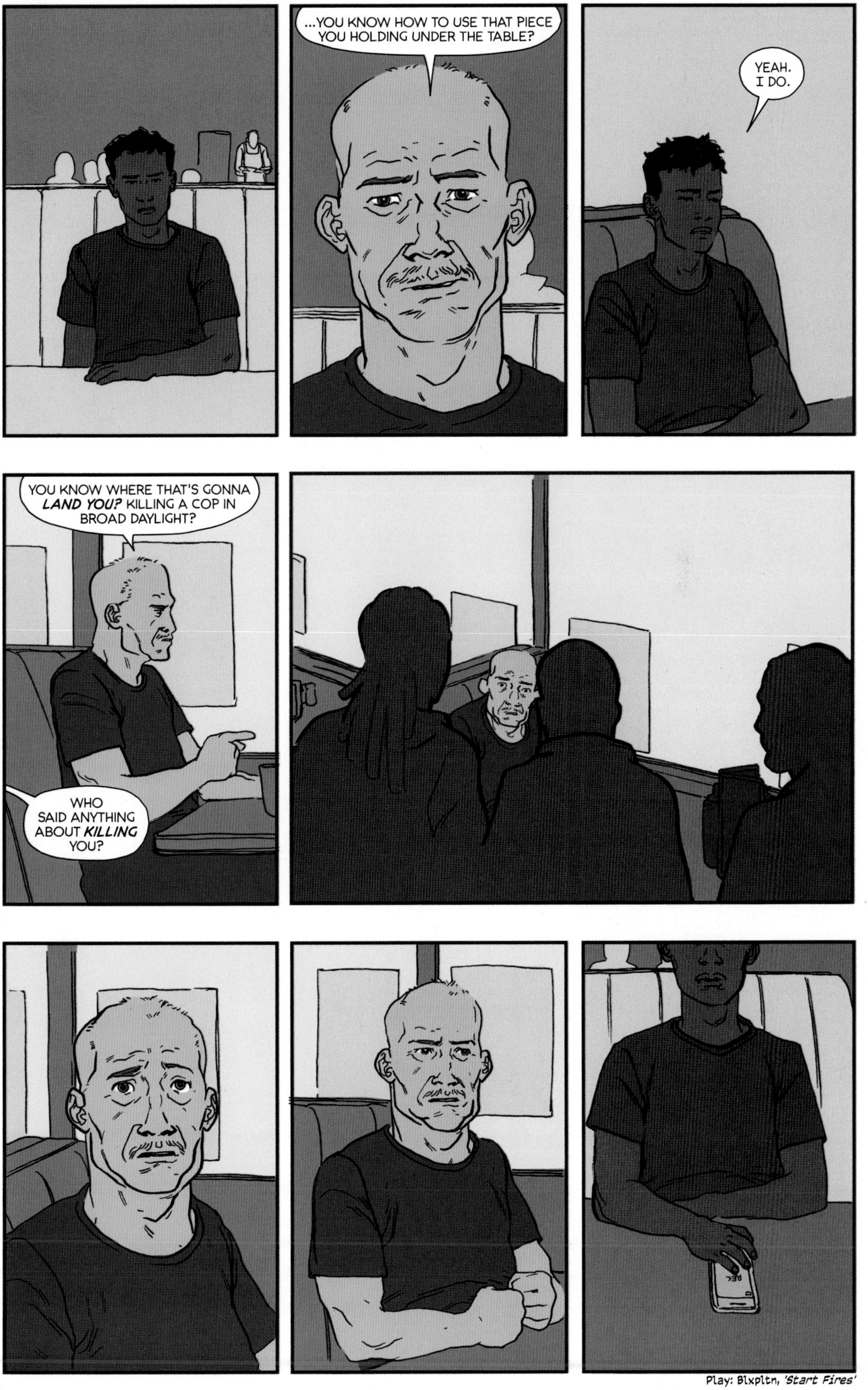
...YOU KNOW HOW TO USE THAT PIECE YOU HOLDING UNDER THE TABLE?
YEAH. I DO.
YOU KNOW WHERE THAT'S GONNA ***LAND YOU?*** KILLING A COP IN BROAD DAYLIGHT?
WHO SAID ANYTHING ABOUT ***KILLING*** YOU?

Play: Blxpltn, *'Start Fires'*

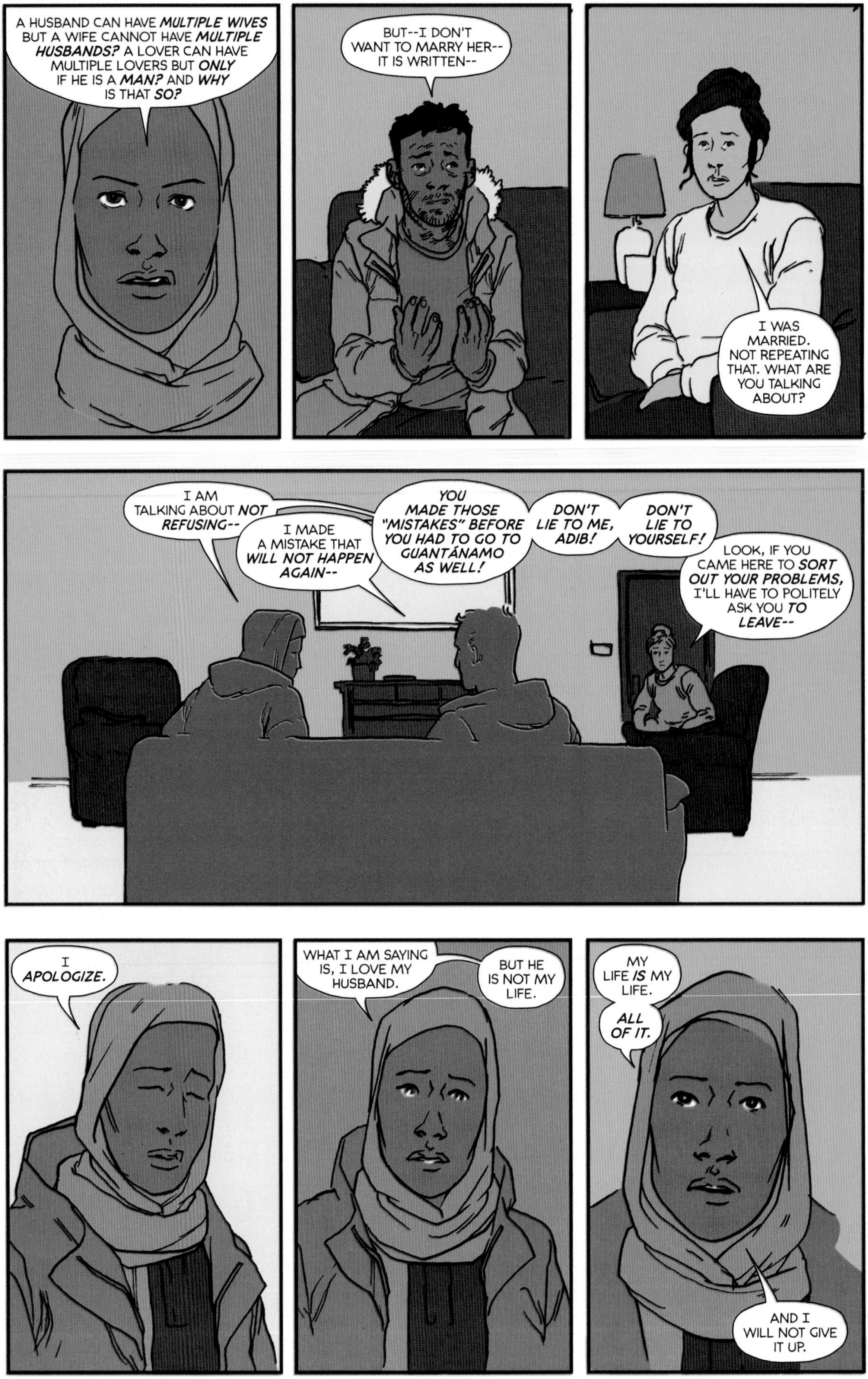
A HUSBAND CAN HAVE MULTIPLE WIVES BUT A WIFE CANNOT HAVE MULTIPLE HUSBANDS? A LOVER CAN HAVE MULTIPLE LOVERS BUT ONLY IF HE IS A MAN? AND WHY IS THAT SO?
BUT--I DON'T WANT TO MARRY HER-- IT IS WRITTEN--
I WAS MARRIED. NOT REPEATING THAT. WHAT ARE YOU TALKING ABOUT?
I AM TALKING ABOUT NOT REFUSING--
I MADE A MISTAKE THAT WILL NOT HAPPEN AGAIN--
YOU MADE THOSE "MISTAKES" BEFORE YOU HAD TO GO TO GUANTÁNAMO AS WELL!
DON'T LIE TO ME, ADIB!
DON'T LIE TO YOURSELF!
LOOK, IF YOU CAME HERE TO SORT OUT YOUR PROBLEMS, I'LL HAVE TO POLITELY ASK YOU TO LEAVE--
I APOLOGIZE.
WHAT I AM SAYING IS, I LOVE MY HUSBAND.
BUT HE IS NOT MY LIFE.
MY LIFE IS MY LIFE.
ALL OF IT.
AND I WILL NOT GIVE IT UP.

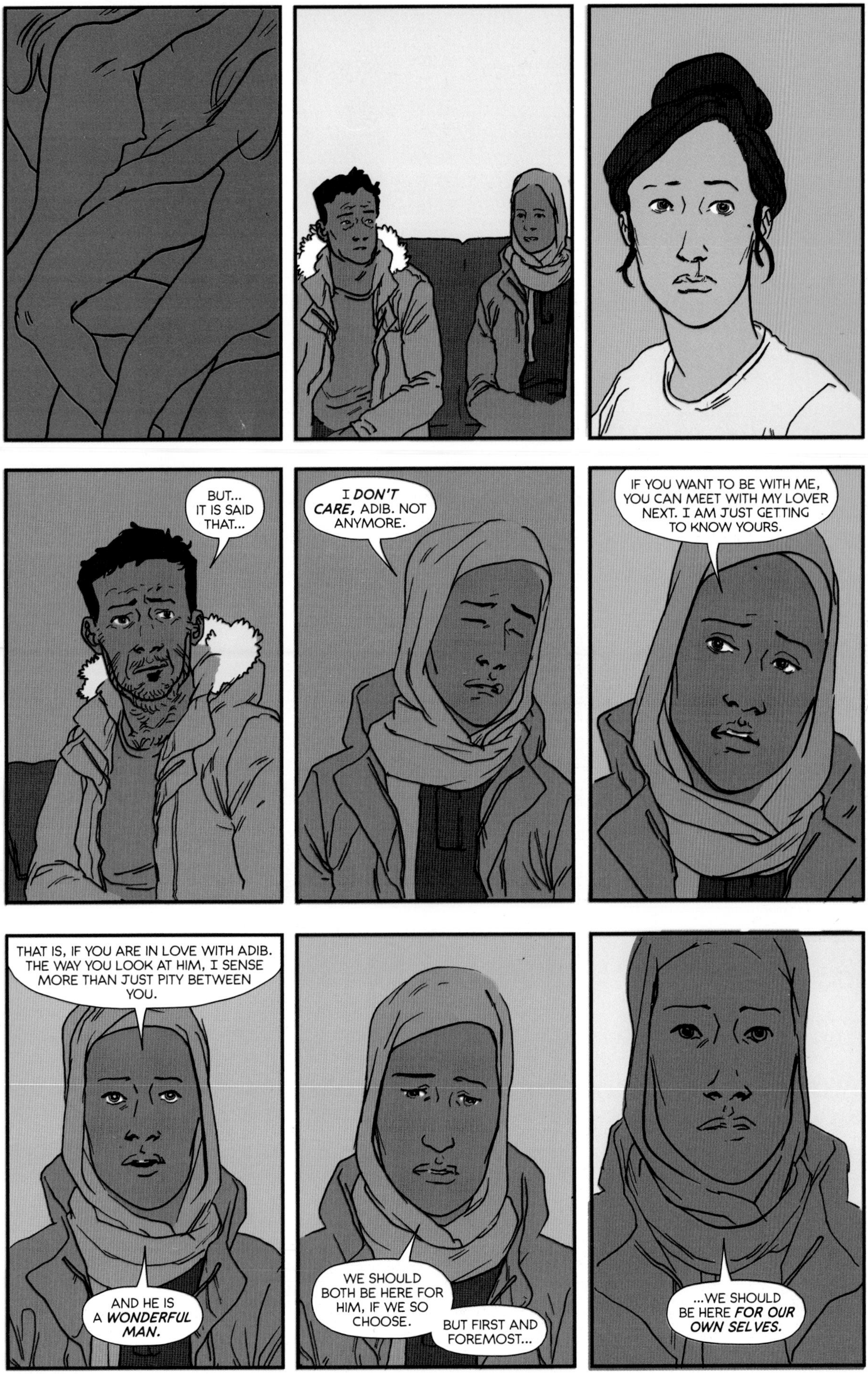
BUT... IT IS SAID THAT...
I DON'T CARE, ADIB. NOT ANYMORE.
IF YOU WANT TO BE WITH ME, YOU CAN MEET WITH MY LOVER NEXT. I AM JUST GETTING TO KNOW YOURS.
THAT IS, IF YOU ARE IN LOVE WITH ADIB. THE WAY YOU LOOK AT HIM, I SENSE MORE THAN JUST PITY BETWEEN YOU.
AND HE IS A WONDERFUL MAN.
WE SHOULD BOTH BE HERE FOR HIM, IF WE SO CHOOSE.
BUT FIRST AND FOREMOST...
...WE SHOULD BE HERE FOR OUR OWN SELVES.

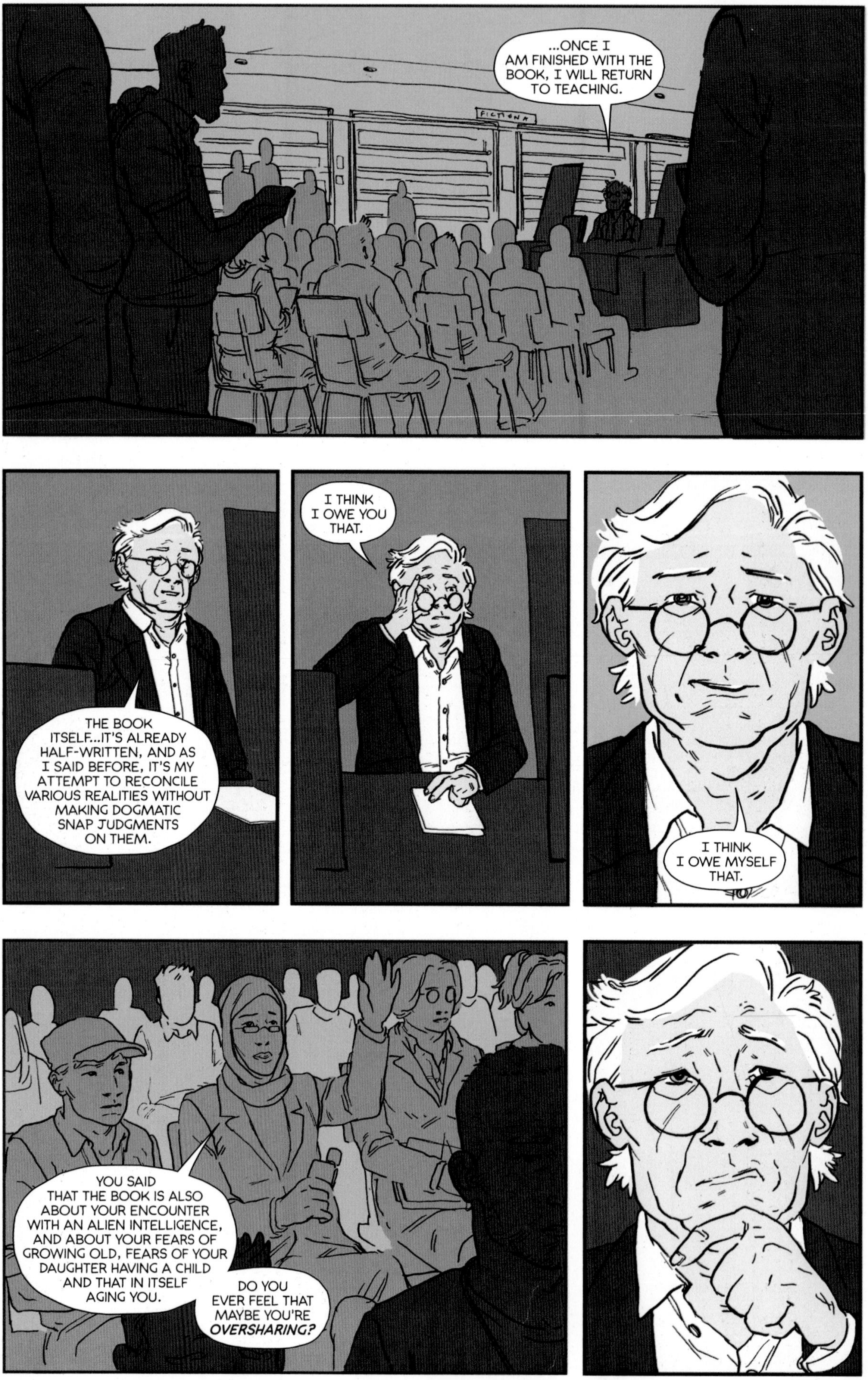
...ONCE I AM FINISHED WITH THE BOOK, I WILL RETURN TO TEACHING.
THE BOOK ITSELF...IT'S ALREADY HALF-WRITTEN, AND AS I SAID BEFORE, IT'S MY ATTEMPT TO RECONCILE VARIOUS REALITIES WITHOUT MAKING DOGMATIC SNAP JUDGMENTS ON THEM.
I THINK I OWE YOU THAT.
I THINK I OWE MYSELF THAT.
YOU SAID THAT THE BOOK IS ALSO ABOUT YOUR ENCOUNTER WITH AN ALIEN INTELLIGENCE, AND ABOUT YOUR FEARS OF GROWING OLD, FEARS OF YOUR DAUGHTER HAVING A CHILD AND THAT IN ITSELF AGING YOU.
DO YOU EVER FEEL THAT MAYBE YOU'RE ***OVERSHARING?***

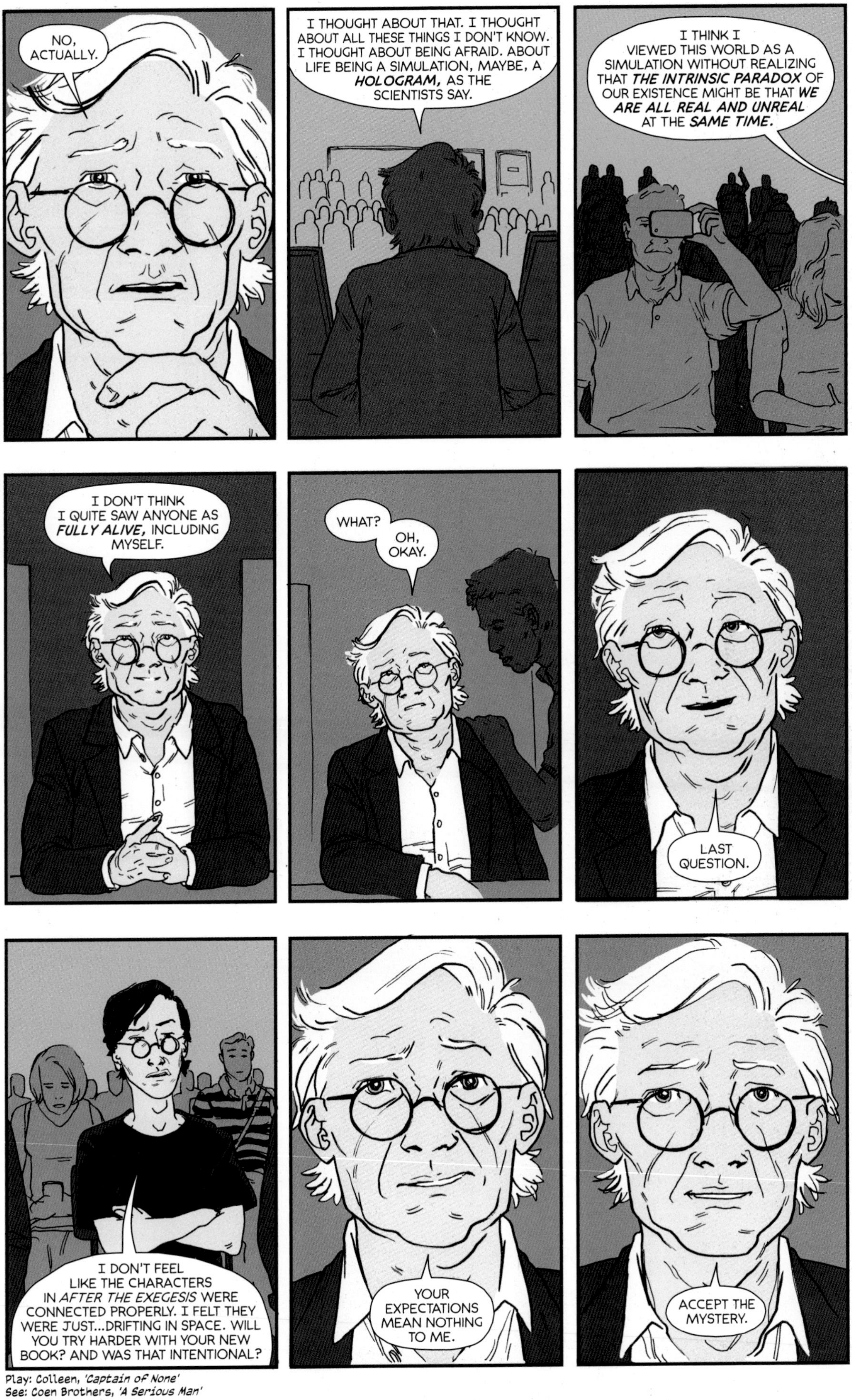
NO, ACTUALLY.
I THOUGHT ABOUT THAT. I THOUGHT ABOUT ALL THESE THINGS I DON'T KNOW. I THOUGHT ABOUT BEING AFRAID. ABOUT LIFE BEING A SIMULATION, MAYBE, A ***HOLOGRAM,*** AS THE SCIENTISTS SAY.
I THINK I VIEWED THIS WORLD AS A SIMULATION WITHOUT REALIZING THAT ***THE INTRINSIC PARADOX*** OF OUR EXISTENCE MIGHT BE THAT ***WE ARE ALL REAL AND UNREAL*** AT THE ***SAME TIME.***
I DON'T THINK I QUITE SAW ANYONE AS ***FULLY ALIVE,*** INCLUDING MYSELF.
WHAT?
OH, OKAY.
LAST QUESTION.
I DON'T FEEL LIKE THE CHARACTERS IN *AFTER THE EXEGESIS* WERE CONNECTED PROPERLY. I FELT THEY WERE JUST...DRIFTING IN SPACE. WILL YOU TRY HARDER WITH YOUR NEW BOOK? AND WAS THAT INTENTIONAL?
YOUR EXPECTATIONS MEAN NOTHING TO ME.
ACCEPT THE MYSTERY.

Play: Colleen, *'Captain of None'*
See: Coen Brothers, *'A Serious Man'*

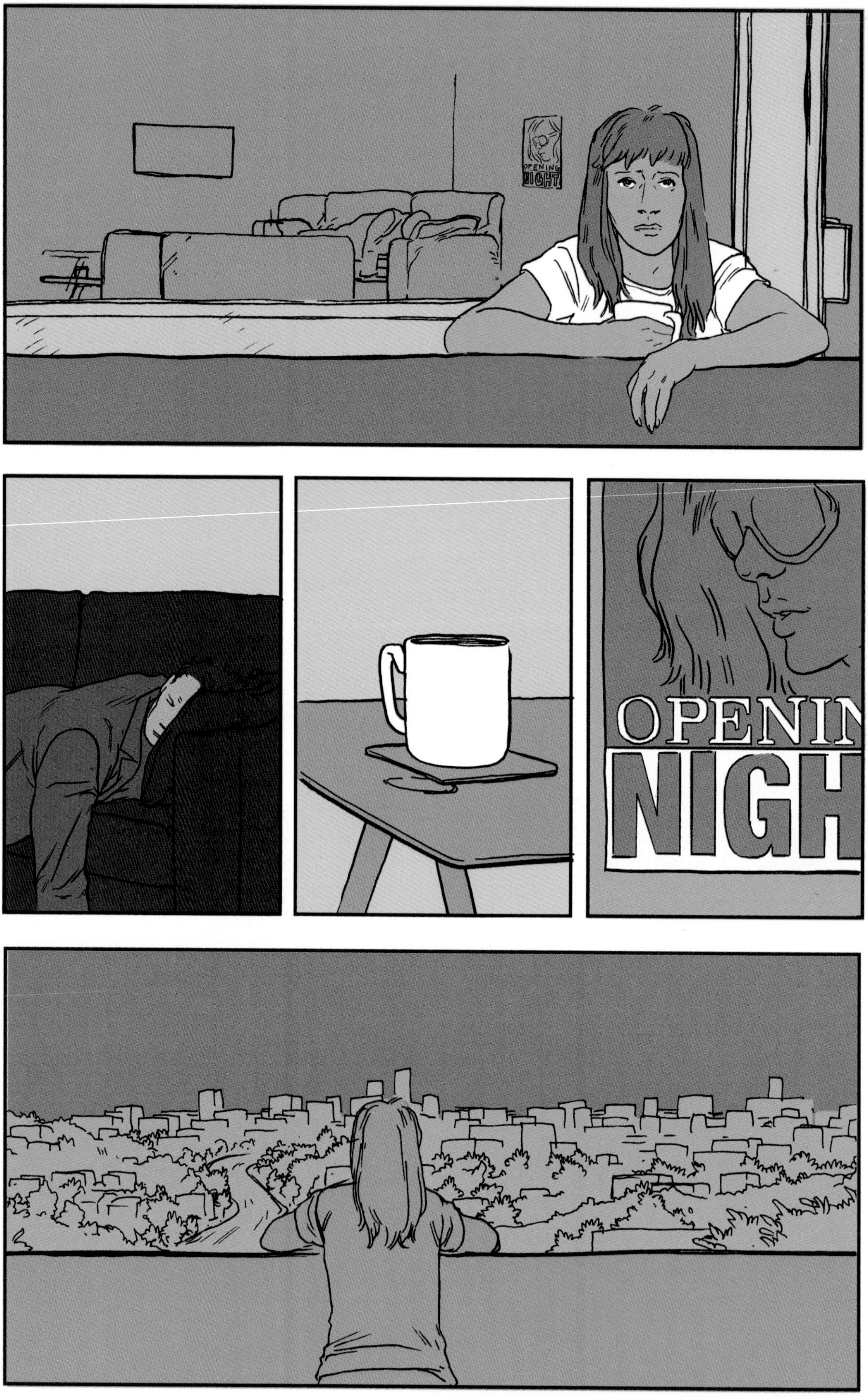
OPENING
NIGHT
OPENIN
NIGH

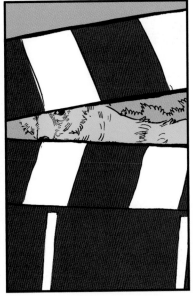

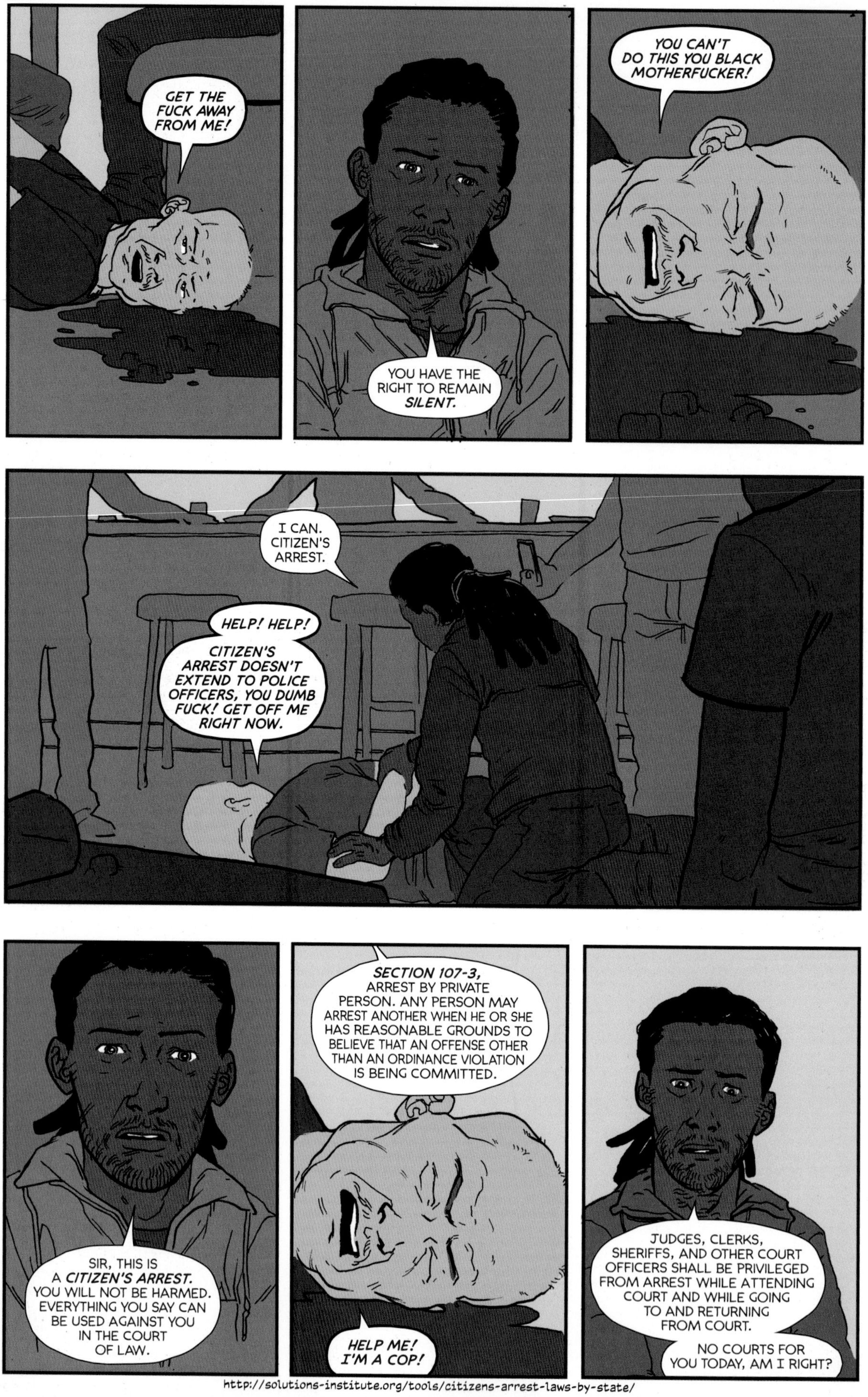
GET THE FUCK AWAY FROM ME!
YOU HAVE THE RIGHT TO REMAIN *SILENT.*
YOU CAN'T DO THIS YOU BLACK MOTHERFUCKER!
I CAN. CITIZEN'S ARREST.
HELP! HELP!
CITIZEN'S ARREST DOESN'T EXTEND TO POLICE OFFICERS, YOU DUMB FUCK! GET OFF ME RIGHT NOW.
SIR, THIS IS A *CITIZEN'S ARREST.* YOU WILL NOT BE HARMED. EVERYTHING YOU SAY CAN BE USED AGAINST YOU IN THE COURT OF LAW.
SECTION 107-3, ARREST BY PRIVATE PERSON. ANY PERSON MAY ARREST ANOTHER WHEN HE OR SHE HAS REASONABLE GROUNDS TO BELIEVE THAT AN OFFENSE OTHER THAN AN ORDINANCE VIOLATION IS BEING COMMITTED.
HELP ME! I'M A COP!
JUDGES, CLERKS, SHERIFFS, AND OTHER COURT OFFICERS SHALL BE PRIVILEGED FROM ARREST WHILE ATTENDING COURT AND WHILE GOING TO AND RETURNING FROM COURT.
NO COURTS FOR YOU TODAY, AM I RIGHT?

http://solutions-institute.org/tools/citizens-arrest-laws-by-state/

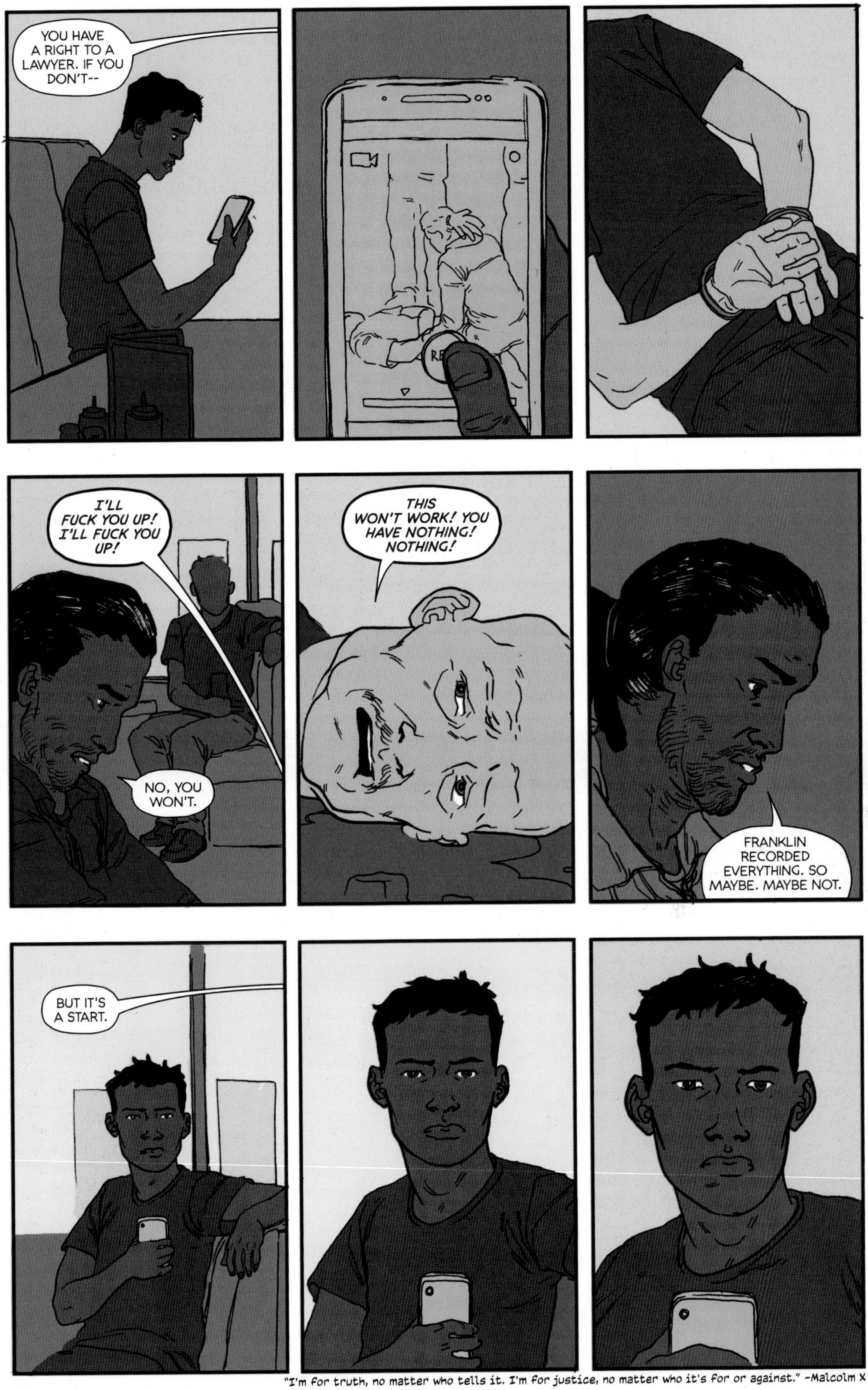
YOU HAVE A RIGHT TO A LAWYER. IF YOU DON'T--
I'LL FUCK YOU UP! I'LL FUCK YOU UP!
NO, YOU WON'T.
THIS WON'T WORK! YOU HAVE NOTHING! NOTHING!
FRANKLIN RECORDED EVERYTHING. SO MAYBE. MAYBE NOT.
BUT IT'S A START.

"I'm for truth, no matter who tells it. I'm for justice, no matter who it's for or against." -Malcolm X

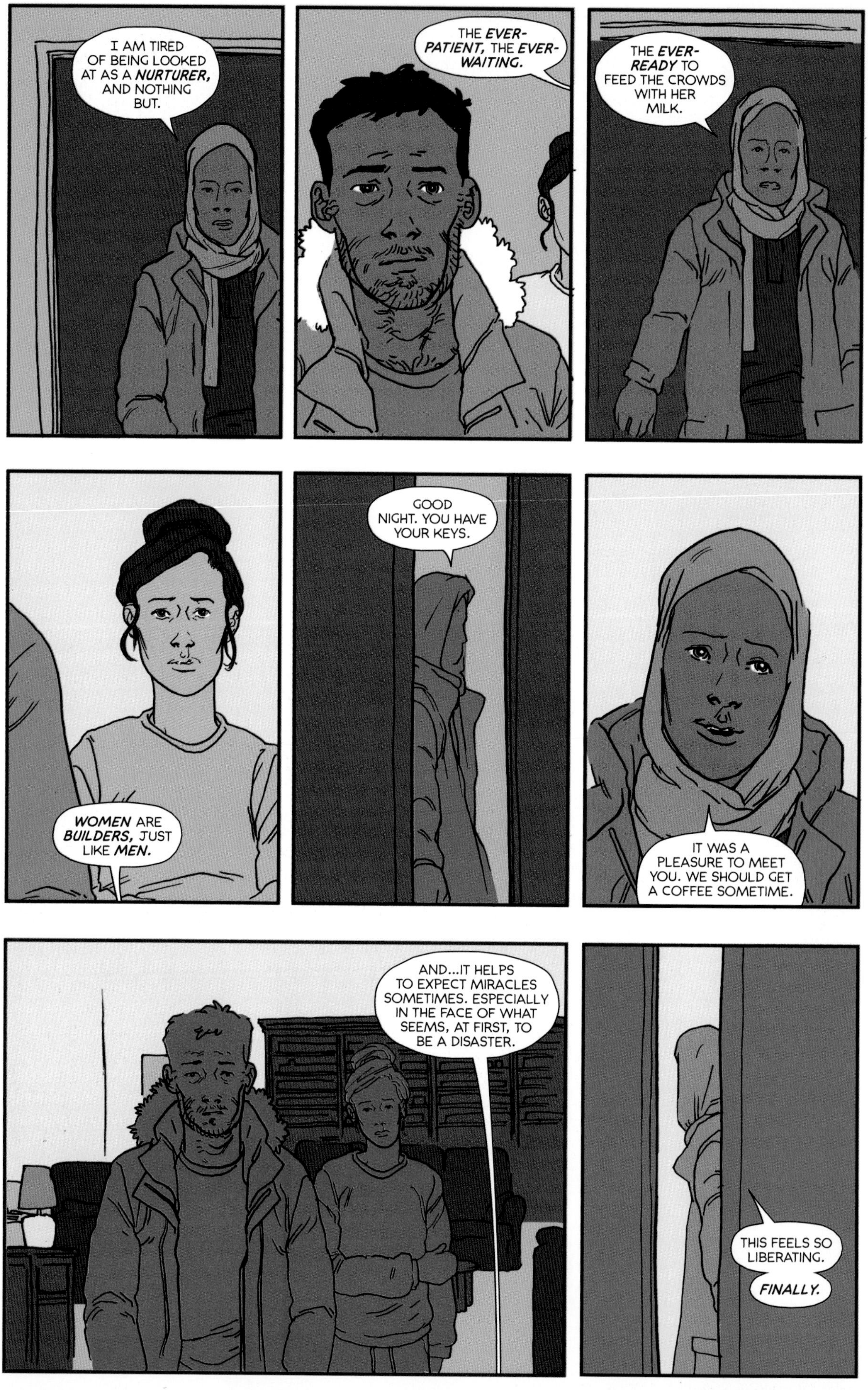
I AM TIRED OF BEING LOOKED AT AS A *NURTURER,* AND NOTHING BUT.
THE *EVER-PATIENT,* THE *EVER-WAITING.*
THE *EVER-READY* TO FEED THE CROWDS WITH HER MILK.
WOMEN ARE *BUILDERS,* JUST LIKE *MEN.*
GOOD NIGHT. YOU HAVE YOUR KEYS.
IT WAS A PLEASURE TO MEET YOU. WE SHOULD GET A COFFEE SOMETIME.
AND...IT HELPS TO EXPECT MIRACLES SOMETIMES. ESPECIALLY IN THE FACE OF WHAT SEEMS, AT FIRST, TO BE A DISASTER.
THIS FEELS SO LIBERATING.
FINALLY.

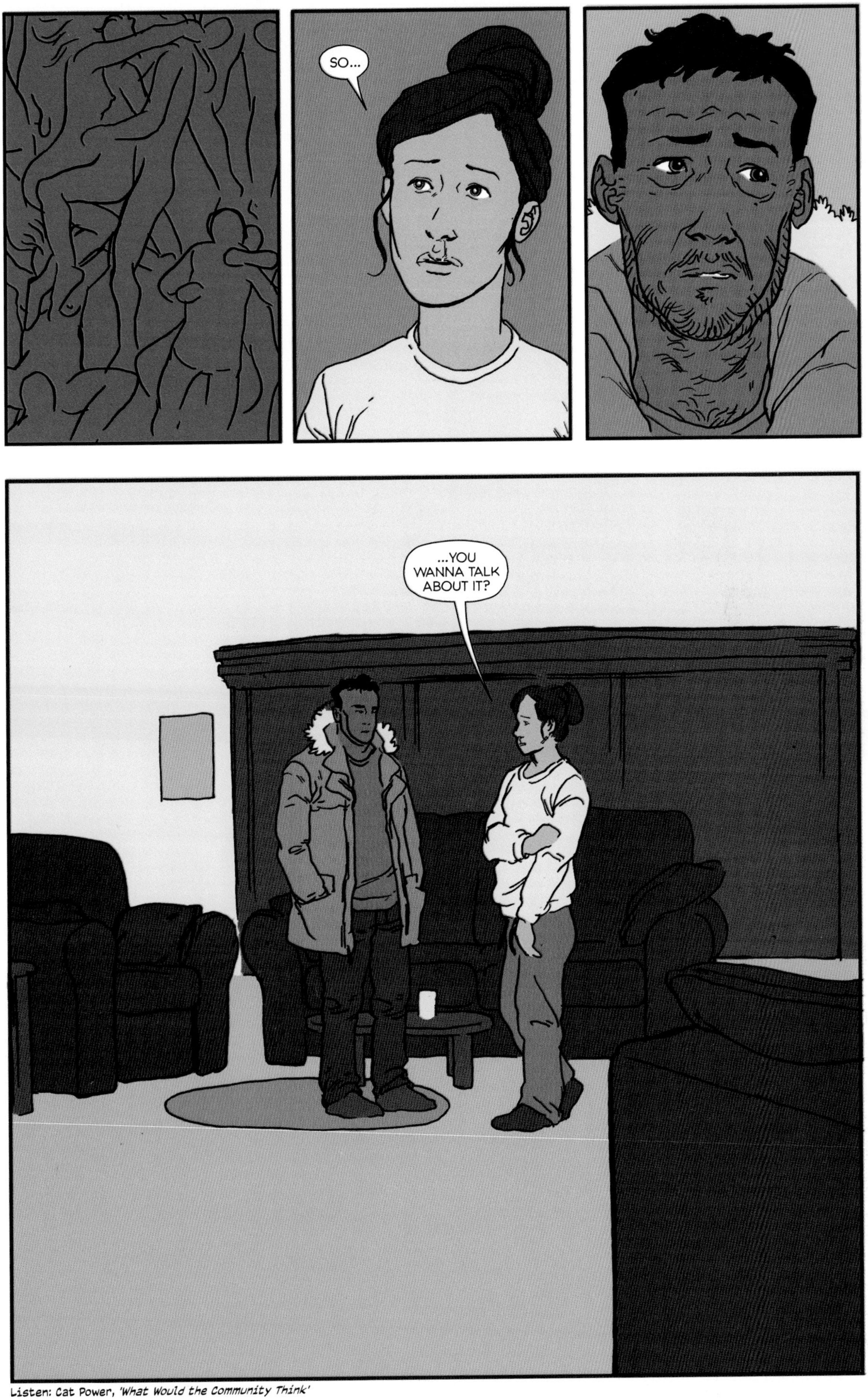
SO...
...YOU WANNA TALK ABOUT IT?

Listen: Cat Power, *'What Would the Community Think'*

Cover Material

Originally published as Material #1—4

The original single issue covers designed and illustrated by **Tom Muller**.

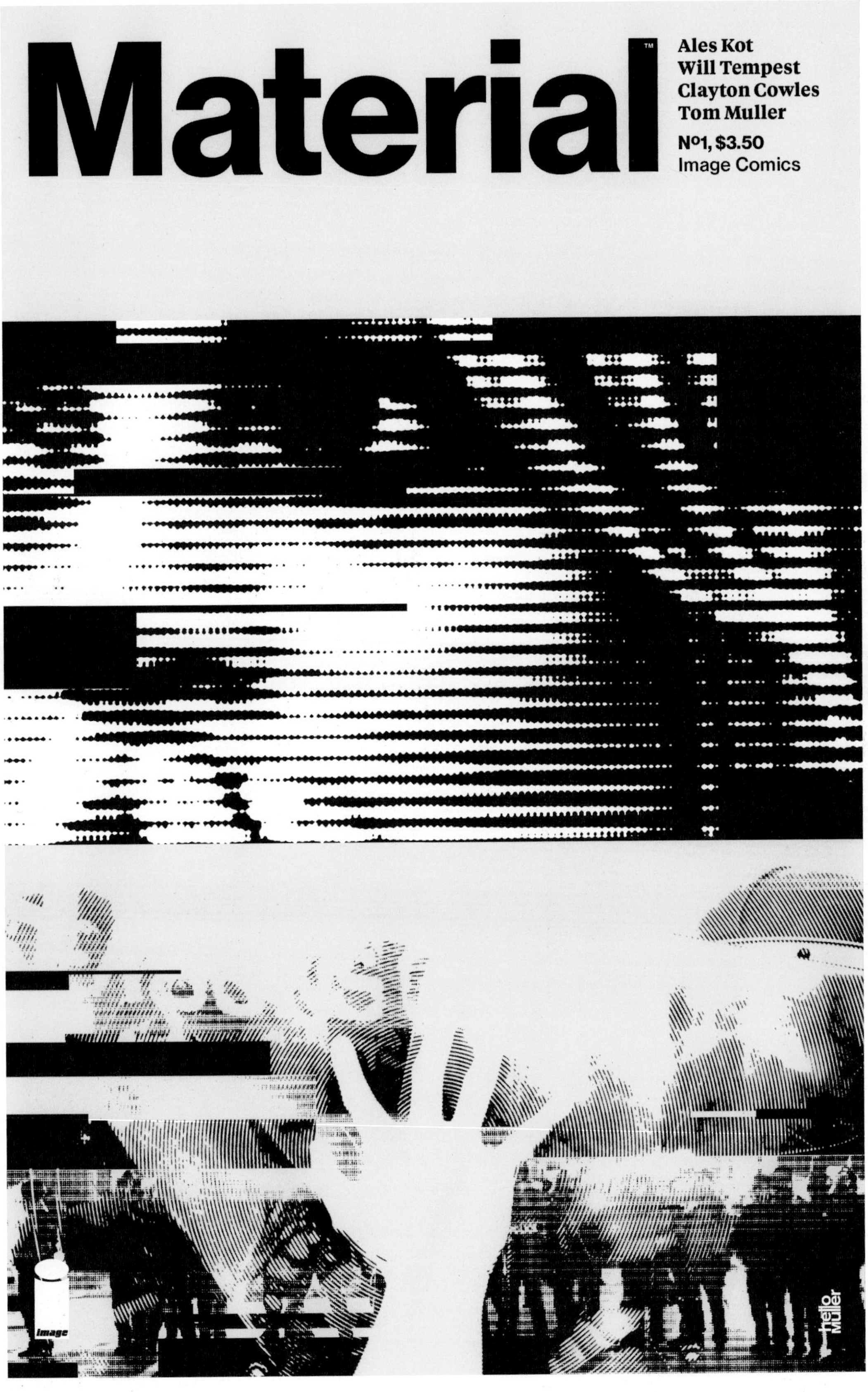
Material™
Ales Kot
Will Tempest
Clayton Cowles
Tom Muller
Nº1, $3.50
Image Comics

Material #1, published May 2015.

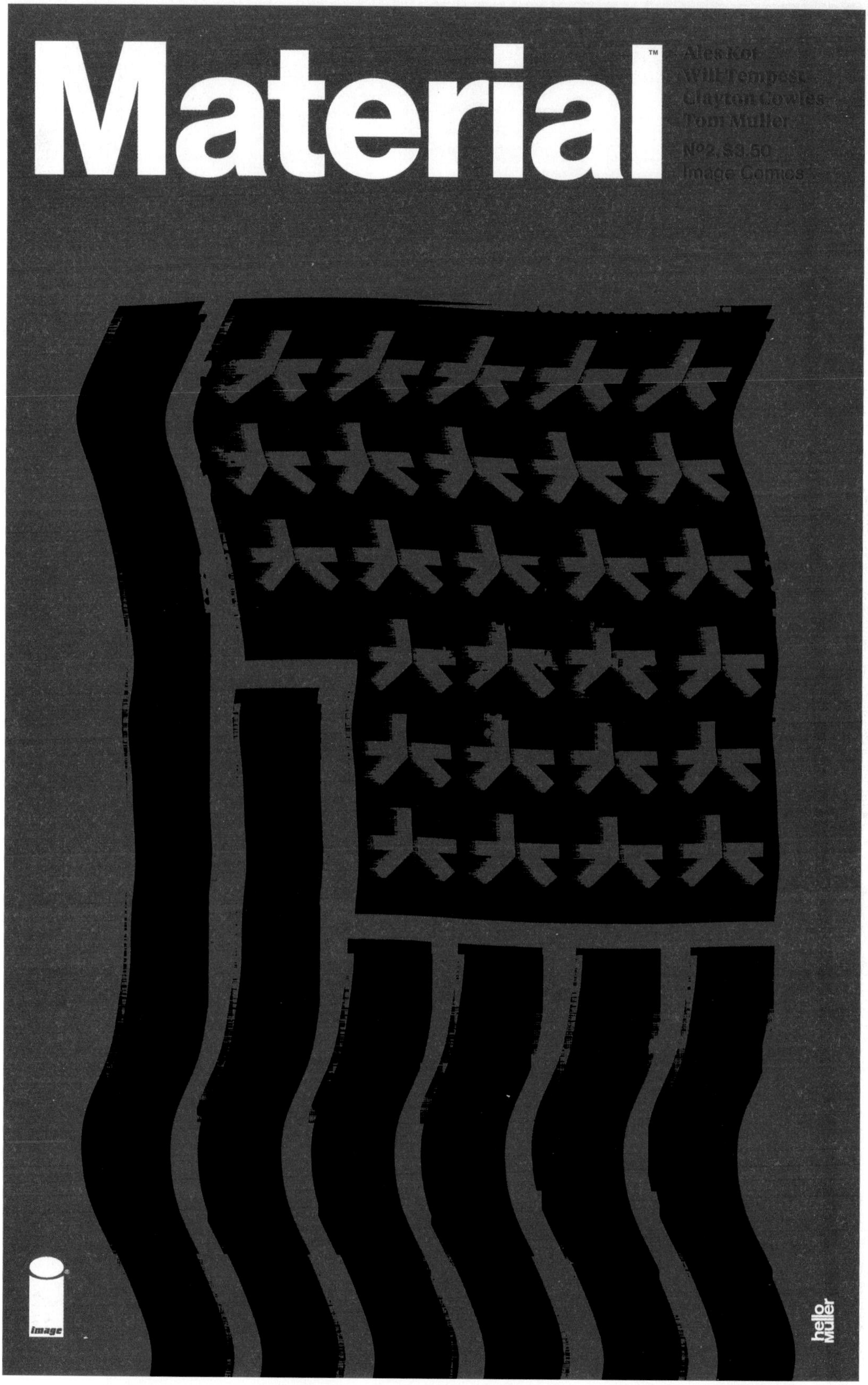
Material™
Ales Kot
Will Tempest
Clayton Cowles
Tom Muller
Nº2, $3.50
Image Comics
image
hello Muller

Material #2, published June 2015.

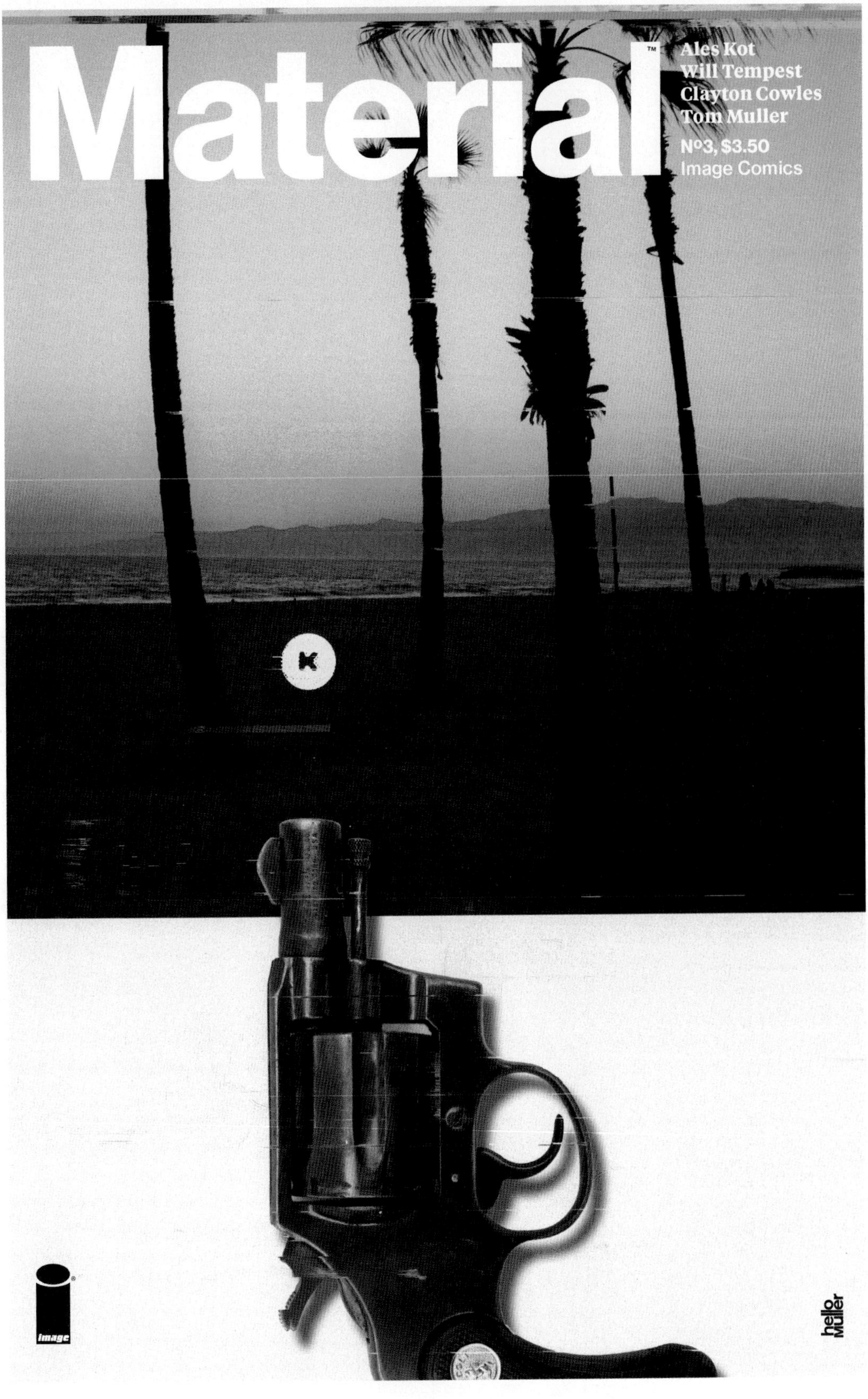
Material™
Ales Kot
Will Tempest
Clayton Cowles
Tom Muller
Nº3, $3.50
Image Comics
image
hello Muller

Material #3, published July 2015.

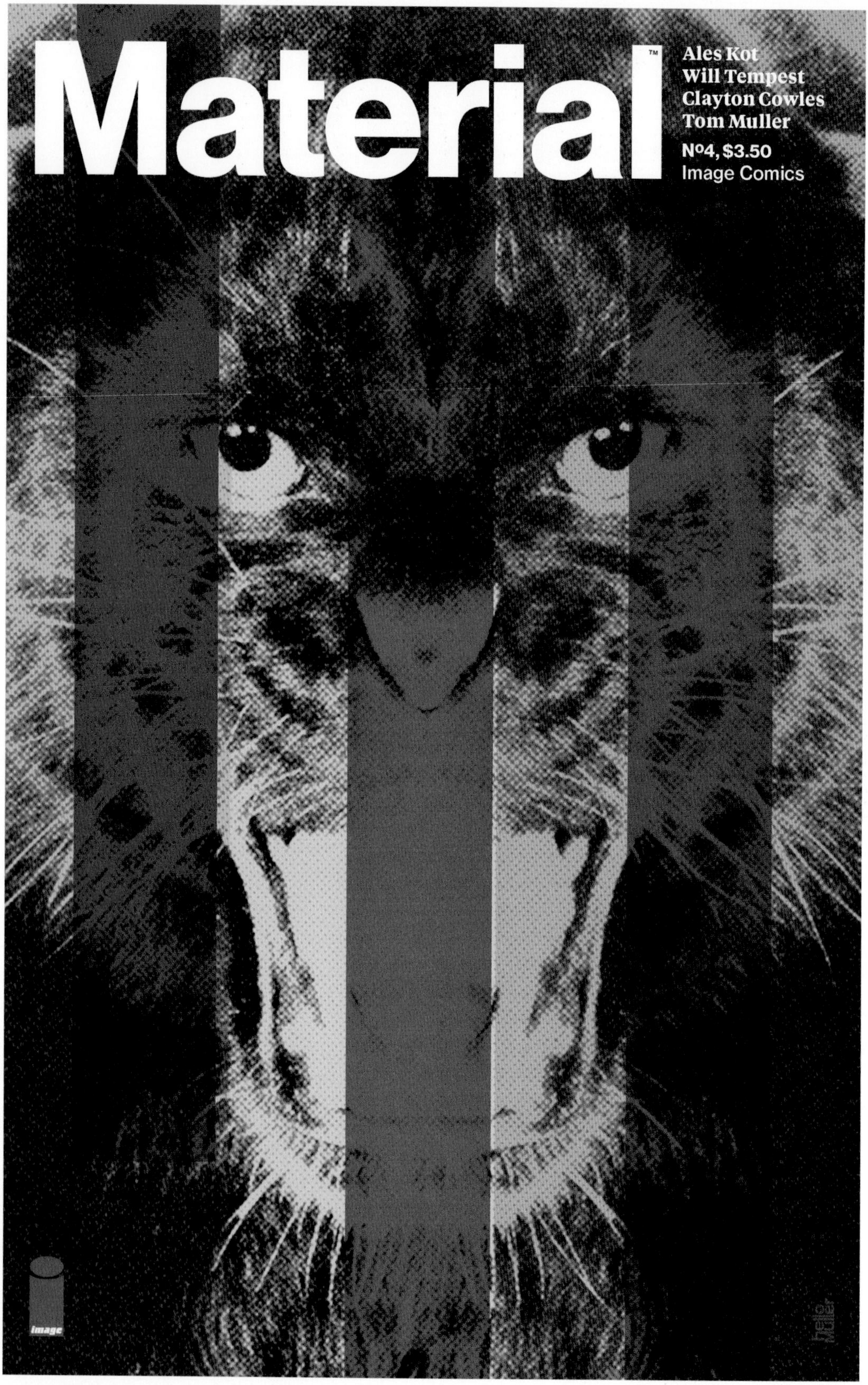
Material™
Ales Kot
Will Tempest
Clayton Cowles
Tom Muller
Nº4, $3.50
Image Comics
image

Material #4, published September 2015.

Material

Bios

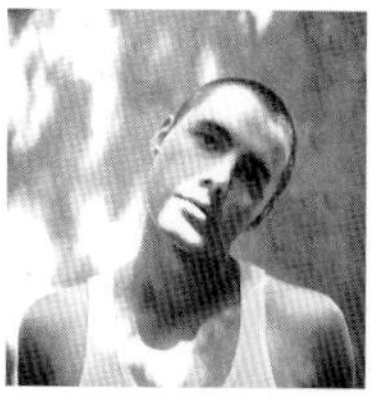

Photo by Clayton Cubitt

Ales Kot invents, writes & runs projects & stories for film, comics, television & more. He also wrote/still writes: *Change*, *Zero*, *Wolf*, *The Surface*, *Wild Children*. **Current body born September 27, 1986 in Opava, Czech Republic. Resides in Los Angeles. Believes in poetry. @ales_kot**

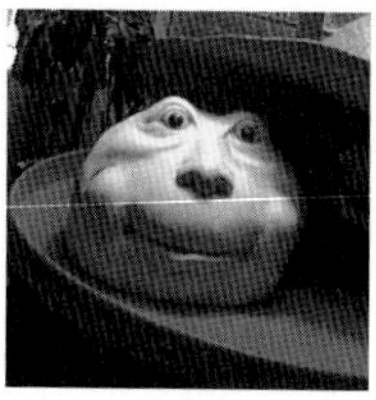

Will Tempest is an artist based in London, England. @Will_Tempest

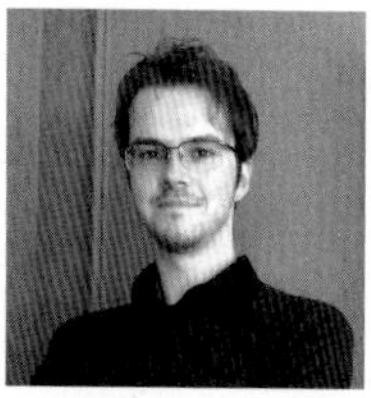

Clayton Cowles graduated from the *Joe Kubert School of Cartoon and Graphic Art* in 2009, and has been lettering for Image and Marvel Comics ever since. For Image, his credits include *Bitch Planet*, *Pretty Deadly*, *The Wicked + The Divine*, **and less than ten others. His Marvel credits include** *Fantastic Four*, *Young Avengers*, *Secret Avengers*, *Bucky Barnes: Winter Soldier* **and way more than ten others. He spends his real life in upstate New York with his cat. @claytoncowles**

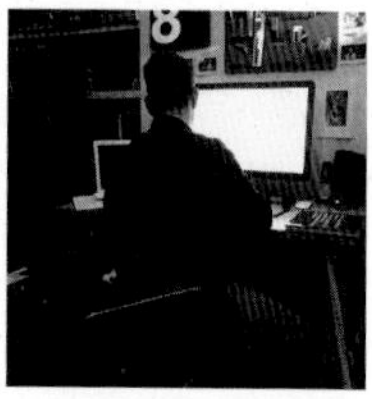

Tom Muller is an Eisner Award nominated Belgian graphic designer who works with technology startups, movie studios, publishers, media producers, ad agencies, and filmmakers. His recent comics design credits include Darren Aronofky's *NOAH*, *Zero*, *The Surface*, *Wolf*, **and** *Drifter* **for Image Comics;** *Constantine*, *Unfollow*, **and** *Survivors' Club* **for DC/Vertigo Comics;** *Divinity* **and** *Book of Death* **for Valiant Entertainment. He lives in London with his wife, and two cats. @helloMuller**

Future Present

By Fiona Duncan

Franco "Bifo" Berardi is an Italian Marxist theorist who bears more than a passing resemblance to *Material*'s opening man — the professor, Julius Shore. Shore's got Bifo's round black-rim glasses, his cloud of white hair, and his shady academic non-style. He's got his gab too, this theoretical preach: this is how it is. Bifo, I love. He's like an intellectual muppet. His long slice of a mouth flops on his choicest word — more! more! more! — eyes bugging under spectacles. He denounces spectacle while embodying it; what a comic.

I first fell for Bifo for his more. In his book *After the Future* (AK Press 2011), Bifo calls for more: poetry, time, pleasure, life. This is his treatment to the ails of accelerated "late hyper-capitalism," which, as Julius Shore explains, has created a kind of dictatorship of time and growth; it wants more material, more profit, yesterday, today, and tomorrow, forever and on, for its own and owner's sake, careless of the masses or Mother Earth.

You know the Miley Cyrus song "We Can't Stop"? It's like that. Addicting, arrogant, corporate, white. "We Can't Stop" was my song the summer I read   .

Heat of 2013, I was revving up to burn out from working too much. I knew it was coming but (I thought) I couldn't stop. Bifo spoke to me like a perennially-unemployed radically-politicked childless uncle might: insisting my exhaustion wasn't my fault, nor my editors' — the system was compelling us to give all of us to the corporations we worked for.

"More life! Less work!" He wrote about the psychopathologies of the "cognitariat," thinking laborers, like myself, a freelance writer — about how American-brand "cognitive capitalism" sought to suck all my mental and psychic energy, all of my time (so that's why I'm depressed and anxious!) (that's why all the vampire movies!). Bifo's good on this: on making you feel not crazy for being mad about the status quo.

What Bifo isn't good on is the good of technology, media, and spectacle. He wanes old man nostalgic. He writes: "The mutation that has infested the post-alphabetical generation, that is, the first generation to learn more words from the machine than from the mother – has deeply eroded the ability to solidarize." He talks about my demographic (I don't buy the word "generation," so market-co-opted) not recognizing that we may be listening. From Bifo, I feel told what's up, somewhat rightly (he's one of few contemporaries writing on subjectivity and capital, the internal affects/effects of technology, media, labor), but then he Others. Man objectifies youth like he does our tools, dismissing both in Ivory Tower prose. Archetypally academic, Bifo talks down.

In Kot's comic, Shore talks up. He stands at the base of an amphitheatre lecturing to hundreds of students. The set-up is like most set-ups of power — somehow one body, through institutional arrangement, is imagined more important than a multitude of others. Julius Shore is detailed down to his pant creases. The students, save for the one who walk outs, are a sketchy mass. This is the scene from Shore's perspective, he's centered. But within the illegible mass of students, you know (flip p.o.v.): there are hundreds of subjectivities.

Maybe their heads are mostly in screens (my experience of lecture halls).

Maybe this looks like "doing nothing" to Shore (my experience of some older people's experience of youth with screens). From all I've read of Bifo, he'd have it so. He presents contemporary screen culture as atomizing and automating. Atomizing: individuals being made lonely for being individuals; that is, defined in opposition to others, bubbled in personalized feeds. Automating: people being programmed by social and technological codes, like (my example) email etiquette, the expectation of a rapid response, which assumes we should always be online, always at work; we turn robotic. Bifo would rather like us to autonomize: to cultivate free thinking and doing. In a 2013 interview, he said that he'd started to believe that, "this precarious generation is unable to start a process of autonomization." This precarious generation being like the "post-alphabetical," we youth who're suffering from, "a sort of psychic frailty produced by precariousness, competition and loneliness." We, according to Bifo, lack autonomy and solidarity and the capacity to get there. So I go — not just! Like the student who interrupts Professor Shore, I wanna speak with Bifo — to tell him what else might be up.

Some highs of a precarious youth: Born in 1987 in Canada to white middle class parents, I am a prototypical Millennial or Gen Y'er or Gen I'er or Gen Me'er or "post-alphabetical" or "precarious" — whatever you want to call me. My name is Fiona. Often, this arrangement of letters — F-I-O-N-A — looks foreign to me, as do my face and body. Because I don't feel like Fiona Duncan, not just. My name is a label meant to make me legible to others, like generational labels aim to. I know, I am more. One more: I feel fluid with screens. Some of my most solid childhood memories are from screens: watching Fresh Prince of Bel Air and 90210 on a 13-inch CRT TV at 6; catching snippets of Cronenberg's Crash at 10, describing it to a crowd at recess the next day; taking undressed selfies with a desktop digital camera at 12, sharing them on ICQ. These memories feel warm, they glow. They're moments of comfort, exploration, and connection. In all, the body is present, on as the tech. My "coming of age" (a forever process I believe but here I'll talk young adulthood) twisted on tech. I learned to come

on a vibrator I ordered online after reading recommendations by Betty Dodson, again online. I learned to write in/for publics online — gained a confidence of voice on, which translated off, where I was before mousy shy. I've met mentors, best friends, and lovers (including the prodigious Ales Kot) online. My text life has improved my sex life. Poetry, Bifo's favorite — I never "got," until I played in exchanging words via screens; how communication is elusive! I'll pause, but there is more — more! more! more...

I have Bifo's email. After I read *After the Future*, I asked around for it. I fantasied cajoling him into a speaking tour.

We'd hit the American colleges first, then Canada, the UK, Europe, Asia...

Bifo would do his podium preach.

He'd speak on how, "the dictatorship of the financial economy... is destroying intelligence, public schools, creativity, the environment, water! Everything has to be sacrificed to an abstract growth of money, of value, of nothing. This is a madness." And on how, "this philosophy of the deregulated economy where everybody is demanded to give ceaselessly in order to survive," is infecting to kill us. He'd go, "STOP WORKING NOW. START LIVING PLEASE." And then there'd be questions, and that's when things would get interesting; he'd be challenged, dialogue would create new meaning, clash and solidarity, perhaps a couple plans to save the world... This plan — evidently — hasn't been enacted. Rather than work to make this happen, I've worked on paying my rent and utilities, on feeding and clothing myself, buying yoga, travel, and weed, the extras that keep me bright. The speaking tour I still stream in my mind's eye, when stress hits. Maybe I'll do it, maybe. I'll find the time, in the future, or after I accept the end of it? For now, at least: I'll mail Bifo this comic.

Fiona Duncan exists to be followed @fifidunks on more than one social media platform.

How the DMV Lost My Change of Addres

How the DMV lost my change of address

By Jarett Kobek

My favorite sections of the Senate Select Committee on Intelligence's Committee Study of the Central Intelligence Agency's Detention and Interrogation Program are on pages 37, 45 and 46, which detail the CIA's use Enhanced Interrogation Techniques on Abu Zabaydah.

Zabaydah, a citizen of Saudi Arabia, was the Patient Zero of torture. His body was the first to experience the techniques. The abuse was developed in concert with his flesh.

It's impossible to say what Abu Zabaydah did to deserve the loss of his eye and his sanity. He might have run a training camp in Afghanistan, and there might've been a tenuous connection with al-Qaeda, but his role was nothing like his original media billing as the organization's #3 or #4 in command. In response to a petition of habeas corpus, The US Department of Justice admitted that the man wasn't responsible for any known terror attack and wasn't part of Al-Qaeda. This was years after the CIA used his body as a canvas for pain.

(By the way, Flagg Miller, who is a professor at UC Davis, has more or less proved that, until 9/11, al-Qaeda didn't exist in anything like the form we envision. Only after Osama bin Laden became an international superstar did the West's concept of the group become a useful organizing principle. American opposition was excellent for marketing. Everyone needs a brand.)

Anyway, I really dig pages 37, 45 and 46. They explain not only how the CIA institutionalized torture but also something true about the human condition. These are the pages in which the inevitabilities of any bureaucracy become manifest.

Basically, members of the CIA back at HQ were receiving cables about the efficacy of torturing Abu Zabaydah. The cables came from a place described as DETENTION SITE GREEN. (Thailand, apparently.) Zabaydah was being tortured at DETENTION SITE GREEN. The cables read: *THIS IS A HUGELY SUCCESSFUL PROGRAM! OUR APPROACH IS WORKING!*

Back at HQ, people began telling each other, and other parts of the US Government, that the Enhanced Interrogation Techniques were a success. They had produced actionable intelligence through torture. Future catastrophes were being prevented. No more 11 Septembers.

But this misrepresented the cables' content. Yes, the people torturing other people were boasting of their success, but their communiqués indicated that, on the ground, the use of torture was not to produce intelligence. It was not to save lives.

To quote page 37: "Rather, the interrogation team believed the objective of the coercive interrogation techniques was to confirm Abu Zabaydah did not have additional information on threats to the United States... the interrogation team later deemed the [techniques] a success, not because it resulted in critical threat information, but because it provided further evidence that Abu Zabaydah had not been withholding the aforementioned information from the interrogators."

A ritual was enacted on Abu Zabaydah, one known well by any writer worth their salt. The CIA had, at long last, achieved the dreams of the world's editorial classes. Fact-checking was conflated with torture.

There is an uncharitable, and easy, interpretation of the disconnect between the cables' content and Langley's belief that torture produced critical threat information. One can argue that members of the CIA, back at HQ, had decided that torture as fact-checking was a valid approach but a method that only the select few could understand. There were two types of people in the world. Hard men who did what was necessary. And everyone else, the weak ones who couldn't understand the problem. Faced with this realization, the CIA adopted a necessary lie.

Maybe this is the true scenario. I have no idea. But I never assume malice in places where I can blame incompetence.

I prefer to posit the following: in the hysteria after 9/11, which included an attack on the five pointed star of Baphomet, there was a rush to find something, anything, absolutely anything which would prevent another attack. Pressure was put on all intelligence agencies. Reorganize or die. So the descendents of the excellently named James Jesus Angleton, people who'd always been tenuous on human rights, decide *okay, sure, torture, why not, let's give it a shot!*

Abu Zabaydah is the first person who falls victim to a pre-existing set of cultural assumptions. He is tortured. The people who are torturing, who are devising the techniques, who are making it up as they go along, know that torture will not gain intelligence. Here is a 2014 quote from James Mitchell, who co-created the program and billed tens of millions of dollars for his efforts: "I would be stunned if [the Senate Committee] found any kind of evidence to suggest that EITs as they were being applied yielded actionable intelligence."

Mitchell and his cohort establish a circumstance in which they define not only the techniques but also the parameters of their own success. They literally can not fail.

The cables go to Langley, where everyone is desperate for something, anything, absolutely anything that will work. They're in new territory. The present challenge exists beyond the traditional borders of the nation state. And here comes intel from DETENTION SITE GREEN. It's pure success. The real stuff. 100%. Gold.

The bureaucracy, always inclined to favor paperwork that recounts an event over the event itself, gets on board. Word goes out: this torture stuff works! But there is, as ever, bureaucratic drift. Nuance is lost.

Six months later, when Khalid Shaykh Mohammad arrives at DETENTION SITE COBALT (near Kabul) he is immediately tortured. There is no chance for him to offer any initial information.

Unlike Abu Zabaydah, KSM was at the center. He was part of awful shit. Presumably there's actionable intelligence in his head. But because he is tortured before any traditional interrogated, there are no facts to check. He's waterboarded at least 183 times. The information he offers is often totally fabricated. He's making it up to get away from the process.

This doesn't matter. The bureaucracy has adopted the process because it works. The purpose of the torture has become the torture itself. Why? Because the process works and has been adopted.

And then all of the broken bodies follow.

So that's why pages 37, 45 and 46 are my to-die for faves. Read them and watch as the consequences of bureaucratic drift are thrown into relief. We are given a primal dose of what emerges whenever human beings attempt to establish order and rule over their fellow human beings.

There are always rings to be kissed. This is always a hierarchy more concerned with its own preservation than with the consequences of its decisions. There are always shibboleths to honor. There's always a new graven idol to which one must genuflect and bow. There's always another meaningless pin affixed to our lapels. There is always the polite response, the empty gesture of solidarity with the mission.

For ourselves, you and me, our goal should be vigilance. Against ourselves. Against our worst impulses. That is the message of pages 37, 45 and 46. Stop assuming. Don't react in crisis. Don't establish complex systems of control.

Don't act as if it can't happen to you.

Because it will.

After all, you know this better than anyone. You're reading this essay in the pages of a comic book, and nothing in American life has hosted as much accidental cruelty as the hierarchies and bureaucratic drifts of the comic book industry.

RIP, Herb Trimpe. RIP, Joe Shuster. RIP, Jerry Siegel. RIP, Dick Sprang. RIP, Jerry Robinson. RIP, Matt Baker. May you never die, Steve Ditko.

RIP, Jack Kirby.

JARETT KOBEK is a Turkish-American writer living in California. His novella *ATTA* has been the subject of much academic writing, been translated into Spanish, and was a recent, and as of yet unexplained, bestseller in parts of Canada.

Lindsay

By Sarah Nicole Prickett

Lindsay Lohan, the real Lolita of Long Island, was born with the middle name Dee and changed it to Morgan. She wanted to be professional, and "Lindsay Morgan Lohan" sounded more like it. As it happened, by the time girls her age were going to prom she'd have exactly as much use for a middle name as Marilyn Monroe had, but that didn't make her professional. It wasn't in her blood.

Morgan does sound professional, I guess, if your profession is witching. While the definition of Morgan is something like "bright sea" in Welsh, the connotation, forged in Arthurian times, is of Morgan Le Fay, a pagan redheaded shapeshifter often mistaken for evil because she tempts. She is sometimes King Arthur's healer and sometimes his curse, sometimes his enemy, sometimes his lover, sometimes his kin. She's his lover and kin in the movie Merlin (1998), her wickedness embodied by a wild, auburn Helena Bonham Carter. "I like the old ways," she says to Merlin. "The old ways made me beautiful." Merlin says her beauty is only an illusion; in this version of the story, she was born deformed. Morgan laughs. "Beauty is always an illusion," she says. I watched the movie in English class, in high school, and that's the only part I remember.

Lindsay likes the old ways, too. In a 2008 cover shoot for New York magazine, she played Marilyn, posing for Bert Stern himself. In a 2013 movie for television, she played Liz. She fared a little better as the blonde of the system, but the real, magic strength—or fate—of the redheaded woman is her congenital resistance to type.

In Hollywood, any woman who isn't this or that might as well be a witch. In Hollywood, unfortunately, it's sink or swim.

Cheryl Blossom goes to Hollywood for the first time in 1996. In a three-issue arc of her Archie spin-off, the foxy rich bitch directs, produces, and stars in her own "vehicle," a pumped-up documentary she calls "Cheryl: A Life." Several residents of Riverdale, where she first appeared at the start of the 1980s, are conscripted into bit parts, the boys more willingly than the girls. Outside Riverdale, readers considered Cheryl too bold for the wholesome world of Archie; inside Riverdale, Betty and Veronica were never better friends than when Cheryl was around.

If "blonde or brunette" is a coin-toss posited as a life choice, redheads are possessed of a different currency, one that has often been valued too much or not at all. Redheads are said to be over-sexed, under-desired, and bad-tempered, to be Satanists, criminals, orphans, aliens, and freaks. Their reputations far exceed their numbers.

"I would be dead if I slept with that many people," Lindsay told NYLON in 2007, addressing the rumors about her and "every older man." Secretly, she was already dating Samantha Ronson, an older woman who looked like a boy her age. "Certain people are true," she said, grinning.

Here's the Archie cast, later in the '80s, on the big question (in even bigger font): Who is Cheryl Blossom?

"I'm not allowed to use that kind of language," says Veronica.
"She's quite indescribable!" says Archie.
"She's a heartbreaker!" says Reggie.

"She's trouble!" says Betty.
"Who cares!" says Jughead, but the answer is everyone, for a while.

The funny thing is, Cheryl doesn't want to be with Archie, let alone breed with him. (It isn't true that gingers are going extinct.) "I don't have a boyfriend. I have Chanel, Hermes, and diamonds," tweeted Lindsay in 2012, sounding a little more Marilyn than Marilyn, more Liz than Liz.

Would you rather be divinely beautiful, dazzlingly clever, or angelically good?

That's one of Anne's favorite questions—Anne as in Anne of Green Gables, Anne whose red hair is a curse. She can never decide between the first two. "It's certain I'll never be angelically good," she says.

Mary Magdalene and Cleopatra have both been depicted as titian again and again, despite the almost indisputable fact that, given their times and places of birth, both were brunette. In Red: A History of the Redhead, Jacky Collis Harvey holds that when we see "Caesar's mistress, lover of Mark Antony, the queen who hazarded a kingdom and chose death over conquest," we can't help but see her hair as red. "What other color would it be?" asks Harvey, who is of course a redhead herself.

Babalon, or the Scarlet Woman, is a goddess in the religion of Thelema, which was taught by Aleister Crowley to a number of Angelenos in the 1940s. Babalon is the name of the divine; the divine is feminine. To Jack Parsons, a Thelemite leader in Pasadena, the divine was his right. He found her in the form of Marjorie Cameron.

Cameron's hair matched the job description, but her beauty surpassed expectations. She was a femme fatale, maybe literally: Seven years after meeting and marrying her, Parsons died at home in a mystery explosion. Two years after that, the girl who grew up a "town pariah" was the toast of Kenneth Anger's Hollywood and the star of his films.

"Marjorie came in and pushed Anaïs Nin out… by magical force," said Anger in a 2013 interview. "She wanted to be the only woman." Others called her a witch, a sorceress, a cover girl, an artist, a fake (beauty is always illusion). She never remarried (certain people are true, after all).

On Mad Men there's a Betty, but no Veronica. She got pushed out. Next to Joan (Christina Hendricks), the newest wives and prettiest models look snipped out of catalogues, pasted onto popsicle sticks. Joan so clearly can't help the way she looks—or the way she is looked at—that it's no surprise she is almost never helped when she's hurt. Women and men alike can't stop seeing her as a threat long enough to see her as vulnerable. But even the sirens, Ariels on the rocks that they are, might sometimes be crying, not singing.

Lindsay's best performance in the last seven years is a fifteen-minute appearance on Letterman. She is promoting something called "Scary Movie Five," but more importantly, to Letterman's tabloid-addled mind, she is days from another stint in rehab. He won't let it go. Is she drinking tonight? Is she shoplifting? What will be different this time? Pained and graceful, she answers some of his questions and admonishes him for others, refusing to play to the image of herself he's holding up: the town pariah, the prodigal daughter-figure, the brat. Eventually she steals his notes, which consist less of jokes than of her expenses, and begins reading the questions herself. "Ask yourself," she says, sweetly mocking everyone in the room including her, "why always in trouble?"

"I'm a target," she answers. "I've always been." She goes on to take "full responsibility," but her quick answers linger. It's insane to feel sympathy, but you do. Before you can heal, says Letterman, "you have to put out the fire." Lindsay says, lightly: "My hair?"

When Cheryl goes to Hollywood, she's met with jeers. "Now, now," she tells the jeering. "Some of us are born to be divine."

(Some of us are born to never be angelically good.)

The other night I looked at Lindsay's Instagram and I wondered if she has a best friend. The night before that I wondered whether she's had more work done or just put on weight or both (she's always been a pathological shapeshifter). In a recent photo, shilling for a new kind of teeth whitener, she smiles with her lips fully closed.

There's something irrepressible and desperate and "who cares!" about this witch that I love, for all the ways she's wasted my time. I guess that's what a spell is.

Although there is no good evidence to support the belief that redheads were burned at the stake, it also doesn't matter to the myth, since beliefs are not beliefs because they're factual but because they're desirable. What does seem true is that it's easy for redheads to be bad, given all the rules they have to break: Don't wear pink. Don't wear red, or red lipstick. Don't go in the sun. Don't be tanned. Never, ever be loud. Don't swim in chlorinated water.

In a 2010 issue of Life With Archie, Cheryl shows up back in Hollywood. We're in a restaurant, and two agents are screaming at her, and it turns out she's waiting tables, broke. The scene is so much meaner than she deserves. She looks amazing in pink, though.

Sarah Nicole Prickett is a writer in New York (*snpsnpsnp.com*) **and the founding editor of Adult** (*adult-mag.com*)**.**

CONVULSIONS AMONG THE LILIES

By Bijan Stephen

"We are a fact-gathering organization only. We don't clear anybody. We don't condemn anybody."
—J. Edgar Hoover, *Look* magazine (14 June 1956).

"All the gods are dead except the god of war."
—Eldridge Cleaver, *Soul On Ice* (Part I: "'The Christ' and His Teachings")

"We shall have our manhood.
We shall have it or the earth will be leveled by our attempts to gain it."
—Eldridge Cleaver, *Soul On Ice*

"On Thursday_____ about 4 o'clock in the afternoon, Matthew_____, 16, was shot in the back and killed by a policeman. The officer had stopped the car Johnson and a friend were riding in: he thought they looked suspicious. The policeman, Alvin_____, 51, ordered the two out of the car and told them to raise their hands. Matthew_____ began to run down a hill with his hands raised. The officer says he fired three warning shots before hitting Johnson. A witness claims that all the shots were aimed at the youth. At the time of the shooting the officer did not know that the car was stolen. The owners reported it as stolen several hours later."

What year is this from? Can you guess?

Not that it matters. Matthew Johnson died on September 27, 1966. The cop, Alvin Johnson—presumably no relation—read out the ending to Matthew's story in the time it took the bullet to find flesh. This is an ending that's so familiar it's banal: Man, sensing his death, attempts to get out from under it; bullet, life's equal and opposite, called once again to active duty, responds. And then there's another body that lies cooling on the ground in the summer heat. We know how the story ends, and we know what the victims of its conclusion look like.

I write to you from another summer. Today, July ____, 20XX, was the hottest so far. And you can feel it in the humidity, in the heat. Don't give them a reason, the indelible lesson my parents taught me, floats across the surface of my thoughts, because it's fighting weather again. It's been years since I've heard the words spoken, but I can still remember their original tone; despite years of warping sun and heat, they haven't lost their original hues.

I wonder what Matthew Johnson's last thoughts were. Did he remember his mother's advice? Or was it pure animal panic, life's animating spirit convulsing one last time in a desperate bid to prolong its existence? I wonder what the heat was like that day. I wonder how humid it was. I can only imagine the gemlike sun, a shard of broken glass in the sky ready to draw blood. I don't believe in time travel but I've put myself there that afternoon; I go there every morning, afternoon, evening, and night that ends the same way. Let me tell you what I see.

In America, hate and history are close bedfellows, and one nourishes the other, motherlike, with the strange black fruit that hangs low and heavy from all different kinds of trees, in every kind of weather. America is not a vegetarian, and she requires many carcasses a day to stay upright. Or perhaps she's not a carrion-eater. Perhaps she's an addict, chasing an eternal high.

But I think I've got it backwards. You can discern truth when your neural chemistry is altered; the filters between you and the everyday unsayable are muted, have disappeared, and you're free to probe the awful nature of things. Maybe America is painfully sober; maybe she's our designated driver. Or perhaps it's that she's in charge of the getaway car, as we rob our memory banks of atrocity and flee.

When I wake up each morning, I thank my heart for beating. I lie on my back and feel it pulse through my chest. I imagine blood rushing through dark veins, the electrical impulses that keep the drumbeat in my chest beating in time. When I contemplate my vitality I imagine the impossibly thin edge that separates me from death. As a black man in America, I am never closer to death than I am always. Get high and think about it. I wish I could put it more simply.

What if Malcolm were still here? How would he and Huey respond? I keep them close. I ask for guidance. They seemed to know the truth of things, to know the secrets of the brutal, peculiarly American disease. Malcolm said "Be peaceful, be courteous, obey the law, respect everyone; but if someone puts his hand on you, send him to the cemetery." You can feel the heat of his sincerity decades later.

But this is all very abstract. I suppose I'm orbiting my point because I can't bear to confront it directly. I'm not strong enough to admit that everything I do, everything I am, is defined skin-first, because it means that the foremost pursuit of my life is convincing Americans that I am, in fact, human. That I am not a monster with my kinky hair, that I am not a demon with a flattened nose. That's the trick of how to survive in this blighted country; that is my advice to you. Force them to grant you personhood. Usually, you have to show them you bleed for them to make them believe you're human.

Before I do anything else, I do this. I bleed. The hearts of Americans are, whether they know it or not, impure. I know they are flawed by their dreams of pure white. They imagine themselves to be like the driven snow, like lilies waving innocently in the breeze. But we, the dark ones, are the soil they grow out of, and they cannot survive without us. Never forget that there are ancient fault lines that cross the globe. Never forget that the massive plates at their edges move imperceptibly against each other in the eternal night of geological time. They do move, though. They convulse and the Earth itself shakes.

Bijan Stephen is an Associate Editor at *The New Republic.*
@bijanstephen

REFERENCES

The Movement, 1966 (PDF)
— bit.ly/TheMovement1966

1966 Hunters Point Rebellion: Recollections of Harold Brooks and Thomas Fleming
— bit.ly/BrooksFleming

Ten-Point Program
— en.wikipedia.org/wiki/Ten-Point_Program

Bobby Hutton
— en.wikipedia.org/wiki/Bobby_Hutton
(Hutton's funeral was held on April 12 at the Ephesians Church of God in Berkeley, California. About 1,500 people attended the funeral and a rally held afterwards in West Oakland was attended by over 2,000 people, including actor Marlon Brando and author James Baldwin.[6][7][8] He was buried at Mountain View Cemetery in Oakland, **but did not have a gravestone until 2003, 35 years after his death**. *[bolding mine])*

Black Armed Guard
— en.wikipedia.org/wiki/Robert_F._Williams#Black_Armed_Guard

'The Kissing Case' And The Lives It Shattered
— n.pr/kwpFxe

The disappeared: Chicago police detain Americans at abuse-laden 'black site'
— gu.com/p/464e7/stw

BOOKS

Encyclopedia of American Race Riots
— bit.ly/AmericanRaceRiots

Negroes with Guns
— wsupress.wayne.edu/books/detail/negroes-guns

Soul on ice
— amzn.to/1N0DCjd

Not in My Neighborhood: How Bigotry Shaped a Great American City
— vox.com/2015/5/10/8578077/baltimore-segregation-pietila
— amzn.to/1T9c7IY

B L X P L T N

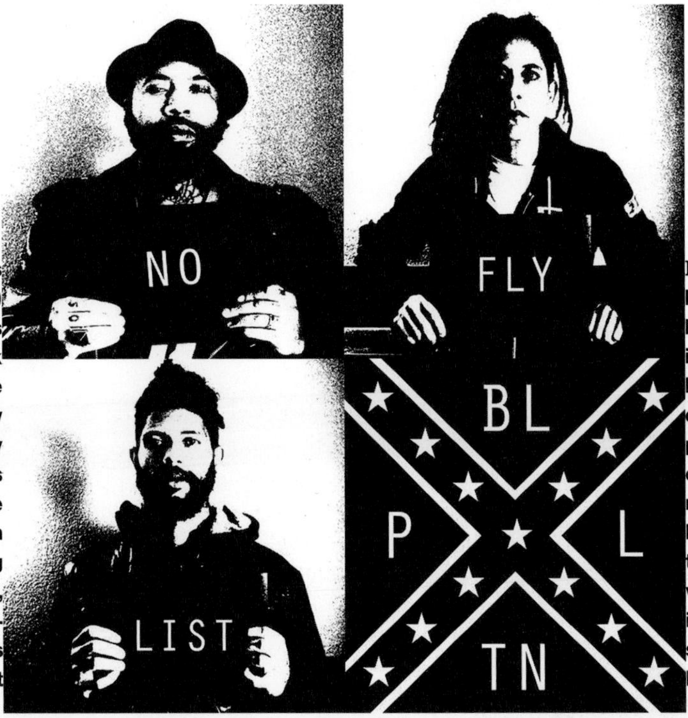
NO
FLY
LIST
BL
P
L
TN

→ **Austin's BLXPLTN (Blaxploitation) has [redacted] been described [redacted] as having a politically-charged — punk industrial sound, "combining the breakneck speed and throbbing low end of Big Black and the hooky politic of prime era UK punk," as one local critic put it. Audience reactions to live shows range from headbanging and [redacted] moshing to [redacted] drop-jawed, drooling disbelief, which has gained these — multi-instrumentalist music [redacted] veterans swift recognition and — support both locally and nationally.**

— The band's debut album, *Black Cop Down,* **was released in October of 2014, featuring production by Autry Fulbright (...Trail of Dead, Vanishing Life) and Elliott Frazier (Ringo Deathstarr), with early tracking from the late Ikey Owens (The Mars Volta, Jack White). The album received recognition from** *The Fader, Vice* **and local publications like the** *Austin Chronicle* **and** *Ovrld,* **the latter of which named album standout "Start Fires" Austin's best song of 2014.**

[redacted] **In 2015, BLXPLTN have already debuted two new tracks from their upcoming record—** *"No Fly List,"* **which addresses racist policies in airports and beyond, and** *"Auf Wiedersehen,"* **an anthemic cry against the injustices faced by people of color-- proving that their sound continues to evolve. They are currently touring, working on their next video release and completing their yet-to-be-titled sophomore album with Autry and Elliott helping them out once again.**

Band site:
— blxpltn.com

Soundcloud:
— soundcloud.com/blxpltn

Newest single *"Auf Wiedersehen"*
soundcloud.com/blxpltn/auf-wiedersehen

Facebook:
— facebook.com/blxpltn

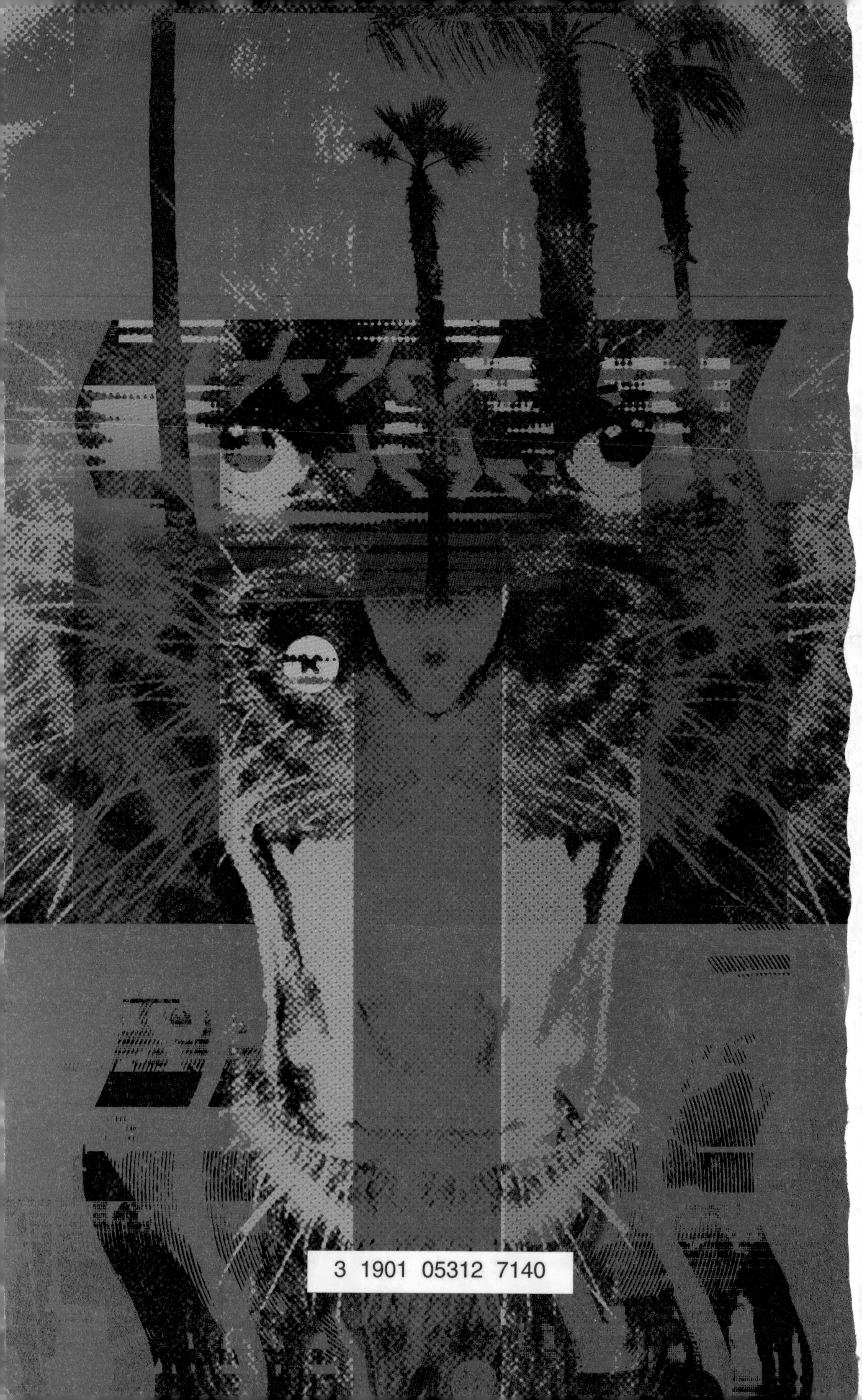